D1187635

PALESTINE
AND
THE GULF

PALESTINE
AND
THE GULF

RASHID KHALIDI and *CAMILLE MANSOUR* (eds.)

Proceedings of an International Seminar
IPS, Beirut

November 2-5, 1981

Institute for Palestine Studies
Beirut
1982

Monograph Series No. 63

DS326
P35
1982

INSTITUTE FOR PALESTINE STUDIES
Anis Nsouli Street, Verdun
P.O. Box 11-7164, Beirut, Lebanon
Telex: MADAF 23317 LE

CONTENTS

JUL 2 4 1984

CONTRIBUTORS

Frank Barnaby *was Director of the Stockholm International Peace Research Institute (SIPRI) from 1971-1981, and is still doing research for SIPRI. He is currently Professor of Peace Studies at the Free University of Amsterdam.*

Marwan Buheiry *is Associate Professor of History at the American University of Beirut and a Research Fellow at the Institute for Palestine Studies in Beirut.*

Shafiq al-Hout *has been the Director of the PLO office in Beirut for many years, and has been a member of the PLO delegation to the UN General Assembly since 1974.*

Rashid Khalidi *is Assistant Professor of Political Studies at the American University of Beirut, and a Research Fellow at the Institute for Palestine Studies in Beirut.*

Oleg V. Kovtounovitch *is a specialist in Contemporary Arab History at the Institute of Oriental Studies of the USSR Academy of Sciences in Moscow.*

Camille Mansour *is a Research Fellow at the Institute for Palestine Studies, Beirut, and is currently Chairman of its Research Department.*

Michalis Papayannakis *is a Research Fellow at the Hellenic Mediterranean Centre for Arab and Islamic Studies in Athens and lectures at the Mediterranean Agronomic Institute at Montpellier.*

Robert J. Pranger *is Director of International Programs at the American Enterprise Institute in Washington D.C., and Adjunct Professor at Johns Hopkins and Georgetown Universities.*

Mohamed al-Rumaihi *is a Professor of Sociology at Kuwait University.*

Elias Shoufani *is a Research Fellow at the Institute for Palestine Studies specializing in Israeli Affairs, and has served as Chairman of its Research Department.*

Michel Tatu *is a Senior Editor at Le Monde, Paris, specializing in East-West and Strategic Affairs.*

Pierre Terzian *is Deputy Director of the Arab Petroleum Research Centre in Paris.*

Introduction

This volume comprises twelve papers written for an international seminar held at the Institute for Palestine Studies in Beirut from 2-5 November, 1981 under the title "The Palestine Question and the Gulf." Nine of the authors presented their papers in person, while the other three, who were unable to attend the seminar, sent their contributions (see list of contributors p. VIII, and programme, p. 345). During the last month of 1981, all of the authors were given the opportunity to revise their papers. These have not been updated since then.

What lay behind the choice of topic for the seminar, at which four researchers from the IPS and eight researchers from outside gave papers? The importance of the relation between Palestine and the Gulf drew the attention of observers during the period 1979-1981, in the wake of the Iranian revolution, the hostages crisis, the Afghanistan intervention, and the Iraq-Iran war. It was underlined by the increased emphasis of the Carter and Reagan administrations, as well as of the USSR, on the strategic significance of the Gulf region. It seemed clear to us that in the perceptions of the main actors in the Middle East, both external and local, there was an important link between developments in the Gulf and the Arab-Israeli conflict.

In the case of the United States and the USSR, this phenomenon is particularly striking. The US has been trying for a number of years to knit together a regional alliance system, either formal or informal, the focus of which would be the protection of the strategic and energy interests of the West in the Middle East, and which would ideally include a number of Arab states as well as the most powerful regional ally of the

US, Israel. In the perception of the US policy-makers, one of the primary stumbling blocks to this scheme, (as well as to earlier fore-runners of it going all the way back to the 1950's) has been the Arab preoccupation with Palestine. Thus, for the United States, the links between Palestine and the Gulf are an inconvenience and a hindrance which prevent a closer relationship with several Arab states of the Gulf. In addition, since the US perceives Israel as a valuable asset, it has rewarded that state by adopting a public posture of calculated indifference to Israel's policies towards the Arabs, while downgrading the significance of the Palestine question.

The effects of all this on US Middle East policy are clear. On the one hand, dealing with major crises in the state-to-state conflict between the Arab states and Israel has frequently (e.g. 1948, 1956, 1967, 1969-70, 1973-74) become a matter of the highest priority for US policy-makers, due to the danger that its escalation might lead to a conflict with the USSR, drive Arab states closer to the latter, or threaten the US position in the Gulf. On the other hand, a comprehensive resolution of the Palestine question itself has failed to receive any sustained American attention, and only lip service was paid to it on those infrequent occasions when oil-producing Gulf states pressured the US, as in 1973-74 and 1977.

The Soviet perception of the importance of the relation between the Gulf and Palestine does not go back as far as that of its super-power rival. Whereas it can be argued that for the US this issue was a matter of concern as long ago as the Roosevelt-Ibn Saud discussions of 1945, for the USSR the link between the two regions seems to have assumed importance only over the past few years. The Soviets have seen that their strongest argument in their intermittent and relatively recent dialogue with Gulf and other strategically-important Arab conservative states has to do with their support for the Palestinians and the Arab states in their confrontation with Israel. The USSR is naturally suspect in the eyes of Saudi

Arabia and its closest allies because of the Afghanistan intervention, as well as for ideological reasons. It is therefore all the more in the Soviet interest to side with the PLO and the Arab confrontation states, a stand which has on occasion earned it the praise of countries such as Kuwait, Jordan and Saudi Arabia.

In addition to these factors specific to each of the two superpowers, there can be added an element common to both, which is that all external actors in the region perceive that there is an important link between Palestine and the Gulf because this is the way local powers such as the Arab states, Israel and Iran see things. These powers see this link because of a number of mundane, but important, objective factors.

The first of these is the simple geographic fact of the proximity of the states of the Gulf to those bordering on Israel. Iraq and Saudi Arabia are the main Arab states of the Gulf. The first has participated twice in wars with Israel (in 1948 and 1973) and its nuclear reactor was bombed by Israel in 1981. The second is separated only by a narrow stretch of Jordanian territory and the Gulf of Aqaba from Israel itself. Not surprisingly, there has been an increasing trend for Israel to consider Iraq and Saudi Arabia potentially hostile powers.* On the other hand, these two Arab states are coming to view Israel as more dangerous to them than ever before. This

* This was brought out in striking fashion in a speech prepared by Israeli Defence Minister Ariel Sharon for delivery at a seminar at the Strategic Studies Institute of Tel Aviv University, but which he could not give due to involvement in the Knesset debate on the annexation of the Golan Heights. It was later published in Ma'ariv (18 Dec. 1981), and describes "the Arab states beyond the confrontation states," such as Iraq, Saudi Arabia and Libya, as falling within the second of three concentric circles to which "Israel must expand her strategic attention" in the 1980's. The Gulf, Sharon added, falls into the third of these circles, which reaches as far as Pakistan and Central Africa. "Israel's security interests", he concluded, are directly affected by the "expanding military potential" of hostile forces in all these areas.

geographical proximity, with all the strategic considerations it engenders, is further emphasized by the fact that the oilfields of Saudi Arabia and northern Iraq are linked to the Mediterranean by pipelines running across the three states bordering Israel on the East (in addition to the newer Iraqi pipeline running through Turkey).

Another fact of importance which further brings out this link is the presence of perhaps 15% of the total Palestinian population in the Arab states of the Gulf, where they contribute both labour power and specialized services to the local economies. To these must be added many hundreds of thousands of citizens of the three Mashriq countries, still technically at war with Israel (Syria, Lebanon and Jordan), who perform similar functions in the Gulf, and who, along with the Palestinians, bring with them a heightened sensitivity to the development of the Arab-Israeli conflict. Yet, their influence is, of course, attenuated by their not being citizens of their host countries and thus not participating directly or formally in the political processes of these countries. On the other hand, this influence is enhanced by their prominent role in education, the media and government service, where they have a powerful impact on the shaping of public opinion. As a result, they constitute a sector of the population which cannot be ignored.

One other objective element in the link between Palestine and the Gulf must be mentioned, although it falls into a different category from those listed above. This is the deep interest shown by Israel in Iran since the time of the Shah, because of its obvious value as a possible counterweight to any tendency among the Arab states of the Gulf, particularly Iraq, to involve themselves too deeply in the Arab-Israeli conflict. On the other hand, since the Revolution, Iran has had an active policy in the Arab world, motivated sometimes by ideology and sometimes by considerations of realpolitik, which generally focuses on the Palestine question and the

Arab-Israeli dispute. Clearly, Iran's alliances, axes and tacit agreements with various Arab states are not all motivated by, or directed towards, the resolution of the Palestine question: indeed in many cases they can best be understood in terms of other regional rivalries and conflicts. Nevertheless, these factors directly affect the Arab-Israeli balance. This was illustrated in striking fashion, as these lines were being written in the spring of 1982, when current developments of the sanguinary Iraq-Iran war seized the attention of Arab and regional powers.

Although falling into the realm of perception as well as objective fact, one more point deserves mention here. This is the view, strongly held by many Palestinians, in particular, that the continuation of the Gulf war represents a painful drain on Arab resources, that it contributes directly and measurably to the deepening of the existing divisions in the Arab world, and that it makes the achievement of a strategic balance with Israel infinitely harder. The reasons for this assessment are many and bear further exposition, but this would take us far from the purpose of this introduction. Suffice it to say that the latest phase of the Iran-Iraq war provides yet another illustration of the close relation between the Gulf and the Palestine question.

This brings us to the difficult and delicate matter of the relation between the Gulf and the process of obtaining a settlement of the Palestine question and the Arab-Israeli dispute, particularly the former.

It has been part of formal Arab strategy for many years to attempt to add the weight of the Arab oil-producing states of the Gulf to the strategic balance with Israel as a means of settling the Middle East conflict. With the notable exception of the 1973 war, these efforts have been almost uniformly futile, for a variety of reasons. In the abstract, the idea of using the "oil weapon" still remains attractive. But it is clear that just as it may be possible to benefit from the enormous potential leverage of the Arab oil producers of the Gulf in order to achieve a just Middle East settlement, so is it equally possible that this leverage could be neutralized, dissipated, or even turned against those attempting to employ it. The sword of the so-called Arab "oil weapon," in other words, cuts both ways. However, the neutralization of this leverage would further highlight the stark contrast between the Arab oil producers' immense potential power, and their actual impotence, in practice. This, in turn, could imperil the internal stability of these countries. Either way, the ambiguity of the oil weapon underlines yet again, and in perhaps the most dramatic manner of all, the vital link between the Gulf and Palestine.

Given the above set of assessments which were (and are) only ours, we were led to consider the Palestine-Gulf connection as the key to understanding regional developments in the eighties. What remained to be done was to test these ideas against the broadest spectrum of opinions and perceptions. What was needed was the objective contribution of experts from various fields, as well as the assessments of analysts from different geographic areas. This brings us to explain the organization of the seminar, and the way in which the organizers initially perceived the place of each paper in it. As the reader will see, in the end various authors developed their papers beyond these initial suggested outlines.

The first group of papers was meant to provide an introduction and general background to the main themes covered by the seminar, specifically Western economic interests in the Gulf, the question of oil, the effect of the international military balance on the Gulf and Arab-Israeli conflict, and questions of social and economic development in the Gulf during the coming decade. This was to be followed by a section on the perspectives of various international actors in the issue, specifically Europe, the NATO alliance, the USSR and US, and then by a third section covering the views of regional actors including the PLO, Israel, and the countries of the Arab Mashriq.

Hence, in planning the Seminar, we envisaged that the first paper, presented by Michalis Papayannakis would deal with Western economic interests in the Arab world, and especially in the oil-producing states of the Gulf. The aim was to obtain an assessment of the competition between Western Europe and the US from the economic point of view, an issue which has generated much controversy in the Arab world. Next came the contribution of Pierre Terzian, who was asked to deal with various aspects of the oil issue, especially questions relating to oil producing countries, such as present and projected production levels, control over production levels, refining and marketing. In addition, the role of the oil companies, projected consumption requirements in the 1980's and the possible production of other regions such as the USSR and Africa were to be dealt with. The paper presented by Frank Barnaby was intended to deal with the super-power strategic balance, insofar as it affects the regions under discussion, including both nuclear and conventional capabilities and the perceptions of both sides. For the final paper in this section, we asked Mohamed Rumaihi to deal with the situation in the Gulf itself: specifically the socio-economic formations, potentials for social change, the labour force, and particularly, the role of Palestinians.

The second section was to open with a paper by Michel Tatu, who was requested to cover the European strategic view of the linkage between the Gulf and the Palestine problem, examining the role Europe envisions for itself and its perceptions of US and Soviet moves in the region. This was then to be followed by a paper on a related topic, the Atlantic alliance and the Middle East in the 1980's, by Marwan Buheiry, covering the way in which the NATO powers have perceived the region, both recently and in the past, with a view to projecting future trends. Next was an analysis of the way in which the Gulf and Palestine are linked in Soviet policy, by Rashid Khalidi, who was to attempt to deal with Soviet policy in this regard from a regional perspective. For the last two papers in the second section, by Robert Pranger and Oleg Kovtounovitch, we suggested that the former write on the US strategic analysis of the relation between Palestine and the Gulf, and the planned approach of the Reagan administration to the problem. The latter was asked to provide a Soviet view on the linkage between the two arenas, and the way they have been treated by Soviet policy in recent years.

The third section included three papers on the regional actors. The first was by Shafiq al-Hout, who was asked to present an analysis of the relation between the Gulf and Palestine from the point of view of the Palestine Liberation Organization, and the strategy followed by the Palestinian resistance movement in this regard. Next, Elias Shoufani was to deal with Israeli strategy and the Gulf, and specifically Israel's view of its role in this region in the future. We planned to end the seminar with an analysis by Camille Mansour of the perspective of the countries of the Arab Mashriq on the relationship between the Gulf and Palestine, touching on Syria, in particular.

As the reader will notice, and as is natural, in many cases the papers as presented and revised often vary in format from our original conception, although not substantially. The result, however, as it represents the views of the various authors, rather than that of the editors or of the IPS, constitutes a rich and diverse collection of views on this important subject from a number of contrasting perspectives.

Many people, aside from the participants themselves, played a role in organizing the seminar and making it a success, and in preparing this volume for publication. Among those who deserve mention here are Mrs. Laila Baroody, who helped at many stages, the indefatigable Alia Tarazi, secretary of the Research Department, Minar Ratib, who assisted with research, and Anne Hilal, Taan Saab and Meric Dobson of the IPS Publications Department.

Although much has changed in the region since members of the IPS Research Department first envisaged the idea for the seminar in early 1981, the editors hope that this book, which emerged from it, will be of interest and value to readers, in view of the continuing relevance and actuality of the themes discussed.

Beirut, May 1982.

R. Khalidi

C. Mansour

I
GENERAL BACKGROUND

1

Western Economic Interests in the Arab World

by Michalis Papayannakis

The notion of "economic interest" is too vague and elastic to permit a brief summary of the recent development of relations between the West and the Arab World. With the general trend towards the internationalization of capital and production which the world economy has experienced at least since the 1960's, it is increasingly difficult to stress one aspect, classic or new, in the whole picture, and to draw definite conclusions as to the position and relative importance of one or other factor, or of one or other partner. A large investment project may be counter-balanced by trading agreements favouring other partners; financial banking ties should not obscure the flow of other sources of finance (remittances, tourism, merchant marine etc.); and massive purchases of a certain product should not conceal the share of the world market obtained over the course of years by others.

Thus we may state that exhaustive studies would be needed in all areas of economic activity in the broadest sense to enable us to appreciate the state and evolution of conflicts of economic interest in a region as vast as the Arab World. This would still leave aside political questions which have their own importance and their own influence on economic relations.

This paper clearly has no such ambitions. It is primarily concerned with drawing the broad lines of the interest that the Arab World presents to the world economy and some trends of development, as they relate to the Arab economy, within the various parts of what is commonly known as the West — which is in fact the whole of the developed capitalist world.

This account has not taken into consideration questions related to oil, which will be dealt with by more expert contributors. Moreover, most of the points dealt with refer to issues of international trade. This is partly due to the need to keep this account brief, but also because it is only in this area that we have at our disposal data that are relatively credible, recent and comparable in time and space. Finally, the period selected for the following remarks covers a recent period of time, starting a little before the so-called "oil crisis," and taking us up to the present day, or at least up to the most recent comparable data.

This span of time is relatively short. We cannot hope to discover in it the major trends which will shape the future. However, it is of interest to study the economic data which may be expected to change at this level, and which have in fact changed during the period. In this lies a further justification for emphasizing trade relations.

That said, the economic relations between the West and the Arab World are longstanding and of prime importance on a global scale. It is unnecessary to recount in detail the history of the opening up of this world of Western capitalism (dating at least as far back as Bonaparte's expedition to Egypt) in order to give a clear indication of this decisive fact in the modern development of the Arab World. The effect of colonialism in all its forms, the discovery of oil and other important minerals (e.g. phosphates) are well enough known in the history of this part of the world. Even more recently, during the post-war period and the period of movements of national liberation and political independence, the West has played an important economic role in the development of the Arab countries, a role which, moreover, has expanded.

Historic ties inherited from the past and the "imperative of development" in most of the Arab countries have been at the bottom of this process. During the 1960's, the sum of trade with Western countries represented for the great majority of Arab countries more than half, three-quarters or more of their total trade. The capital invested in the modern sectors of their economy and more generally the financing of all kinds of development came for the most part from the West. Large numbers of emigrant workers (especially from the Maghrib) worked in the West, mainly in Europe.[1] Even at that time, there occurred shifts and important struggles for influence in the economic development of these countries, in relation to the exterior.

Several movements and trends could be studied in a given country or region of the Arab World. The most important of these, during this period, seem to be the relative deterioration in the position of the former colonial powers in favour of more diversified exchanges with the rest of the world, and a significant effort on the part of the United States and (to a lesser degree) the USSR to take the place of the European countries.[2] By the 1960's, the positions of the United Kingdom and of France were seriously threatened or had been totally undermined to the benefit of, for example, West Germany. Meanwhile American trade and investment, apart from oil, progressed, as did the Soviet presence by means of aid and trade, especially in the Western Mediterranean.

---

[1] Mahmoud Allaya, *Les Migrations Internationales des Travailleurs du Bassin Méditerranéen et la Croissance Economique* (Montpellier: IAM, No. 1, Juin 1974).

[2] Michalis Papayannakis, "Crise et Construction Hégémonique d'un Nouvel Ordre Economique International en Méditerranée," *The Greek Review of Social Research*, No. 26-27, Athènes.

These facts are relatively well known and it is unnecessary to stress their significance. We may, however, underline the fact that despite the strategic importance of the region, there was no case of massive economic intervention which could have transformed part or all of it into a development zone comparable with that of South East Asia or even certain Latin American countries. The relative homogeneity and potential of the Arab World, its own resources which it was a question of "recycling" and which have not yet been used fully on behalf of the Arab World itself, the conflicts of interest (East-West, North-South, West-West...) and the resulting uncertainty, especially political uncertainty, explain this phenomenon, surprising as it is for the uninformed observer. Table 1 shows (no doubt in too cursory a fashion) the relatively modest place of the Arab group of countries in international investment, and indirectly in other parameters of international economic activity.

Only 3.5% of direct Western investments were made in Arab countries up until 1977, of which 1.2% were in Gulf countries and 2.3% in other Arab countries. These percentages are clearly inferior to the economic importance of these countries, however this may be defined. Moreover, the percentages for the cumulative sum of grants awarded by the West to the Arab countries amounted to 17.2% of the total channelled towards the Arab world, of which 0.8% went to the Gulf countries and 16.4% to the other Arab countries. This difference shows that until very recently the Arab world, except of course the oil-rich countries, was seen mainly as a partner to be assisted rather than an associate in production. However, all the indications are that this type of relationship is undergoing a rapid process of change.

The "oil crisis" considerably strengthened the economic importance of the Arab World as far as the rest of the world was concerned, in particular the "developed countries" (the

TABLE 1. Cumulated Stock of External Resources at the End
of 1977 ($ million)

Arab Gulf countries	Grants	Direct foreign investments	Debt	Debt service (1977)
Bahrain	203	200	217	39
Iraq	144	130	1625	668
Kuwait	11	160	194	109
Oman	303	50	578	128
Qatar	7	100	371	143
Saudi Arabia	56	215	1537	1046
UAE	57	150	1188	310
Other Arab countries				
Algeria	2903	360	10065	1409
Egypt	4722	217	8140	1058
Jordan	2162	70	864	51
Lebanon	383	100	144	49
Libya	265	530	694	458
Morocco	1283	325	3608	307
Sudan	674	55	117	x
Syria	1812	70	1551	137
Tunisia	1170	260	2005	190
Yemen AR	734	–	315	8
PDR Yemen	441	–	307	6
Total developing countries	*100657*	*84996*	*264422*	*41227*

Source: OECD, Development Cooperation, 1979 Review, Paris.

heading which denotes the Western capitalist world in international statistics). Table 2 shows the sharply growing share of
the whole of the Arab League in world trade in the very short
span of 8 years. If the Arab countries' share in

TABLE 2. Weight of the External Trade of the Arab League Countries

	1970	1978
Exports of the A.L. as % of international exports	5.0	9.0
Imports of the A.L. as % of international imports	3.0	7.0
Percent share of the A.L. in industrial countries exports	3.0	8.2
Percent share of the A.L. in EEC exports	5.9	14.2
Percent share of the A.L. in A.L. exports	6.0	5.3
Percent share of the A.L. in industrial countries imports	5.1	12.6
Percent share of the A.L. in EEC imports	11.7	18.5
Percent share of the A.L. in A.L. imports	9.3	7.3

Source: Deduced from Eurostat, *Analysis of Trade Between the European Community and the Arab League Countries,* Luxemburg 1980.

world exports has been increasing for a simple reason, i.e. the substantial rise in the price of oil, their share in world imports, even more important in relative terms, has been brought about by more complex considerations. It was natural enough to expect a significant rise in the imports of oil-exporting countries, if only as a result of a domestic consumer boom, the expenses of social transfers, arms etc. — or in order words, current public expenditure and the purchase of products almost immediately transferable on the soil of the importing country. But two other phenomena of unequal importance have manifested themselves. Their significance is still a subject for discussion: the extremely swift launching of very ambitious development plans and the financing of imports of all kinds (consumer goods and various kinds of equipment) from other non-oil Arab countries. Thus we may see in Table 3 that with certain exceptions (Lebanon, South Yemen, Sudan), all the Arab countries have experienced a growth in their imports

TABLE 3. Arab Countries Imports (1970-1979)

Arab Gulf countries		Imports $ million	As % of total imports		Average annual increase 1970-1979
			Food	Machinery	
Bahrain	1970	247	10.4	20.0	31.4
	1979	2300	8.0	21.6	
Iraq	1970	509	17.7	28.8	33.2
	1979	5000	15.0	48.4	
Kuwait	1970	625	19.8	35.9	32.1
	1979	5359	12.0	45.5	
Oman	1970	29	39.3	25.0	50.5
	1979	1387	17.4	38.5	
Qatar	1970	64	24.1	30.8	43.6
	1979	1425	11.5	53.5	
Saudi Arabia	1970	692	32.8	32.7	56.1
	1979	27736	12.7	41.2	
UAE	1970	267	15.6	25.6	48.5
	1979	6960	10.9	40.2	
Other Arab countries		Imports $ million	As % of total imports		Average annual increase 1970-1979
			Food	Machinery	
Algeria	1970	1257	12.8	36.5	28.5
	1979	8200	16.6	45.3	
Egypt	1970	787	32.2	26.6	28.3
	1979	3837	26.2	33.9	
Jordan	1970	184	31.0	16.9	32.8
	1979	1949	21.4	30.1	

Other Arab countries (contd.)		Imports $ million	As % of total imports		Average annual increase 1970-1979
			Food	Machinery	
Lebanon	1970	567	25.1	19.9	13.7
	1979	2400	17.6	35.5	
Libya	1970	554	22.6	29.7	31.7
	1979	7898	16.6	41.6	
Morocco	1970	686	20.7	31.7	23.9
	1979	3807	19.8	30.5	
Sudan	1970	325	21.3	26.6	18.3
	1979	1000	19.0	35.8	
Syria	1970	357	28.6	18.1	30.3
	1979	3307	17.8	29.8	
Tunisia	1970	305	27.9	26.2	29.3
	1979	2838	14.7	27.4	
Yemen AR	1970	32	62.6	8.6	58.2
	1979	1400	40.9	25.8	
PDR Yemen	1970	201	–	–	17.1
	1979	480	–	–	

Source: UNCTAD, *Handbook of International Trade and Development Statistics,*
Supplement 1980.

which greatly exceeds the world average (about 20 percent a year) over a comparable period of time (1970-79). In the same table it may be seen that a general characteristic of these imports is the relative and strongly growing importance of all kinds of capital goods. The growth of this kind of imports has been so marked that it makes the share of food imports (apart from in Algeria and Egypt) appear to be declining in relative terms. Food imports, however, as we know elsewhere, constitute one of the most dynamic sectors of overall Arab imports.[3]

From the foregoing, we may infer the growing importance of the Arab World in relation to the world economy. It is one of the few zones in the world to display this dynamism at a time when the world economy is in crisis and when a so-called "trade war" is developing. This constant threat sometimes takes the form of the urge towards protectionism and sometimes that of wild competition. The economic and political consequences are still hard to discern. Its extension into the region of the Arab World was and remains an essential phenomenon in the latter's evolution. On the other hand, the reorientation of this dynamic market towards new types of imports, such as capital goods, puts more cards into the hands of the countries which export such goods, above all the developed capitalist countries, but at the same time brings them into even sharper competition. The production of capital goods for the purpose of export represents a crucial element in the economies of these countries: it constitutes a decisive part of their overall industrial production, employment and total trade; it is necessary so that these economies may maintain an adequate rhythm in the development of research and technology, since it is exports which make this process profitable. A country's capacity to produce exportable goods is decisive in the struggle to keep or improve its place in the massive shake-up which is emerging or will emerge from the current crisis, in what has already been termed the "new international

---

[3] Michalis Papayannakis, "L'Agriculture et le Développement des Etats Méditerranéens" in Institut d'Etudes Européennes – Université Libre de Bruxelles, *La Grèce et la Communauté* (Bruxelles: Editions de l'Université de Bruxelles, 1978).

division of labour", and the "new international economic order."

This explains the exceptional effort being made by all the Western countries to maintain, reoccupy or gain important positions in Arab imports. It is perhaps still too early to make a definite judgement on the result of these efforts. However, certain changes can already be seen clearly. We have summarized these in Tables 4 and 5. Table 4 shows the geographical pattern of the imports of each Arab country for 1970 and 1979 (or adjacent years, when data for 1970 was not available). The Gulf countries have been distinguished from the other Arab countries, in order that certain trends may be better perceived. In the columns of Table 4 appear the six leading suppliers of each Arab country and the percentage (in decreasing order) that each supplier country provides to the total imports of the Arab country in question.

With this crude data we may appreciate certain changes which have recently taken place in the region. For the purposes of a more systematic appreciation, a "mark" decreasing from 6 to 1 has been attributed to the first six suppliers of each Arab country, and the total of these "marks" has been added up. The result indicates the overall performance of each country in relation to the Arab World as a whole. The figure finally attributed to each supplier is to be used with care. It is no more than a relative indicator which allows a qualitative comparison over time; it has *no* absolute value. Moreover, the index obtained in this way does not take into account either the relative importance of each Arab country in world trade or the relative distribution of imports, in absolute figures, of each Arab country. Nor does it take into consideration the proportion represented in the imports, by the first or second supplier and so on. Thus, this index cannot be used to measure the absolute importance of each supplier in Arab trade. On the other hand, it does give a general idea of the main rankings that occur among the suppliers as a whole.

TABLE 4. Main Suppliers of the Arab Countries and Their Rankings in the Imports of Each Arab Country (in %)

Arab Gulf countries		Suppliers ranking											
		1st		2nd		3rd		4th		5th		6th	
Bahrain	1970	UK	31.1	JAP	12.4	US	7.3	CHINA	5.1	NL	4.8	IND	4.2
	1978	UK	19.9	JAP	14.4	US	11.7	FRG	8.1	AUSTR	5.6	I	3.9
Iraq	1970	USSR	11.9	UK	9.1	CND	6.6	AUSTR	6.2	F	6.2	CZH	5.0
	1978	JAP	18.8	FRG	16.5	UK	7.2	F	5.5	I	5.3	US	4.9
Kuwait	1970	JAP	15.2	US	13.2	UK	11.8	FRG	8.4	I	4.8	F	4.8
	1978	JAP	19.5	US	13.2	UK	10.2	FRG	9.1	I	6.2	F	3.7
Oman	1970	UK	20.7	UAE	18.5	JAP	10.4	IND	6.0	AUSTR	5.7	NL	5.1
	1978	UK	20.7	UAE	15.7	JAP	15.5	FRG	6.4	US	6.3	IND	4.4
Qatar	1970	UK	24.2	US	10.1	JAP	9.3	LEB	6.5	IND	6.1	FRG	5.6
	1978	JAP	19.8	FRG	18.6	UK	15.7	US	10.0	F	7.3	I	4.6
Saudi Arabia	1970	US	17.8	LEB	11.3	JAP	9.8	FRG	9.8	UK	7.2	I	4.5
	1978	US	20.9	JAP	15.4	FRG	10.8	UK	7.4	I	7.1	NL	4.4
UAE	1970	UK	17.7	JAP	16.9	US	9.2	SW	8.6	IND	5.8	HK	3.4
	1978	JAP	12.6	UK	11.5	US	6.8	FRG	4.7	IND	2.4	NL	2.0

Other Arab Countries		1st		2nd		3rd		4th		5th		6th	
Algeria	1970	F	42.4	FRG	10.0	US	8.0	I	7.3	USSR	3.6	BL/LX	3.5
	1978	F	18.1	FRG	17.8	I	10.9	JAP	9.1	US	6.7	SP	4.6
Egypt	1971	USSR	13.5	FRG	7.0	I	5.6	US	5.6	F	5.2	IND	4.8
	1977	US	16.4	FRG	10.7	I	8.9	F	6.3	UK	5.8	USSR	5.6
Jordan	1971	US	23.6	UK	9.0	LEB	6.9	FRG	5.9	JAP	5.5	S A	5.5
	1978	FRG	13.1	S.A.	9.4	UK	7.9	US	7.3	JAP	6.7	I	6.6
Lebanon	1970	SW	12.1	UK	11.5	US	9.9	F	9.4	FRG	8.8	I	6.6
	1977	SW	16.8	I	10.4	F	9.7	FRG	8.1	US	6.4	UK	6.4
Libya	1970	I	21.6	US	13.8	UK	9.4	FRG	9.1	F	6.4	JAP	5.6
	1977	RFA	13.9	F	8.5	US	6.7	UK	6.5	JAP	6.0	BL/LX	4.9
Morocco	1971	F	30.7	US	14.2	USSR	7.6	I	5.9	UK	4.1	USSR	4.0
	1978	F	26.1	SP	10.3	US	8.4	FRG	6.9	I	6.6	NL	3.4
Sudan	1970	UK	14.4	IND	13.0	I	7.6	FRG	7.2	JAP	5.1	EGY	4.9
	1975	UK	22.3	JAP	14.7	F	12.4	FRG	12.4	IND	10.6	I	9.5
Syria	1970	USSR	7.7	FRG	6.8	I	6.5	IRAQ	6.4	LEB	6.3	JAP	5.8
	1978	FRG	10.7	I	8.3	F	7.5	IRAQ	7.0	RUM	7.0	JAP	5.0
Tunisa	1970	F	34.7	US	16.9	FRG	8.5	I	7.2	UK	2.9	AUS	2.3
	1978	F	33.2	FRG	11.7	I	10.0	US	4.6	GRE	4.0	SP	3.0

Other Arab Countries (contd.)		1st	2nd	3rd	4th	5th	6th
Yemen AR	1970	PDRY 24.8	USSR 9.9	AUSTR 9.8	UK 8.4	F 7.6	JAP 7.5
	1978	S A 15.9	JAP 12.7	F 5.7	FRG 5.7	PDRY 5.6	I 5.2
PDR Yemen	1970	IRAN 18.4	KUW 13.3	JAP 10.6	UAE 5.5	UK 5.5	IND 4.2
	1978	UK 13.3	JAP 10.5	KUW 9.4	NL 9.0	CHI 7.1	THAI 5.9

UK   : United Kingdom
JAP   : Japan
US   : United States
CHI   : China
NL   : Netherlands
I   : Italy
IND   : India
AUSTR   : Australia
CND   : Canada
CZH   : Czhechoslovakia
F   : France
LEB   : Lebanon

GRE   : Greece
UAE   : United Arab Emirates
SW   : Switzerland
BL/LX   : Belgium/Luxemburg
SP   : Spain
SA   : Saudi Arabia
EGY   : Egypt
RUM   : Rumania
THAI   : Thailand
AUS   : Austria
KUW   : Kuwait
HK   : Hong Kong

Source: Our calculations deduced from the *Middle East and North Africa* (London), No. 8, (1979).

TABLE 5. Distribution of the Main Suppliers of the Arab Countries According to Their "Global Performances"

	1970			1978		
	Gulf	Other	Total	Gulf	Other	Total
United Kingdom	35	29	64	32	26	58
US	24	27	51	25	24	49
France	3	27	30	6	38	44
FRG	7	34	41	26	45	71
Italy	3	24	27	8	22	30
Japan	28	11	39	38	23	61
USSR	6	24	30	—	1	1
China	3	—	3	—	2	2
Netherlands	3	—	3	2	4	6
India	8	7	15	3	2	5
Canada	4	—	4	—	—	—
Australia	5	4	9	2	—	2
UAE	5	3	8	5	—	5
Lebanon	8	6	14	—	—	—
Switzerland	3	6	9	—	6	6
Belgium/Luxemburg	—	1	1	—	1	1
Saudi Arabia	—	1	1	—	11	11
Egypt	—	1	1	—	—	—
Iraq	—	3	3	—	3	3
PDR Yemen	—	6	6	—	2	2
Iran	—	6	6	—	—	—
Kuwait	—	5	5	—	4	4
Spain	—	—	—	—	7	7
Rumania	—	—	—	—	2	2
Greece	—	—	—	—	2	2
Thailand	—	—	—	—	1	1
Austria	—	1	1	—	—	—
Hong Kong	1	—	1	—	—	—
Czechoslovakia	1	—	1	—	—	—
EEC	51	117	168	74	138	212

Source: Our calculations (See Table 4).

That said, Table 5 charts the evolution of the performances of the main supplier countries for the two benchmark years indicated for the whole of the Arab World and within it, for separate regions. The main suppliers are those which occupied one of the first six places at least once in 1970 and/or 1978. The trends indicated by this arrangement of the data may be summarised as follows:

1. The member countries of the EEC have achieved a general expansion in the Arab market during this period. Their penetration is the most significant and promising. This development is due primarily to the dynamism of West Germany, which has made a remarkable come-back in the Gulf countries. France's performance has also been substantial. It has strengthened its positions in the area of "other Arab countries." By contrast, the United Kingdom, once the main Gulf supplier, has lost ground.

2. Paradoxically, at least for those who are obsessed with oil and arms, the relative importance of the United States has remained static and it has shown little commercial dynamism.

3. The third Western "power," Japan, has achieved a leap as spectacular as that of West Germany: it has strengthened its traditional positions in the Gulf, while at the same time increasing its relative importance in the "other Arab countries."

4. Four other interesting trends are also worth mentioning:

(a) The collapse of the USSR as a trading partner even with those countries with which it still enjoys good political relations. This fact may be in the final analysis attributable to the non-correspondence of the Soviet economy and trade with the new need for imports following the oil boom (as much for consumer goods as for capital goods).

(b) The relative decline of inter-Arab relations. This fact was already apparent in the data shown in Table 2. Here it may be seen how the Arab countries supplying their neighbours disappeared from the top six places. They were probably rendered marginal for the same reasons as in the preceding case. This trend is clearly the most significant in the eyes of all who believe that there cannot be an Arab political power on the international scene without an economic base (production and trade) in the process of unification. The method used here gives only a dim picture of the relative decline of inter-Arab trade since it only takes into account the main suppliers. Other analyses[4] can give a more detailed idea of this development. In 1979, exports to other Arab countries represented 0.1% of Algeria's exports, 3.9% of Morocco's, 6.2% of Tunisia's and 2.9% of Libya's. Exports to other Arab countries were relatively important only for Syria (12.5%) and Egypt (8.3%). Recent figures for Lebanese exports are not available. The figures are a little higher for the imports of the above-mentioned countries, but they include oil and therefore do not necessarily demonstrate a form of economic cooperation different in quality to what had gone before. Finally, it may be added that the percentages given above are in nearly every case lower than those for the mid-1960's.

(c) The relative decline of other underdeveloped countries which were present in the region, such as India, no doubt for the same reasons.

(d) The arrival of new suppliers in the form of small but industrially dynamic countries favoured by proximity or history, such as Spain, Greece, and Rumania.

5. The trends delineated above confirm those which had already been observed at the beginning of the 1970's[5] not only in the Arab World but also throughout the Mediterranean region. Moreover, analagous trends have been observed in other areas bordering the region, such as Africa on the one

---

4 See for example, Eurostat, *Analysis of Trade Between the European Community and the Arab League Countries*, Luxemburg, 1980, pp. 23-28.

5 Michalis Papayannakis, "Evolution Récente des Echanges Méditerranéens", *Options Méditerranéennes*, No. 30, Paris.

hand and Eastern Europe on the other. They all correspond to the redistribution of international economic power begun in the 1960's and confirmed since then; the European Economic Community, now the leading trading power in the world, exerts its influence and attraction particularly in the Euro-Mediterranean and even the Euro-African zones. The objection might be raised that, despite these quantitative observations, the qualitative aspects of trade are playing an expanding role, with the United States and Japan occupying a dominant position in sectors which are strategic for the development of all the Arab countries. This may be especially true in the military or electronics fields, but the game of competition is increasingly open to almost any kind of product, (aeronautics, nuclear energy, automation, agro-industry, modern transportation etc.).

Elsewhere, it is claimed that this competition is of little general significance if it is compared with the particular significance of military and strategic influences in the region. The EEC is not a considerable military power, in strategic, i.e. nuclear, terms. It has neither the infrastructure nor the outlook that would give it credibility as a force of intervention and protection or of military arbitration on the spot. But this is a fringe argument, one that considers the contradictions and conflicts of the region as simple out-growths of the East-West strategic confrontation and therefore soluble only by the logic of confrontation within this framework. Thus there is an overly political tone to the analysis of international relations which greatly reduces the importance of various factors in the evolution of the region, whether these are of local or more general significance. If it is accepted that "last case" analyses are also (given the world strategic balance) analyses of the final stage of world history, it can be better understood that in the meantime it is the other, non-strategic, factors which are of more importance. Hence our interest in the economic and geographic differentiation of trade and development in the region.

The evolution of the economic relations of the Arab countries with the West appears in the final analysis to be fairly positive, given the structure of these countries. This appears to follow logically from the directions and choices which have been adopted since the 1950's with regard to the foreign policy of most of the Arab countries. Foreign policy, however, bore little relation to the social quality and economic coherence of the choices concerning each country's internal development strategy, and the development strategy of the area as a whole.

In the foregoing analysis, we might also have expounded the structural transformations undergone by exports from the Arab countries, but this would only have confirmed the picture already outlined.

As for other changes in these countries' foreign economic relations, the same characteristics appear in the majority of cases. It would clearly be of interest to make a more detailed analysis of movements of capital, but this is rather difficult at present[6] : we do not have recent, systematically arranged and comparable data available. Moreover, Western capital is playing its part in the transformation of Arab economies by different means than in the past. It is no longer direct investment in the productive sectors which is playing the main role. Local capital (state or private) and capital from other Arab countries is more frequently financing accumulation. In contrast, Western capital is playing a coordinating, stimulating or guiding role in the economic activity of quite a few Arab countries by various means, such as cooperation, triangular operations, technology transfer, organization, sharing of international markets, sub-contracting etc. Since these Arab countries have been involved

---

6 See however, Joseph Sasson, "Labour and Capital in the Mediterranean Area," *Lo Spettatore Internazionale*, XI, 1, Jan.-March 1976, Rome.

in the development process by increasingly clear participation in the international division of labour and of the world market, such links are not surprising. And in this area there have also been important shifts in recent years, in terms of sectors and the whole. However, a detailed study of them is possible only country-by-country, and sector-by-sector. We know, for example, that European capital is playing an increasingly important role in investments designed to strengthen exports to Tunisia and that, in contrast, the "game" is very open with regard to the other investments: Japanese cooperation in chemicals, French in car manufacturing, German in electronics, Arab in chemicals and tourism, etc. Similarly, we know that in the automobile sector there is at present a high-powered assault by the Japanese at the expense of the Europeans and the Americans. In general, leaving the oil industry and certain Gulf countries aside, it is European capital which is more active, although we are not in a position to specify the share of strictly transnational corporations in these activities.

By examining Table 6, however, we may get a general idea of the relations between the financial resources from various sources which are at the disposal of Arab countries. The sum of "total receipts "includes direct investments, but also (and in particular) financing of different kinds: grants, aid, long-term loans, commercial credits. This table partly confirms the preceding arguments. However, it introduces a new factor, namely finance coming from OPEC member countries, essentially Arab countries in the cases considered here. Their importance in financing certain economies (Jordan, Sudan, Syria) is decisive. This fact balances the remarks made about the weakness of trading relations. If the phenomenon lasts, it is to be hoped that it will have repercussions on trading relations. This, however, is not a foregone conclusion, particularly since the models of development prevailing in the Arab countries will continue to be designed in terms of relations

TABLE 6.   OECD, Geographical Distribution of Financial Flows to Arab World (million dollars) (% in paranthesis)

Countries	Total	Receipts	EEC		OPEC		Multilateral		USA	
	1976	1979	1976	1979	1976	1979	1976	1979	1976	1979
Iraq	−54.6 (100)	24.9	26.7	25.3	1.2	−2.0	24.4	12.5	−2.0	−1.0
Algeria	1832.4 (100)	1552.0 (100)	1282.6 (70.0)	907.0 (58.4)	33.8 (1.8)	−2.3 (−)	71.2 (3.9)	73.7 (4.7)	64.0 (3.5)	148.0 (9.5)
Egypt	2323.5 (100)	1930.1 (100)	332.2 (14.3)	538.1 (27.9)	1270.4 (54.7)	32.4 (1.7)	414.4 (17.8)	417.0 (21.6)	216.0 (9.3)	624.0 (32.3)
Jordan	557.4 (100)	1057.1 (100)	61.8 (11.1)	52.5 (5.0)	390.6 (70.1)	878.4 (83.1)	23.5 (4.2)	71.2 (6.7)	82.0 (14.7)	44.0 (4.2)
Lebanon	24.9 (100)	132.4 (100)	0.5 (2.0)	62.7 (47.4)	8.1 (32.5)	34.7 (26.2)	10.3 (41.4)	41.1 (31.0)	7.0 (28.1)	6.0 (4.5)
Morocco	657.0 (100)	774.0 (100)	385.4 (58.7)	491.8 (63.5)	101.4 (15.4)	16.5 (2.1)	70.6 (10.7)	189.6 (24.5)	95.0 (14.5)	12.0 (1.6)
Sudan	636.6 (100)	643.1 (100)	155.5 (24.4)	124.5 (19.4)	301.5 (47.4)	290.8 (45.2)	116.4 (18.2)	167.9 (26.1)	−5.0 (−)	22.0 (3.4)
Syria	587.7 (100)	1414.4 (100)	66.0 (11.2)	−15.4 (−)	458.7 (78.0)	1272.6 (90.0)	50.8 (8.6)	92.8 (6.6)	19.0 (3.2)	71.0 (5.0)
Tunisia	383.3 (100)	474.7 (100)	192.7 (50.3)	324.9 (68.5)	41.0 (10.7)	48.0 (10.1)	69.0 (18.0)	72.5 (15.3)	4.0 (1.0)	3.0 (0.6)
AR Yemen	253.8 (100)	268.7 (100)	17.2 (6.8)	99.8 (37.1)	190.6 (75.1)	115.0 (42.8)	48.8 (19.2)	45.3 (16.9)	(−) (−)	9.0 (9.3)
PDR Yemen	164.6 (100)	88.0 (100)	2.0 (1.2)	32.6 (37.0)	135.1 (82.0)	10.4 (11.8)	20.9 (12.7)	43.9 (49.9)	6.0 (3.6)	(−) (−)

only with already "developed" countries, even in competition with other Arab countries.

7. These recent developments, combined with the foregoing analysis concerning trade, offer certain objective advantages for any eventual attempt on the part of any country or group of countries to make their own choices as far as development strategy and politics are concerned. There is a gap between the trends in international politics in the world and the region, and the trends in the world economy in and because of its current crisis. The former trends arise from the logic of East-West relations, but apparently to an increasingly small degree. The latter are formed within the logic of a network of multi-polar relations, which in spite of all American efforts, do not obey the former. The possibility is therefore open to those who are willing and able to exploit these contradictions. But will and power are essentially, though admittedly not exclusively, internal questions.

2

The World Energy Balance
and the Gulf

by Pierre Terzian

To discuss a subject like the position of the Gulf in the world oil balance at a seminar which is to deal mainly with political and strategic issues, might appear a thankless task. Indeed, it presupposes having recourse to fairly extensive statistical data and constant reference to all types of projections, whose principle characteristic is that they are often belied by the facts. But this handicap is minor compared to the difficulty the Gulf presents in the political and strategic problems you are to examine. So I consider, without reservation, that this is the least hazardous job of the whole seminar.

What is the Gulf's position in the present world oil balance? Who needs oil from this area now? Who will still need it tomorrow? Will the pattern of oil interdependence of the past 10 to 20 years continue? Or will it change? Where will the Gulf be on the oil scene by the year 2000? These are some of the questions I will try and look at here.

The Past

First a few brief words on the past. The main statistics which seemed important to me in distinguishing the development over the past 20 years are given in Table 1. Here I would like to pinpoint four significant figures:

TABLE 1. Position of Gulf Area[a] in World Oil Balance 1960-1980

		1960	1970	1980	Change 1960-80
Proven Crude Oil Reserves	Gulf (million b)	182,700	345,993	360,020	
	World (million b)	300,987	611,397	648,525	
	Gulf/World (%)	60.7	56.6	55.5	− 5.2
Crude Oil Production	Gulf (thousand b/d)	5,265	13,717	18,180	
	World (thousand b/d)	20,961	45,719	59,740	
	Gulf/World (%)	25.1	30.0	30.4	+ 5.3
Oil Exports[b]	Gulf (thousand b/d)	4,794	12,957	16,879	
	World (thousand b/d)	11,142	31,332	39,339	
	Gulf/World (%)	43.0	41.3	43.7	+ 0.7
Reserve/Production Ratio	Gulf	94.8	69.1	54.2	−40.6
	World	39.2	36.6	29.7	− 9.5
	World (Gulf excluded)	20.6	22.7	20.0	− 0.6

a Gulf: Bahrein, Iran, Iraq, Kuwait, Oman, Qatar, Saudi Arabia and UAE.
b Crude oil and refined products.

Source of basic data: OPEC, Oil and Gas Journal, World Oil, Arab Oil & Gas Directory.

• The Gulf's share ·of world crude oil proven reserves fell 5.2 points between 1960 and 1980, although the area's share of oil production rose 5.3 points over the same period;
• The crude oil reserve/production ratio declined 40.6 points in Gulf countries, but only 0.6 points in 20 years throughout the rest of the world.

In other words, the oil effort demanded of the Gulf increased by more than 10 points, while its relative oil capacity dropped 43% between 1960 and 1980.

Let us now take a look at the pattern of Gulf nations' share of world oil demand over the past ten years. Table 2 shows the Gulf's importance as regards oil compared to the OECD area, Latin America, Africa and Asia (excluding Japan). There as well it can be seen that after having risen either in absolute or relative terms between 1970 and 1978, the Gulf's share of these countries' oil demand declined in 1979-80. Data for the first half of 1981 reveals that this fall continued.

Is this development transitory or, on the contrary, does it herald a pattern which will carry on and intensify in the future? This is undoubtedly the most important question. To answer it, we must examine the oil prospects of the six countries or areas listed in Table 2. However, this analysis would be incomplete without also taking account of the Soviet Union's energy outlook. Much has been said about the Soviets' concern for their energy future and here we must establish the position on the matter.

Let us begin with the United States, the dominant military and industrial power in the Gulf area.

The Position of the United States

The United States is in the process of reducing considerably its dependence on imported oil in general and Gulf oil in particular. This cutback is being achieved through energy savings, the use of substitute energy sources and above all through the development of domestic crude oil exploration

TABLE 2. Gulf's Share in World Oil Demand[a] (thousand b/d)

	1970			1978			1980		
	Total Demand	Imports from Gulf	%Gulf/ Demand	Total Demand	Imports from Gulf	%Gulf/ Demand	Total Demand	Imports from Gulf	%Gulf/ Demand
United States	14,697	225	1.5	18,847	2,115	11.2	17,030	1,666	9.8
Western Europe	12,528	5,928	47.3	14,448	8,112	56.1	13,944	6,783	48.6
Japan	3,847	3,133	81.4	5,142	3,740	72.7	4,993	3,088	61.8
Latin America	2,673	300	11.2	4,158	1,176	28.3	4,609	916	19.9
Africa	705	594	84.2	1,290	426	33.0	1,414	281	19.9
Asia and Far East[b]	2,346	1,134	48.3	3,698	2,296	62.1	4,014	2,267	56.5

[a] Data not available for socialist countries.

[b] Except Japan

Source of basic data: OPEC, *Annual Statistical Bulletin*, various years.

and production. The linchpin of this three-pronged course of action is a policy of high oil prices, both within America and abroad.

In a major speech delivered in London at a seminar held on September 28 and 29, 1981 by the *International Herald Tribune* and *The Oil Daily*, US Energy Secretary Mr James Edwards said: "Within a few years, we hope to become far less dependent on imported energy." He added: "Within not too many years, we may achieve energy self-sufficiency."[1]

The US Energy Secretary's statement is reminiscent of the ambitions of another Republican Administration, that of President Richard Nixon, as set forth in "Project Independence," which failed dismally. Because of this precedent, the NEPP (National Energy Policy Program) could be regarded with a certain scepticism, although this time the intentions expressed do correspond to concrete facts. What are these facts?

They were pointed out by Mr Edwards in his speech in London. "We are proud of the accomplishments we've made as a nation during the first eight months of the [Reagan] Administration. Last week, there were 4,249 drilling rigs at work in the US, more than at any time since the oil industry began keeping records," he said.[2]

This fact deserves further explanation. Drilling is a capital element, determining the full oil cycle. In this respect, the United States has always held a position of overwhelming superiority; during the 1970's, about 80% of the wells drilled throughout the world were located in America, while the Gulf's share stood at scarcely more than 1%.

In 1980, some 65,000 wells were drilled in the United

---

[1]   James Edwards, "Reagan Administration Energy Policy"; speech given at Oil and Money in the Eighties seminar, London, September 28 and 29, 1981; stencilled text, pp. 2 and 3.

[2] *Ibid.*, p. 1.

States, double the 1974 number, and this figure is expected to reach 75,000 in 1981.[3] Towards the end of this year or at the beginning of 1982, the number of rigs operating in the United States will touch the 5,000 mark, whereas the average in 1980 was only 2,910.

"Contrary to the prophecies of the doomsdayers, we believe that there are still enormous quantities of oil and gas waiting to be discovered and added to world reserves," said Mr. Edwards, announcing proudly that an American firm had just developed a rig capable of drilling to the amazing depth of 50,000 feet, or 15,240 meters.[4] At this depth, the structure explored is still virgin, so the geological prospects are inestimable. Furthermore, the American outer continental shelf (OCS) has scarcely been explored. The Energy Secretary recalled that, of the 1.1 billion acres over which the OCS stretches, only 20 million have been leased as oil concessions so far. American oil potential, therefore, is still enormous. The most evident sign of American companies' interest in this potential is the huge scale of investment they plan to devote to exploration. The Bankers Trust Company forecasts that American companies will invest $811.7 billion in crude oil exploration and development in the United States between 1980 and 1990, against $73.3 billion in the nuclear cycle, $46.5 billion in coal, $10 billion in synthetic fuels and only "minor" sums in solar energy.[5]

It is undoubtedly these figures which permit the Reagan Administration, in its NEPP, to project a decline in American oil imports to 4.8 million b/d in 1990 and to only 1.2 million b/d in the year 2000, compared to 6.3 million b/d in 1980 and 8.6 million b/d in 1977. At the same time, American consumption is expected to fall to 12.3 million b/d by the year 2000,

---

[3] *Energy Week* (Dallas), VII, 9 (January 26, 1981), p. 1.
[4] J. Edwards, *op. cit.,* p. 1.
[5] *Oil and Gas Journal* (Tulsa), October 12, 1981 pp. 48-49.

against 16.9 million b/d in 1980.[6]

As at January 1, 1981, US proven oil reserves were estimated at 26.4 billion barrels, which at the 1980 production rate would be sufficient for just over eight years' extraction. So, for the NEPP objectives to be met, over 40 billion barrels of crude oil would have to be discovered or developed by the year 2000. Such an effort can be sustained only if an adequate financial return is assured. The NEPP therefore estimates that the world crude oil price will rise from $37/b on average in 1980 to $52/b in 1990 and to $70/b by the year 2000, all expressed, of course, in constant 1980 dollars.

Far from abandoning its expensive oil policy worked out in the early 1970's, the United States will thus continue it even up to the end of the century; and once again, OPEC will certainly be blamed for the price rises.

The American oil companies make implementation of the NEPP contingent on this price increase. One of these companies' most eminent spokesmen, Mr John Lichtblau, Executive Director of the Petroleum Industry Research Foundation of New York, made it very clear last September. Also speaking at the "Oil and Money in the Eighties" seminar, he endorsed entirely the NEPP oil import target for 1985. But he refused to commit himself for the longer term, declaring that for 1990, all would depend on the pattern of oil prices in real terms, that is to say the increase in prices. With remarkable frankness, Mr Lichtblau said:

> The business community has of course no choice but to take the appropriate action to protect its investments and earnings. But could their and Administration actions carry with them the seed for another sharp real oil price increase in the late 1980's? I submit that while such a course is by no means inevitable, nor even the most likely, it cannot be dismissed as an unrealistic possibility.[7]

6 *Oil and Gas Journal* July 27, 1981, p. 97.

7 John Lichtblau, "US Oil Requirements in the 1980's"; speech given at Oil and Money in the Eighties seminar, London, September 28 and 29, 1981; stencilled text, p. 5.

As can be seen, Mr Lichtblau is really suggesting a joint Federal Government-oil companies programme of action.

The optimism of these forecasts contrasts strongly with all others established before the sharp oil price increases of 1979 and 1980. We know that between 1974 and 1979, organizations of all kinds indulged in an "orgy" of energy projections, which are estimated to have numbered about 150. There is obviously no question of mentioning them all. Happily for us, two American economists, Robert Stobaugh and Daniel Yergin, examined some 90 of these study forecasts and presented their conclusions in the Spring 1979 issue of *Foreign Affairs*.[8]

On the basis of these projections, the United States should be importing 14 million b/d of crude oil by the late 1980's, while the Reagan Administration's NEPP predicts imports of only 4.8 million b/d at that time. The difference is vast. To help reduce this dependence on imported oil, Stobaugh and Yergin advocated the accent being placed on energy savings, the development of alternative sources to oil and an increase in the recovery rate of oil in place, which is now around 50% in the United States, the highest in the world.[9] There is only one way to attain these objectives: real price increases. Everyone needs high oil prices, concluded Stobaugh and Yergin.[10]

It would also be interesting to compare the NEPP to the Carter Administration's last oil forecasts. Deputy Energy Secretary at the time, Mr John Sawhill, presented a statement to the American Senate Foreign Relations Committee in February 1980 on the importance of Gulf oil to the United

---

[8] Robert Stobaugh and Daniel Yergin, "After the Second Shock: Pragmatic Energy Strategies" in *Foreign Affairs* (New York), VII, 4, (Spring 1979) pp. 836-871.

[9] In some OPEC countries, the recovery rate of oil in place is only 18%.

[10] R. Stobaugh and D. Yergin, *op. cit.*, p. 869.

States.[11]   Mr Sawhill's thesis was greatly opposed to that of the NEPP. According to him, American demand for imported oil would reach 8.2 million b/d in 1985 (NEPP: 6.3 million b/d), of which the Gulf would supply 2.9 million b/d. This area's share of US oil imports would thus rise to 34% from 31% in 1979, leading to greater dependence on that area.

What conclusions can be drawn?

The Sawhill projections suffer from a double disadvantage:

• They have been overtaken by events and are starting to be belied by the facts. Since these forecasts were made, OPEC oil prices have risen by about 23% and the number of rigs has doubled in the United States. The Gulf's share of American oil imports amounted to no more than 26% in 1979 and 1980 (Sawhill predicted 31%) and OPEC supplied 22.5 million b/d to the "free world" in 1980, instead of the 29 million b/d the American official expected.

• They were established in a climate of extreme antagonism between the Carter Administration and the American oil companies, especially over taxation of windfall profits.

However, their pessimism gives them the advantage of indicating the lower limit of American possibilities and thus of supplying us with more or less the lower level of a forecast range.

In contrast, a faithful reflection of the Reagan Administration's attitude, the NEPP could suggest the upper level of the American forecast range. In its favour, nonetheless, several facts must be recognized.

• The climate of relations between American oil companies and banks on one side and the Federal Government on the other have never been so glowingly warm. And for good reason: the philosophy of the Reagan Administration fits in

11 The text of this statement was published in a special supplement entitled "US Assesses Vital Persian Gulf Oil Role," in *Petroleum Intelligence Weekly* (*PIW*), (New York), March 10, 1980, 7 pages.

exactly with the interests and aspirations of the American oil and banking worlds.

• For once, the Federal Government and oil companies seem to offer each other the means of achieving their declared aims, thanks to the increase in oil prices, the extraordinary acceleration in drilling activities and the mobilization of the necessary funds. Even the high American interest rates do not appear to be a major handicap; Bankers Trust opportunely recalls that due to domestic oil price decontrol and the rise on world markets, the American oil industry should be able to maintain and even improve its present self-financing margin, which already exceeds 65%.[12]

It seems, therefore, that the current overall balance in Gulf-United States oil relations can be expected at least to remain stable up to 1985, while the American position will probably improve considerably from 1985-1990.

So much for the United States. What about the other super-power, the Soviet Union?

The Position of the USSR

Projections on the Soviet Union's oil prospects have changed dramatically since the first CIA public report on the "International Energy Situation," published in April 1977 in Washington. It should be recalled that the report's deeply pessimistic forecasts were subsequently amended by the CIA itself and have been contradicted by several other sources.

The report stated that the USSR's oil production would soon level out, possibly in 1978 and certainly no later than at the beginning of the 1980's. Before 1985, the USSR would probably no longer be supplying oil to Eastern and Western Europe on the same scale as it had been doing and would even have to import OPEC oil for its own use. The authors

[12] *Oil and Gas Journal,* October 12, 1981, p. 48.

estimated that the Soviet Union and Eastern Europe would have to import at least 3.5 million b/d of oil by 1985. At worst, the fall in production could boost import needs to 4.5 million b/d, added the report.[13]

The CIA renewed its claims in August 1979. In a new eighty-page report, entitled "The World Oil Market in the Years Ahead," the US agency said: "The Soviet Union and the Eastern Bloc will no longer be net exporters of oil within three to four years," predicting that Soviet oil production would plateau in 1979 and 1980 and then fall "sharply."[14]

This thesis was taken up five months later in Davos, Switzerland, by Saudi Petroleum and Mineral Resources Minister Mr Ahmed Zaki Yamani. Speaking at the "European Management Forum" on February 7, 1980, Mr Yamani said: "The USSR will definitely become a net importer of oil in the 1980's" and added: "Should the USSR ever try to advance to the Gulf, this would create a military response from the US and its allies and lead to a Third World War."[15]

These predictions were contradicted in May 1980 by the Swedish Malmoe-based firm Petrostudies. "There is no danger whatsoever that the USSR will be forced to become a net importer of oil in this decade, and highly improbable it will become so in the 1990's," asserted Petrostudies, which gave the following explanation: for 13 years the benchmark prices of Soviet crude oil were maintained by the Plan at $0.75-$1.50/b, curbing costly development and recovery operations. In April 1981, affirmed the Swedish firm, these prices would rise to $17-$20/b, making way for a substantial increase in Soviet output.[16]

---

13 Taken from a French translation of the report, prepared by the Arab Petroleum Research Center, Paris, pp. 15 and 17, stencilled text.

14 "Oil Supply Risks Loom for Consumers in 1980's CIA warns," in *PIW*, September 3, 1979.

15 *PIW*, February 18, 1980, p. 9.

16 "CIA, Swedish Group Differ in Assessing Future of Soviet Oil," in *PIW*, May 19, 1980, pp. 6 and 7.

Almost simultaneously with the publication of the Petro-studies report, the CIA Director, Admiral Stansfield Turner, made a statement to the American Senate Energy Committee, modifying extensively the agency's previous projections. Admiral Turner said that Soviet oil production would reach a ceiling of 12 million b/d in 1980 and would then fall, not "sharply," but "steadily," so that by 1985, the USSR would be a net importer of at least 1 million b/d, 2.5 million b/d less than the first report forecast. The CIA Director was also pessimistic about the OECD area's oil outlook; this double evolution, according to him, would "set the stage for an East-West competition for Middle Eastern oil." He concluded that the "struggle for energy supplies will ... create a severe test of the cohesiveness of both the Western and Eastern alliances."[17]

Nine months later, Saudi Minister Yamani also changed his tune. In a lecture given on January 31, 1981 at the Petroleum and Minerals University in Dammam, he said that the USSR "will definitely be importing oil sometime in the eighties, most probably in 1987," suggesting the figure of 1 million b/d for the volume of these imports and drawing the same conclusion as Admiral Turner: "At this point, the dangers of East-West confrontation will multiply." Mr Yamani added: "The main area of such a struggle will be the oil sources."[18]

In summer 1981, came a new dramatic turn. This time it was the Defense Intelligence Agency (DIA) itself, which took an opposite stance to that of its counterpart, the CIA. The DIA report was presented on July 8, 1981 to the American Congressional Joint Energy Committee by the agency's Deputy Director, Major-General Richard Larkin, but was not made public

---

[17] "The CIA Reassesses the Geopolitics of Oil," in *PIW*, May 19, 1980; special supplement, pp. 1-4.

[18] "Yamani Takes a Look at the Future for Oil," in *PIW*, March 9, 1981; special supplement, pp. 1-4.

until the following September 3. The DIA predicted that the "Soviet Union will continue to be the world's largest oil producer and remain a net oil exporter for the foreseeable future." Noting that the USSR had met its 1980 production target of a little over 12 million b/d, the DIA said output could reach 12.4 million b/d to 12.9 million b/d in 1985, stabilize towards the end of the 1980's and start rising again from 1990.[19]

The latest available document in this series of forecasts for the USSR is the paper given at the end of September 1981 in London, by Mr Anthony Scanlan of the British Petroleum International, during the seminar "Oil and Money in the Eighties."[20] Mr Scanlan gave a detailed analysis, area by area and sometimes field by field, of Soviet oil potential. He considered it "premature" to forecast "a decline" in the USSR's oil production and even said: "The prospect for another super giant field in Western Siberia... cannot be ruled out." Mr Scanlan believes the oil targets of the Soviet Eleventh Plan could be reached; the plan calls for production of 620 to 645 million tons of crude oil by 1985, which would leave an exportable surplus of 80 to 155 million tons. The author himself advanced some projections for 1990; he suggested that the USSR would then be able to produce 600 to 675 million tons of crude and would therefore be able to export 30 to 150 million tons/year. In conclusion, he stressed the USSR's determination "to remain self-sufficient in energy, in each major type of primary energy."

So it seems that the present status quo in Gulf-USSR oil relations can be expected to be maintained overall, with

[19] "US Study Sees Rise in Soviet Energy Output," in *USICA Wireless File* (Paris), Nos. 172, 173, pp. 15-21.

[20] Anthony Scanlan, "Outlook for Soviet Oil" speech given at Oil and Money in the Eighties seminar, London, September 28 and 29, 1981; stencilled text, 11 pages.

Moscow purchasing crude oil from time to time under barter deals, three-way transactions including oil, or possible support to a "client" state through crude liftings. The USSR will probably not "vitally" need Gulf oil, as has been the case historically for several industrialized or developing countries, and will remain at least self-sufficient in oil, if not a net exporter.

As far as the socialist countries regarded as a bloc are concerned, for several years they have imported about 350,000 b/d of crude oil produced in the Gulf. A slight increase in this quantity cannot be ruled out, but its share will remain negligible, as it represents barely 1.5% of the Gulf nations' present export capacity.

Western Europe, Japan and Developing Countries

Forecasts on the oil prospects for Western Europe and Japan are much less divergent and contradictory. All sources agree that the two areas will remain greatly reliant on oil imports and that the Gulf will cover more than half of them.

The most consistent projections concern Japan. Those established by Mr John Sawhill in early 1980, discussed earlier,[21] give the country an oil import level of 6.3 million b/d in 1985, of which 73% or 4.6 million b/d would be covered by the Gulf. The latest available document from the International Energy Agency (IEA), published in April 1981 in Paris,[22] predicts that Japan will be importing 6.5 million b/d of oil by 1985. The IEA expects this level of imports to be maintained up to 1990, but gave no particular detail on the Gulf.[23] Japan has no domestic oil production and depends entirely on

---

[21] See footnote 11.

[22] International Energy Agency, "Energy Policies and Programmes of IEA countries," *1980 Review*, Paris; OECD, 1981.

[23] *Ibid*, p. 16. Original IEA figures, supplied in metric tons, have been converted into b/d on the basis of 50 tons/year per 1 b/d.

imports to meet its oil needs.

The divergences are more serious in the case of Western Europe. Mr Sawhill expects the region's oil imports to amount to 12.5 million b/d by 1985, of which 7.8 million b/d (62%) would come from the Gulf, against 12.8 million b/d and 8 million b/d (63%) in 1979 respectively. According to the IEA, Western Europe's oil imports in 1985 will be lower, neighboring the 10 million b/d mark, against 12.2 million b/d in 1979. For 1990, the IEA estimates West European imports at 11.4 million b/d. In addition, the Agency forecasts that the United Kingdom and Norway will supply 0.7 million b/d of oil to the rest of Western Europe in 1985, but that this volume will fall to 0.2 million b/d by 1990, when only Norway will continue to export to other European countries.

Western Europe's own oil potential will probably remain modest in coming years. The American firm Hughes Tool, an authority on the subject, said recently that only 209 rigs were in operation on June 29, 1981 in this area, against 181 on June 30, 1980, which is negligible compared to the United States.[24] The magazine *World Oil* predicts that some 962 wells will be drilled in Western Europe in 1984, whereas the figure for the United States should then approach 86,000.[25]

Now we come to the developing countries (LDCs), which are not OPEC members and are located outside the Gulf area. In this group, oil demand continued to rise between 1978 and 1980, while it declined in all industrialized nations. Table 2 shows that oil demand in the United States, Japan and Western Europe dropped by 6.4% from 1978 to 1980, whereas in Africa, Latin America and Asia, it increased by 9.7%,

The Gulf supplied 3.5 million b/d of oil to these three areas

[24] "International Active Rig Tally Climbs to 5,601," in *Oil and Gas Journal*, August 3, 1981, pp. 68 and 69.

[25] R.E. Carlile, "Forecasting Worldwide Seismic Activity," *World Oil (Houston)*, February 15, 1981, p. 36.

in 1980, against 3.9 million b/d in 1978. But its share in covering their oil demand slid from 42.6% to 34.5%, while production of the three areas under review rose meanwhile by more than 40%, thanks notably to the contribution of countries such as Mexico and Egypt.

Indications are that developing countries' oil consumption during the next 10 to 20 years will increase in line with their economic development efforts. Developing nations' oil consumption remains extremely low; in 1978 it hardly reached 0.45 barrel per capita, against 16.3 barrels per capita in Japan and 31.5 barrels per capita in the United States. Although these two countries cannot necessarily serve as development models for LDCs, a comparison between their oil consumption indices and those of under-developed nations speaks for itself.

The IEA also predicts a relatively fast increase in Third World countries' consumption between now and 1985-1990.[26] This consumption (OPEC included) would rise from 10.2 million b/d in 1979 to 14.4 million b/d in 1985 and 18.3 million b/d in 1990. It can therefore be estimated that non-OPEC developing countries' oil consumption could reach 11.3 million b/d in 1985 and 14.4 million b/d in 1990.

What about their own production? LDCs' oil potential is undoubtedly the least exploited in the world. So, all depends on the scale that oil exploration will (or will not) assume in these countries during coming years. However, these prospects are extremely uncertain. If we take Africa as an example, the least developed continent in the oil sphere, according to the World Oil study already quoted,[27] the number of drillings in this area should jump 86% between 1977 and 1984, against only 20% in the Middle East. However, despite renewed activity over the past few years, a levelling off can be noted

[26] See IEA, *1980 Review,* p. 18.
[27] R.E. Carlile, *op.cit.*

between 1980 and 1981. According to statistics of the Hughes Tool Company, the number of rigs remained unchanged or even fell slightly between the end of June 1980 and the end of June 1981.[28] In fact, faced by countries extremely short of technical capacity as well as financial means, the oil companies consider themselves in a strong position to market their services to the hilt, demanding production terms incomparably more profitable for them than in other regions, such as the Gulf or North Sea. Last September, Mobil Oil Corporation President Mr William Tavoulareas openly threatened Third World countries that his company would cut back on oil exploration if these countries persisted in demanding revenues per barrel as high as in the OPEC area.[29] Mr Tavoulareas omitted to say that in 1980, while the government's receipt per barrel of oil produced reached an average of $27 in OPEC countries, it remained lower than $16 in nations such as the Congo.

The IEA estimated that non-OPEC LDCs' oil output could rise from 5.2 million b/d in 1979 to 8.7 million b/d in 1985 and to 10.5 million b/d in 1990. Exxon suggests the figure of 12 million b/d for 1990,[30] while the US State Department gives a production range for 1985 of 7.2 to 9.4 million b/d.[31] Between 1985 and 1990, LDCs should thus import 2 to 4 million b/d of crude oil to cover their needs.

Return to the Gulf

In summary, it could be said that the role of the Gulf in the

[28] "International Active Rig Tally Climbs to 5,601," *Oil and Gas Journal, Op. cit.*

[29] William Tavoulareas, "Some Unresolved Problems in Foreign Oil Development"; speech given at Oil and Money in the Eighties seminar, London, September 28 and 29, 1981; stencilled text.

[30] "World Energy Outlook," in *PIW* special supplement, March 24, 1980, 8 pages.

[31] "US Assesses," in *PIW op. cit.*

OECD and LDCs' oil supplies will probably remain important up to 1985 and to the end of the decade. From 1990, however, the United States could start to be much less dependent on this area as regards oil. Furthermore, it is very unlikely that the USSR will have vital need of Gulf oil in the foreseeable future.

During the last decade of this century, we may find ourselves confronted by a totally paradoxical situation: Western Europe, Japan and, to a lesser extent, LDCs, may remain heavily dependent on the Gulf for their oil imports, while militarily the area could come under increasingly antagonistic pressure from both the United States and the USSR.

But these considerations make us lose sight of the essential point: no-one is more dependent on Gulf oil than the Gulf itself. The countries bordering this strip of water draw 70% to 95% of their budget revenues from oil exports. Less than a year ago, Mr Walter Levy was worried that 60% of Gulf oil was exported from only three ports, with eight pumping stations regulating the flow of oil to these ports.[32] Today, 70% of Gulf oil is exported from one port alone – Ras Tannura.

Security concerns have prompted the countries of the area to launch immense projects in order to increase the number of sea outlets for oil and to establish them as far away as possible from the Gulf and the Strait of Hormuz. Iraq was the first to build a strategic oil pipeline, enabling the country to move its oil either to the Gulf, the Syrian-Lebanese coast or the Turkish port of Ceyhan. Saudi Arabia has laid a pipeline – Petroline – linking the fields in its eastern province to the Red Sea; it is now planning the construction on the same coast of a giant 1.5 billion barrel underground storage facility, capable of withstanding air raids. Kuwait and Iraq are also considering

---

[32] Walter Levy, "Oil and the Decline of the West," *Foreign Affairs*, Summer 1980, pp. 999-1015.

TABLE 3. Drilling of Oil Wells: a Gulf/United States Comparison

		World Total	United States Wells	% of Total	Gulf Wells	% of Total
1972	Exploration	10,540	7,539		52	
	Total	36,501	28,755	78.8	386	1.0
1973	Exploration	10,974	7,466		33	
	Total	36,586	27,602	75.4	525	1.4
1974	Exploration	11,699	8,619		36	
	Total	41,815	32,893	78.7	589	1.4
1975	Exploration	12,180	9,214		35	
	Total	45,959	37,235	81.0	539	1.2
1976	Exploration	12,959	9,234		65	
	Total	52,136	41,455	79.5	585	1.1
1977	Exploration	n.a.	n.a.		n.a.	
	Total	57,428	46,479	80.9	569	1.0
1978	Exploration	15,248	10,677		n.a.	
	Total	61,122	48,513	79.4	529	0.9

Source: *International Petroleum Encyclopedia,* various editions.

pipeline projects to give them access to the Red Sea by crossing Saudi territory.

Finally Iran, said to have learnt from the experience of its war with Iraq, and in order no longer to depend almost exclusively on the Kharg installations, is believed to be considering the possibility of building a new oil terminal further south, either at the same level as the Lavan field or below the Strait of Hormuz towards the Indian Ocean.

It goes without saying that none of these extremely costly facilities have had, or ever will have, any economic justification whatsoever, just as over 50% of Gulf countries' oil exports have no economic justification, from the point of view of these nations' financial needs.[33] Former US Ambassador to Saudi Arabia, Mr James Akins, said recently that the Kingdom could easily finance its development plans from crude oil production of 3 million b/d.[34] The "authorized" oil output ceiling is officially 8.5 million b/d, but Riyadh often allows the level to go beyond 10 million b/d, when crises arise or when it wants to exert pressure on its OPEC partners. For his part, Mr Akins stated that Saudi Arabia raised its output to such a high level simply because the United States asked it to do so.[35] It is known that this policy is increasingly contested even in Saudi Arabia itself. Not all the Saudis understand the point of depleting their country's main natural resources in this way, while inflation erodes the buying power of their financial investments. At the same time, it can be argued that expending oil revenues on military gadgets and luxury expenditures threatens social peace, which is particularly risky while the Palestinian question has still not been settled.

For several years, the Saudi leaders have delighted in talking about the "sacrifice" the country has made to meet world oil needs and to help Western economies check price increases. According to Mr Akins, only a third of Saudi oil production would be enough to cover Riyadh's financial needs; the remaining two-thirds are therefore "sacrificed." But even if we estimate that "only" 50% of crude output is "sacrificed," this

---

[33] Adnan al-Janabi, "The Supply of OPEC Oil in the 1980's," *OPEC Review* (Vienna), Summer 1980.

[34] James Akins, "The Influence of Politics on Oil Pricing and Production Policies,"; speech given at Oil and Money in the Eighties seminar, September 28 and 29 1981, London; stencilled text p. 3.

[35] *Ibid.* p. 4.

gives the fantastic figure of 11 billion barrels of oil reserves depleted between 1974 and 1980 for the sake of political altruism. On the basis of the 8.5 million b/d "authorized" production level, this 50% would become a total of 42 billion barrels in 25 years. As a point of comparison, 42 billion barrels are equal to all the oil discovered so far since the start of the oil era in a country the size of Iraq or Venezuela.

Let us now look at the other aspect of the Saudi sacrifice — the low crude oil pricing policy. This policy started in January 1977, so as to create a gap between Saudi oil prices and those charged by the other OPEC member countries and the North sea producers. Its cost is colossal. Between January 1 1977 and June 30, 1981, the Saudi loss in earnings resulting from this policy exceeded $20 billion, equal to the combined oil revenues of two countries the size of Indonesia and Algeria in 1980.[36] Mr Yamani justified this policy on the grounds of preventing oil being replaced too quickly by alternative energy sources, which would definitely occur, according to him, if oil prices rose too far and too fast. "If we force Western countries to invest heavily in finding alternative sources of energy, they will," he told students at the Dammam University of Petroleum and Minerals in January 1981. "This would take no more than seven to ten years and would result in reducing dependence on oil as a source of energy to a point which would jeopardize Saudi Arabia's interests," added Mr. Yamani.[37]

This reasoning was denied strongly by Mr. Akins, who claims to know well Saudi leaders' thinking. In his speech in London, already mentioned, Mr. Akins said: "The Saudis know they will be able to sell the oil for as long as they have it. Attempts to frighten them by the spectre of their sitting in

---

[36] Pierre Terzian, "Saudi Arabia's Loss in Earnings Amounts to Over $20 Billion As a Result of Its Pricing Policy," *Arab Oil and Gas* (Paris), No. 236 (July 16, 1981, pp. 20-22.

[37] "Yamani Takes a Look," in *PIW, op. cit.*

pools of oil forever are not successful in Saudi Arabia.... Many countries in the world, including major industrialized nations (France, Germany, Japan, Italy) will need to import liquid hydrocarbons for as long as the Saudis will have them."[38] Moreover, Mr. Yamani himself said in February 1980 in Davos, Switzerland: "No alternative in sight can quantitatively replace oil."[39] One can only speculate as to the intention behind the minister's statements to students at the University of Petroleum in Dammam.

Whatever the case, it would be naive for the countries which depend so heavily on Gulf oil to consider the present Saudi policy as eternal, irrespective of whichever regime is in power in Riyadh. This issue is particularly important as none of the other major producers in the area − Iran, Iraq or Kuwait − seems to be endowed with a spirit of sacrifice that even distantly resembles that of the Saudi Kingdom. If they had had such a spirit, moreover, the American press would have discouraged it long ago. As a *Washington Post* editorialist wrote in July 1979: "It is enough for the United States to pay once (for Saudi oil), in dollars. It is bad policy to accept uncritically the notion that it must pay a second time, in 'friendship'." He added, bluntly: " 'Friendship' is a poor foundation for policy."

[38] James Akins, *op. cit.*, p. 5.
[39] *PIW*, February 18, 1980, p. 9.

3

The Global Arms Build-up

by Frank Barnaby

The Soviet-American arms race is about to take yet another great leap forward. This new spiral in the arms race will be by far the most dangerous to date. It may move the nuclear arms race so far out of the control of the political leaders that it will be exceedingly difficult to bring it back under control, even given the political will to do so.

For one thing, large numbers of nuclear weapons will be deployed which will be seen as useful for fighting a nuclear war but useless for nuclear deterrence. Military technology is also developing a number of weapons systems which will strengthen the perception that nuclear war is fightable and winnable.

The USA and the USSR have become very nervous about the situation in the Middle East and Persian Gulf areas. The USA, for example, believes that it may have to bolster up some of the regimes there by military force, and may even have to use military force to defend the West's oil supplies. The US is, therefore, building up a rapid deployment force which, at a time of crisis, could be transported to a trouble spot. A number of ships are being pre-positioned at appropriate locations, like Diego Garcia in the Indian Ocean, so that they can sail to crisis areas to meet the troops flown in from the US. The ships are loaded with munitions, supplies and heavy weapons.

All of this costs money. As indeed does the purchase of new conventional weapons in general. The US has convinced itself that it must rearm to counter what Washington believes is a newly-acquired Soviet military superiority. And anxiety over the situation in Poland and Afghanistan has increased demands for more military spending. It is hardly surprising, then, that the American military budget will rise sharply over the next few years.

Having achieved what for all intents and purposes is military parity with the West, it is not likely that the USSR will allow itself to slip behind again in military power and risk another humiliation like the one it experienced during the 1962 Cuban missile affair. We can,therefore, be sure that any significant rise in American military spending will be more or less matched by an increase in Soviet military spending.

Third World military spending has been rising fast in recent years, albeit from a relatively low base. In fact, during the 1970's, the Third World (excluding China) share of total world military expenditure increased from about 4 per cent to 16 per cent. There is no reason to believe that this rate of increase will ease off. For the next few years, then, total world military expenditure can be expected to increase sharply.

World Military Spending

For many years now, world military spending, in real terms, has increased at a rate of about 2 per cent a year. During the past decade, according to SIPRI figures, the world has spent on military activities about $4 million million (in constant 1978 prices, to take inflation into account). World military spending is now in excess of $500 thousand million a year.

NATO

NATO countries have committed themselves to a 3 per cent annual real growth in military spending. But most NATO European countries (with the exception of the UK, Luxemburg, and Portugal) have failed to reach this goal.

According to US Defense Secretary Caspar W. Weinberger, this year's US military budget ($162,000 million) will be 12 per cent higher, in real terms, than last year's budget and next year's budget will be 15 per cent higher, in real terms, than this year's. The proposed 1986 budget — a whopping $343,000 million a year — will be about 43 per cent higher, in real terms, than this year's budget. These increases are unprecedented in peace-time.

It seems that one of President Reagan's ambitions is to expand rapidly the US Navy. The Navy wants a 600-ship fleet headed by fifteen aircraft-carrier battle groups, instead of today's fleet of 530 ships headed by twelve carrier battle groups. The Reagan Administration may well give the Navy what it wants. Altogether eighteen new ships will be added to the US fleet in Fiscal Year 1981 and thirty-three new ones, including reactivated vessels, in 1982.

According to Admiral Holcomb, the director of the US Navy's programme planning, the Navy would have to buy about seventeen ships and 330 aircraft each year, at a cost of $16,000 million a year, just to maintain today's fleet. Throughout the past decade the Navy has, on average, bought fifteen ships and 247 aircraft a year.

The purpose of huge surface battleships in today's world is puzzling. They are such enormous targets that they would be very soon destroyed in war by anti-ship missiles, which are now very accurate and reliable. Presumably, the super-powers go in for big fleets of large warships simply to be able to project their political power worldwide during peacetime.

America is increasing its military strength at the expense of its economic strength. This may prove to be a very foolish move. Not only will it increase tensions with American society but an economically weak America will have much less influence worldwide, irrespective of its military power.

High levels of military spending fuel inflation and increase unemployment. American labour productivity is alarmingly low, mainly because a large fraction of America's top scientists and engineers work only on military science. This year, military research and development will be funded by nearly $17,000 million, almost as much as the government will give for peaceful research.

THE WARSAW TREATY ORGANIZATION

The Soviet Union may also be having difficulty in persuading its allies in the Warsaw Treaty Organization (WTO) to "share more of the defence burden." The only other WTO country which shows any willingness to increase its military spending significantly is the German Democratic Republic. Over the last three years, from 1977 to 1980, East German military expenditure appears to have risen, in real terms, by some 25 per cent. The figures for the other countries seem roughly constant − except for Poland, where there may have been a fall.

The military budget of the USSR itself remains a mystery, due to Soviet secrecy about most military matters. On the one hand, there is the CIA dollar estimate, which claims that Soviet military expenditure is about 50 per cent higher than that of the United States. On the other hand, there is the Soviet official figure in roubles which, when converted into dollars at the official exchange-rate, implies that Soviet military spending is about one-fifth that of the United States. Neither of these figures gives a credible comparison of the military spending of the two countries. Given the roughly equal size of their arsenals, the best assumption is that they each spend about the same on the military.

MIDDLE EAST MILITARY SPENDING

During the past decade Middle East countries have increased their military spending by a factor of about 3.4, in real terms. The region is spending about $350 per capita a year on the military. This is about three times the world figure.

Some Middle East countries spend much more than the average on the military. According to SIPRI figures, Saudi Arabia spends annually about $2,700 per capita, the United Arab Emirates about $1,700, Oman about $1,200, Kuwait about $950, and Israel about $700.

The military expenditures of Egypt and Israel are about the same now, in real terms, as they were ten years ago. Iran increased its military budget nearly six times between 1971 and 1979. But since 1976 it has more than halved its military spending. Iraq increased its military spending 2.8 times between 1971 and 1979. Kuwait is spending about 2.6 times more on the military as it did ten years ago. Oman has increased its military budget by a factor of 19 during the decade, and Saudi Arabia and Syria have increased theirs by a factor of about 9. But the record goes to the United Arab Emirates which has increased its budget by 56 times since 1974.

The Middle East contains less than 3 per cent of the world's population. But it accounts for more than 8 per cent of total world military expenditures.

Arms Production and Trade

According to SIPRI figures, the international trade in conventional armaments increased dramatically over the past decade. New suppliers and recipients entered the arms market, the weapons supplied became more sophisticated and expensive, and the chances of controlling the arms trade diminished even further. For all intents and purposes, the global arms trade is out of control.

About 140 wars or armed conflicts have taken place in the world since World War II. Approximately fifty of these took place during the past decade. These wars were fought almost exclusively in the Third World and, with few exceptions, using weapons supplied by the industrialized countries.

About $130,000 million a year is being spent on arms worldwide. The arms business is the world's second biggest, following oil. Some $35,000 million worth of arms are traded globally.

The major suppliers of arms are the United States and the Soviet Union. They alone accounted for some 75 per cent of the total export of major weapons (aircraft, missiles, armoured vehicles and warships) during the 1970's. But the share of the other arms suppliers is steadily increasing. France, Italy, West Germany and the United Kingdom accounted for approximately 22 per cent of the total arms exports during the past decade — a substantial increase compared to previous post-war decades.

Another new trend is a marked increase in production in and export from Third World countries. Licence production agreements with industrialized countries and various forms of technological assistance allowed some Third World countries to acquire the design capacity necessary for large-scale arms production. The main Third World weapon producers are currently Israel, India, Brazil, South Africa and Argentina.

At present, the Third World contribution to the global export of major arms is small — 2 or 3 per cent of the total. But the share is rising. Due to relatively small production costs, major arms produced in Third World countries are particularly attractive to other Third World countries. Third World countries (such as Argentina, Brazil and Israel), therefore, usually export arms to other Third World countries.

The bulk (about 75 per cent) of the arms exported by the industrialized countries go to the Third World. The Middle East was by far the largest arms importing region, accounting

for 48 per cent of total Third World arms imports over the
past decade. In this region, conflicts coincide with great-power
strategic interests and competition for the oil resources of the
region. The oil wealth of many Middle East countries facil-
itates the purchase of the most sophisticated weapon systems.
Six of the eight largest Third World major-weapon importing
countries during the decade are in the Middle East.

The Far East and Africa each account for another 20 per
cent or so of Third World arms imports during the past decade.
The value of the weapons imported by African countries is
increasing particularly rapidly.

The Soviet and American Nuclear Arsenals

American *strategic* nuclear forces carry about 9,800 nuclear
warheads, with a total explosive power equivalent to that of
about 3,400 million tons of high explosive. Soviet strategic
nuclear forces would deliver about 8,000 nuclear warheads,
with a total explosive power equivalent to that of about 4,200
million tons of high explosive. In the tactical nuclear arsenals
there are probably about 35,000 nuclear warheads –
about 20,000 American and about 15,000 Soviet – each on
average several times more powerful than the Hiroshima bomb.
These add another 4,500 or so million tons of high-explosive
equivalent to make a grand total of about 12,000 million
tons – the equivalent of about 1,000,000 Hiroshima bombs, or
about three tons of TNT for every man, woman and child on
earth.

Strategic nuclear weapons are deployed on intercontinental
ballistic missiles (ICBM's), submarine-launched ballistic missiles (SLBM's), and strategic bombers. Soviet and American
ICBM's have ranges of about 11,000 km, modern SLBM's have
ranges of about 7,000 km., and strategic bombers have ranges
of about 12,000 km. Range is the main distinguishing feature
between strategic and tactical nuclear weapons – the former
having long (intercontinental) ranges.

Some ballistic missiles carry multiple warheads. Modern multiple warheads are independently targetable on targets hundreds of kilometres apart. These are called multiple independently targetable re-entry vehicles or MIRV's.

Strategic bombers carry free-fall nuclear bombs and air-to-ground missiles fitted with nuclear warheads. The most modern of these missiles is the American air-launched cruise missile (ALCM) which can fly over a range of about 2,500 km.

The United States now has 1,653 ballistic missiles (1,053 ICBM's and 600 SLBM's) of which 1,070 (550 ICBM's and 520 SLBM's) are fitted with MIRV's. Some 340 B-52's are operational as long-range strategic bombers.

The Soviet Union has deployed 2,348 ballistic missiles (1,398 ICBM's and 950 SLBM's), of which about 1,010 (818 ICBM's and 192 SLBM's) are MIRVed. About 150 of its long-range bombers are probably assigned strategic roles.

Tactical nuclear weapons are deployed in a wide variety of systems – including, howitzer and artillery shells, ground-to-ground ballistic missiles, free-fall bombs, air-to-ground missiles, anti-aircraft missiles, atomic demolition munitions (land mines), submarine-launched cruise missiles, submarine-launched ballistic missiles, torpedoes, naval mines, and anti-submarine rockets. Land-based systems have ranges varying from about twelve km. (artillery shells) to a few thousand km. (intermediate range ballistic missiles). The explosive power of these warheads varies from about 100 tons to about a megaton.

The US deploys tactical nuclear weapons in Western Europe, Asia, and the United States, and with the Atlantic and Pacific fleets. The USSR deploys its tactical nuclear weapons in Eastern Europe, in the Western USSR, and East of the Urals.

FUTURE DEVELOPMENT IN THE NUCLEAR ARSENALS

Although, according to present plans, there will be signi-

TABLE 1. US Strategic Delivery Capability (mid-1981)

Vehicle	Number of delivery vehicles deployed	Number of warheads per delivery vehicle	Total delivery capability (number of warheads)	Total yield per delivery vehicle (Mt.)	Total delivery capability (Mt.)	Estimate CEP (m.)
MIRVed vehicles						
Minuteman III	450	3	1,350	0.51	230	300
Minuteman III (Mk 12A)	100	3	300	1.05	105	200
Poseidon C-3[a]	320	10[b]	3,200	0.4	128	500
Trident C-4[a]	200	8	1,600	0.8	160	500
Sub-total	1,070		6,450		623	
Non-MIRVed vehicles						
B-52 (SRAMS + bombs)	150[c]	12[d]	1,800	5.6	840	180
B-52 (bombs)	190[c]	4[d]	760	4	760	180
Titan II	53	1	53	9	477	1,300
Minuteman II	450	1	450	1.5	675	400
Polaris A-3[a]	80	3	240	0.6	48	900
Sub-total	923		3,303		2,780	
TOTAL	1,993		9,753[e]		3,423	

[a] SLBM

[b] Average figure

[c] Including heavy bombers in storage, etc. there are 573 strategic bombers.

[d] Operational loading. Maximum loading per aircraft may be eleven bombs, each of about one megaton.

[e] Of these, 7,033 are independently targetable warheads on ballistic missiles (2,153 on ICBM's and 4,880 on SLBM's.) Ballistic missiles carry 53% of the megatonnage, 43% on ICBM's and 10% on SLBM's, and bombers carry 47%.

ficant increases in the number of warheads in the Soviet and American arsenals over the next few years, mainly because of the deployment of more MIRVed ICBM's and SLBM's and cruise missiles, the most important development in nuclear weapons in the foreseeable future will be qualitative improvements. There are so many nuclear weapons in the arsenals that any further increases in numbers will, in any case, make no sense, from a military or from any other point of view. This has been true for years now.

The most important qualitative advances in nuclear weapons are those which improve the accuracy and reliability of nuclear weapon systems.

MODERNIZATION OF US AND SOVIET STRATEGIC NUCLEAR WEAPONS

The accuracy of a nuclear warhead is normally measured by its circular error probability (CEP), the radius of the circle centred on the target within which a half of a large number of warheads, fired at the target, will fall. In both the US and the USSR, the CEP's of ICBM's and SLBM's are being continually improved. In the US, for example, improvements are being made in the computer of the NS-20 guidance system in the Minuteman III ICBM's, involving better mathematical descriptions of the in-flight performances of the inertial platform and accelerometers, and better pre-launch calibration of the gyroscopes and accelerometers. With these guidance improvements, the CEP of the Minuteman III will probably decrease from about 350 to about 200 metres. At the same time the Mark-12 re-entry vehicle and the W62 170-kiloton nuclear warhead are being replaced with the Mark-12A re-entry vehicle and the W78 350-kiloton nuclear warhead. The plan is to put the new warheads on 300 of the existing 550 Minuteman III missiles. The Mark-12A will have roughly the same weight, size, radar cross-section and aerodynamic characteristics as the Mark-12.

Mark-12A warheads with the higher accuracy will be able to

TABLE 2.   Soviet Strategic Missile Delivery Capability (mid-1981)

Vehicle	Number of delivery vehicles deployed	Number of warheads per delivery vehicle	Total delivery capability (number of warheads)	Total yield per delivery vehicle (Mt.)	Total delivery capability (Mt.)	Estimated CEP (m.)
MIRVed vehicles						
SS-17	150	4	600	2	300	300-600
SS-18	308	8	2,464	5	1,540	300-600
SS-19	360	6	2,160	3	1,080	330-450
SS-N-18[a]	192	3	576	0.6	115	550-1,000
Sub-total	1,010		5,800		3,035	
Non-MIRVed vehicles						
SS-11	230	1	230	1	230	1,000-1,800
SS-11 (MRV)	290	3	870	0.6	174	
SS-13	60	1	60	1	60	
SS-N-5[a]	18	1	18	1	18	
SS-N-6[a]	166	1	166	1	166	1,000-2,500
SS-N-6[a] (MRV)	272	3	816	0.6	163	1,400
SS-NX-17[a]	12	1	12	1	12	500
SS-N-8[a]	290	1	290	1	290	1,000-1,500
Sub-total	1,338		2,462		1,113	
TOTAL	2,348		8,262[b]		4,148	

[a] SLBM

[b] Of these, 7,138 are independently targetable (5,804 on ICBM's and 1,334 on SLBM's). ICBM's carry 81% of the total megatonnage, and SLBM's carry the remaining 19%.

destroy Soviet ICBM's in silos hardened to about 1,500 psi (pounds per square inch) with a probability of about 57 per cent for one shot and about 95 per cent for two shots. Superior arming and fuzing devices will provide more control over the height at which the warhead is exploded and, hence, the damage done.

The upgraded land-based ICBM force will significantly increase US nuclear-war fighting capabilities. These will be further increased by the MX missile system, now under development.

The MX system includes both a new ICBM and a related basing scheme. The guidance for the MX missile will probably be based on the advanced inertial reference sphere (AIRS), an "all-attitude" system which can correct movements of the missile along the ground before it is launched. A CEP of about 100 m. should be achieved with this system. If the MX warhead is provided with terminal guidance, using a laser or radar system to guide the warhead on to its target, CEP's of a few tens of metres may be possible.

No decision has yet been made about the yield and other characteristics of the MX warhead but each missile will probably carry ten warheads.

The launch-weight of the MX will probably be about 86,000 kg., about 2.4 times more than that of the Minuteman III, and the throw-weight about 3,500 kg. The three MX booster stages will use advanced solid propellants, very light motor cases, and advanced nozzles to produce nearly twice the propulsion efficiency of the Minuteman.

The MX missile, by design, could fit into the existing Minuteman silos. But, if deployed, a mobile basing system will probably be used. The first missiles will probably be operational in 1986.

The most formidable Soviet ICBM is the SS-18, or the RS-20 in Soviet terminology. This is thought currently to have a CEP of about 500 m. This accuracy will probably improve to about 250 m within a few years. Each SS-18 warhead probably has an explosive power equivalent to about 500 kilotons. With the higher accuracy, the warhead will have about the same silo-destruction capability as the new US Minuteman III warhead.

The USSR also has the SS-19 ICBM (the RS-18). This is thought to be more accurate than the SS-18 and to be equipped with a similar warhead. Some of both the SS-18 and -19's are MIRVed. So far, a total of 668 SS-18's and -19's have been deployed. If these are MIRVed to the extent allowed by the SALT II Treaty, they are equipped with a total of about 4,500 warheads. The other Soviet MIRVed ICBM, the SS-17 (or RS-16), has been tested with four warheads. So far about 150 SS-17's have been deployed. According to US sources, the USSR is developing at least two new types of ICBM.

The Soviet MIRVed strategic missile force is clearly an increasing threat to the 1,000-strong US Minuteman ICBM force as the accuracy and reliability of the Soviet warheads are improved and their number increases.

STRATEGIC NUCLEAR SUBMARINES

The quality of strategic nuclear submarines and the ballistic missiles they carry is also being continuously improved. In the US, for example, the present Polaris and Poseidon strategic nuclear submarine force is being augmented, and may eventually be replaced, by Trident submarines. The Polaris submarines now operating will be phased out by the end of 1982. Thirty-one Poseidon submarines are now operating.

Trident submarines will be equipped with a new SLBM, the Trident I, the successor of the Poseidon C-3 SLBM. Yet another SLBM, the Trident II, is currently being developed for eventual deployment on Trident submarines.

In the meantime, Trident I missiles will also be deployed on Poseidon submarines. The first of twelve Poseidons to be modified to carry Trident I missiles went to sea in October

1979; the others should be ready by 1984.

The first Trident submarine, the *USS Ohio* will become operational in 1981. According to current plans, at least eight Trident submarines (these have already been ordered) will become operational during the 1980's. But the ultimate size of the Trident fleet has yet to be decided.

The Trident displaces 18,700 tons when submerged. The enormous size of the Trident can be judged from the facts that it is twice as large as a Polaris/Poseidon submarine, which has a submerged displacement of about 8,300 tons, and it is as large as the new British through-deck cruiser (displacement 19,500 tons).

Each Trident submarine will carry 24 SLBM's. The Trident I SLBM is designed to have a maximum range of 7,400 km. when equipped with eight 100-kiloton MIRVed warheads. Even longer ranges can be achieved if the missile has a smaller payload. The Poseidon SLBM, which it replaces, can carry up to fourteen 40-kiloton MIRVed warheads, but has a maximum range of only 4,600 km. With the longer-range missile, Trident submarines will be able to operate in many times more ocean area and still remain within range of their targets. The long-range missiles will also allow Trident submarines to operate closer to US shores and still reach their targets, giving the submarines greater protection against Soviet anti-submarine warfare (ASW) activities.

Trident I, a two-stage solid propellant rocket, is provided with a stellar-aided inertial guidance system to provide mid-course corrections. The CEP of the Trident SLBM is probably about 500 m. at a maximum range, whereas that of the Poseidon SLBM is about 550 m., and that of the Polaris I SLBM is about 900 m. The development and deployment of mid-course guidance techniques for SLBM's and the more accurate navigation of missile submarines will steadily increase the accuracy of the missiles.

SLBM warheads may eventually be fitted with terminal

guidance, using radar, laser or some other device to guide them on to their targets after re-entry into the Earth's atmosphere. This could give CEP's of a few tens of metres. SLBM's will then be so accurate as to cease to be only deterrence weapons aimed at enemy cities and become nuclear-war fighting weapons.

The most modern Soviet SLBM is the 7,400 km. range SS-N-18, equipped with three 200-kt MIRV's. So far, 192 SS-N-18's have been put to sea, sixteen on each of twelve Delta-class submarines, the most modern Soviet strategic nuclear submarines. The other main Soviet SLBM is the SS-N-8, with a range of 8,000 km and a single 1-Mt warhead. Two hundred and ninety SS-N-8's are deployed on twenty-two Delta-class submarines.

The USSR also operates about thirty Yankee-class strategic nuclear submarines, each carrying sixteen SS-N-6 SLBM's, a 3,000 km. range missile carrying either a 1-Mt warhead or two 200-kt warheads. In all, the USSR has 950 SLBM's, 192 of them MIRVed.

The USSR is developing a new ballistic-missile firing submarine — the Typhoon — which is apparently even bigger than the American Trident. A new SLBM, the SS-NX-20, is also under development, presumably for deployment on the Typhoon.

Soviet SLBM's are less accurate than are US ones. The SS-N-6 is thought to have a CEP of about 1,000 m. But one can expect that the accuracy of Soviet SLBM's will be steadily improved and that more Soviet MIRVed SLBM's will be deployed.

Current US ballistic missiles carry 7,033 independently targetable warheads. Of these missile warheads, 4,880 are sea-based. US ballistic missiles have a total explosive yield of about 1,820 megatons (Mt.), of which about 330 Mt. are carried by SLBM's. US sea-based strategic nuclear forces account, therefore, for about 70 per cent of the missile warheads. If all US strategic warheads, on bombers and missiles, are included, the sea-based forces account for about 50 per cent of the number.

Almost all Soviet strategic nuclear warheads are deployed on ballistic missiles; the USSR operates no more than 150 strategic bombers and there is no evidence that they are assigned an intercontinental role. There are said to be about 7,140 independently targetable Soviet missile warheads. Of these, about 1,300, or 20 per cent, are probably carried by SLBM's, while the rest are on ICBM's. The SLBM warheads probably have a total explosive yield of about 770 Mt. out of a total missile megatonage of about 4,100 Mt. According to US sources, the Soviet Union normally has only about one-seventh of its strategic submarines (about ten boats) at sea at any one time. The land-based ICBM force is, at present, therefore, by far the most important component of the Soviet strategic nuclear arsenal.

CRUISE MISSILE

The US strategic bomber force, the third component of America's strategic triad, will be modernized by equipping B-52 strategic bombers with air-launched cruise missiles (ALCM's). The ALCM is a small, long-range, sub-sonic, very accurate, nuclear-armed, winged vehicle. ALCM's can be launched against Soviet targets by bombers penetrating Soviet defences or from outside Soviet territory.

According to current plans, ALCM's should become operational in December 1982, when the first B-52G squadron is loaded with cruise missiles under the aircraft's wings. Full operational capability is planned for 1990, when all 151 B-52G aircraft will be loaded, each with twelve ALCM's under the wings and eight in the bomb bays. ALCM's will about double the number of nuclear weapons these aircraft carry.

NEW TACTICAL NUCLEAR WEAPONS

Many of the 7,000 or so tactical nuclear weapons in NATO countries in Western Europe were put there during the late 1950's and early 1960's. Since nuclear weapons have a lifetime of about 20 years, these are about due for replacement. In the meantime, new types of nuclear weapons have been developed and the plan is to replace the old nuclear weapons with some of these new types.

Among the new types of nuclear weapons planned for NATO are Pershing II missiles and ground-launched cruise

TABLE 3.   Strategic Arsenals of Other Major Nuclear Powers[a]

Weapon	First deployed	Maximum range[b] (km)	No. of re-entry vehicles	Yield	Number deployed
FRANCE					
IRBM S-2[c]	1971	3,000	1	150 kt.	18
SLBM M-20[d]	1977	3,000	1	1 Mt.	80
Aircraft Mirage IV-A	1964	3,000	1 nuclear weapon per aircraft		33
BRITAIN					
SLBM Polaris A-3[e]	1967	4,600	3	200 kt.	64
Aircraft Vulcan B-2[f]	1960	6,500	2 nuclear weapons per aircraft		48
CHINA					
MRBM CSS-1	1966	about 1,200	1	about 20 kt.	about 40
IRBM CSS-2	1971	about 3,000	1	about 1 Mt.	about 50
ICBM CSS-3[g]	1978	about 6,000	1	about 3 Mt.	about 2
Aircraft Tu-16	1968	about 3,500	1 nuclear weapon per aircraft		about 75

MRBM: medium range ballistic missile
IRBM: intermediate range ballistic missile
ICBM: intercontinental ballistic missile
SLBM: submarine launched ballistic missile
kt.: kiloton
Mt.: megaton

---

[a] The total nuclear-weapon stockpiles are larger than is implied here because of reserves and tactical nuclear weapons. China probably has about 300 or 400 nuclear weapons, and France and the UK roughly the same. Fighter aircraft could be used to deliver tactical nuclear weapons. France has 32 PLUTON ground-to-ground missiles, each of which carries a warhead with a yield of about 20 kt and has a range of 120 kilometres.

[b] For aircraft the operational range which would allow the aircraft to reach the target and return to base is less than a half of the maximum range.

[c] Being replaced with the S-3, which has the same range but a 1.2 Mt warhead.

[d] Carried on 5 nuclear submarines, each having 16 SLBM's. One more strategic nuclear submarine is being built. The M-4 SLBM, carrying 6 or 7 multiple independently targetable re-entry vehicles each with a yield of 150 kt., is being developed. The M-4 will have a range of 4,000 kilometres.

[e] Carried on 4 nuclear submarines, each having 16 SLBM's. The British may replace their Polaris submarines with Trident submarines.

[f] These aircraft will probably soon be retired.

[g] An ICBM, the CSS-4, has been tested to a range of about 12,000 kilometres. It will probably soon be deployed.

---

missiles. These weapons are so accurate as to be perceived as nuclear-war fighting weapons. In December 1979, NATO decided to deploy 108 Pershing II's and 464 cruise missiles, starting at the end of 1983.

Although less accurate than the American weapons, the Soviet SS-20 intermediate-range ballistic missile — a new type of Soviet tactical nuclear weapon — is accurate enough, or will soon be made so, to be regarded as a nuclear-war fighting weapon, given the large explosive yield of its warhead. About 250 were deployed in mid-1981, about 60 percent targeted on Western Europe and the rest targeted on China.

The SS-20

The Soviet SS-20, a two-stage mobile missile, was first deployed in 1977. The missile carries three MIRV's. With these warheads its range is said to be about 5,000 km.

The yield of each SS-20 warhead is estimated by Western sources to be between 150 and 500 kilotons and the CEP is said to be about 400 m.

The Pershing II Missile

The Pershing II missile will replace the Pershing I missile, first deployed in 1962.

Pershing II will use the same rocket components as Pershing I. But there the similarity ends. Pershing II will be provided with a formidable new guidance system called RADAG. In the terminal phase of the trajectory, when the warhead is getting close to the current, a video radar scans the target area and the image is compared with a reference image stored in the computer carried by the warhead before the missile is launched. The computer operates aerodynamic vanes which guide the warhead on to the target with accuracy unprecedented for a ballistic missile with a range of about 1,700 km. The CEP of Pershing II is about 45 m.

Pershing II has double the range of Pershing I (750 km) because it has new rocket motors and uses a new highly efficient solid fuel. The missile is the only NATO ballistic missile able to penetrate a significant distance into the USSR — it could, for example, reach Moscow from the Federal Republic of Germany.

The Ground-launched Cruise Missile (GLCM)

The GLCM's to be deployed in Europe will carry light-weight 200-kt, nuclear warheads. These missiles are not only very accurate, with CEP's of about 40 m., but, although flying at sub-sonic speeds, are relatively invulnerable, having a very small radar cross-section.

The replacement of existing tactical nuclear weapons with new types is likely to reduce somewhat the total number deployed but the reduction is unlikely to be very significant. Over the next few years, the number deployed in NATO countries in Western Europe may, for example, decrease from about 7,000 to about 6,000. A similar reduction may occur on the Warsaw Pact side.

THE INCREASING PROBABILITY OF A NUCLEAR WORLD WAR

As we have seen, the world's arsenals contain tens of thousands of nuclear weapons, probably topping 50,000. The total explosive power of these weapons is equivalent to about one million Hiroshima bombs. If all, or a significant portion of them, were used, the consequences would be beyond imagination.

All the major cities in the Northern Hemisphere, where most nuclear warheads are aimed, would be destroyed (on average, *each* is targeted by the equivalent of some 2,000 Hiroshima bombs). Most of the urban population there would be killed by blast and fire, the rural population by radiation from fallout. Many millions of people in the Southern Hemisphere would be killed by radiation. And the disaster would not end even there. The unpredictable (and, therefore, normally ignored) long-term effects might well include changes in the global climate, severe genetic damage and depletion of the ozone layer that protects life on earth from excessive ultraviolet radiation. No scientist can convincingly assure us that human life would survive a nuclear world war.

Utterly catastrophic though a nuclear world war would be, its probability is steadily increasing. Symptoms of the current drift to a nuclear world war include the recent propaganda campaign to try to convince us that nuclear war may not be so bad after all, that limited nuclear wars are not only possible but may in some circumstances even be militarily effective, that civil defence measures could reduce casualties to an "acceptable" level, that essential industry should be protected against nuclear blast, that the Warsaw Treaty Organisation will soon militarily overwhelm NATO (and, no doubt, the opposite is said in the East), and so on. The current hawkish mood seems to be worldwide, or at least to extend throughout official circles in most of the Northern Hemisphere.

There are a number of reasons for the drift to war. The most obvious are related to international politics. Others are connected with advances in military technology.

The escalation of a regional conflict to a general nuclear war is perhaps the most likely way in which a nuclear world war would start; more likely than a direct nuclear attack by one Superpower on the other, although the danger of its starting by accident or miscalculation is ever present. A local conflict in, say, a Third World region (like the Persian Gulf) might begin as a conventional war and then escalate to a limited nuclear war, using the nuclear weapons of the local powers. This could in turn escalate to a general nuclear war involving the Superpowers, especially if the Superpowers supplied the conventional weapons for the original conflict. And that is why both the international arms trade, now totally out of control, and nuclear-weapon proliferation are so dangerous.

We seem to be on the threshold of a new round of nuclear weapon proliferation, with Pakistan the next probable nuclear power. The widening access to nuclear-weapon technology goes hand in hand with the spread of peaceful nuclear technology, itself a spin-off from military programs. The more nuclear reactors there are generating electricity around the world, the greater will be the number of countries acquiring the skills and the capability to produce the fissile material to make nuclear weapons. As the number of countries with nuclear weapons increases, the probability of nuclear war will increase.

The Demise of Nuclear Deterrence

Nuclear deterrence depends on the belief that the enemy will not attack pre-emptively if he knows that most of his people and industry will be destroyed in retaliation. Cities are the hostages to deterrence. If the enemy stops fearing that his cities are at risk, nuclear deterrence no longer works. This will happen as accurate and reliable missile warheads are deployed.

Remember that deterrence is essentially a matter of psychology. What the enemy believes is all-important. It is, therefore, impossible to maintain a policy of nuclear deterrence with accurate weapons simply because the enemy will assume, willy-nilly, that the other side's warheads are targeted on his military forces and not on his cities. Accuracy, in other words, kills deterrence. Nuclear war-fighting, based on the destruction of hostile military forces, will then become the only credible and, therefore, feasible policy.

Nuclear-war fighting perceptions are being strengthened by a whole range of first-strike technologies. The most dangerous are those related to anti-submarine warfare. Now that land-based ballistic missiles are vulnerable to a first (i.e. pre-emptive) strike by hostile land-based missiles, nuclear deterrence depends solely on the continuing invulnerability of strategic submarines. In fact, if strategic nuclear submarines do become vulnerable (and this may, given current research efforts, be only a matter of time) a first strike may be seen as desirable and even essential to prevent the enemy from himself acquiring a first-strike capability.

Other first-strike technologies currently being developed or deployed include: navigational systems, providing unprecedented three-dimensional accuracies; anti-satellite warfare systems; ballistic missile defence systems; early-warning-of-attack systems; command, control, communications, and intelligence systems; and reconnaissance systems. Of these mostly space-based technologies, much current attention is focussed on ballistic missile defence.

Great Power Rivalry in the Middle East

The Middle East has become the world's most unstable region. The world of Islam is increasingly anti-American. Fuelling this attitude is the threat of US military intervention to secure and protect the West's vital sources of oil in the Gulf.

About half of the world's energy comes from the consumption of oil, over a third of which comes from five Middle Eastern countries (Iran, Iraq, Kuwait, Saudi Arabia, and the United Arab Emirates). In fact, the Middle East is the only world region in which oil production significantly exceeds consumption.

Countries vary considerably in their dependence on oil. Oil accounts for roughly half the total energy consumed by the US, Western Europe and South Korea, but as much as about three quarters of that consumed by Japan and Taiwan. Gulf oil supplies a significant fraction of the total energy used by these countries – ranging from about one tenth for the USA to over half for Japan.

By contrast, oil accounts for about a third of the total energy used by the Soviet Union which currently produces more oil than it consumes. But, according to some American sources, the USSR will become a net importer of oil by the mid-1980's. Soviet oil exports to its East European allies and the West will then dry up and the USSR will compete for Gulf oil.

Great power rivalry in and near the Gulf region has been intensifying for some time now. This will not only greatly complicate oil supplies in the 1980's but will make much more acute any crisis brought on by a significant interruption in the flow of oil.

It is therefore hardly surprising that the US is drawing up military plans for such a contingency.

US RAPID DEPLOYMENT FORCE

Serious thinking about military action to secure Gulf oil

supplies began in October 1973 when the Arabs started their five-month oil embargo against the United States. In January 1974, US Defence Secretary James R. Schlesinger publicly warned that it was "feasible" for the US to "conduct military operations [in the Gulf area] if the necessity should arise." The US is in the process of setting up a Rapid Deployment Force of about 200,000 men.

The Rapid Deployment Force would be equipped by ships pre-positioned at Diego Garcia in the Indian Ocean. They would carry supplies and heavy weapons for troops trans-ported from the US. The force would use facilities provided by countries in the area, if necessary. Specifically, military faci-lities are being prepared in Oman and Egypt, as well as in Somalia and Kenya.

In Oman, the US will be allowed the use of facilities at the ex-British air base on Masirah Island. About $75 million worth of improvements are planned for these facilities. Facilities at the airfield at Seeb will also be available to the US.

The Egyptian base at Ras Banas will provide air and naval facilities, and $100 million worth of improvements are planned there. The runways at the air base will be extended for use by jet fighters and transport aircraft.

Logistics and communications would be major obstacles to any US military action in the Middle East. Distances from the US to the Gulf are large — about 16,000 kilometres by sea around the Cape.

The mainly desert area containing the oilfields is large — essentially a rectangle about 600 kilometres wide and 1,200 kilometres long. The area contains about sixty major oilfields, about thirty-eight of them onshore, with about 2,800 oper-ating wells and about twenty refineries, about 20,000 kilo-metres of pipeline and loading terminals in about twenty-four ports. Just the 800 or so Saudi oil wells and their facilities stretch over a distance of 500 kilometres, and are connected by about 5,000 kilometres of pipeline.

According to John M. Collins and Clyde R. Mark, two senior specialists of the US Library of Congress Research Service, each oilfield consists of a bewildering complex of installations, including "wells, gas-oil separator stations, stabilizer plants, gas and water injection plants, pipelines, pumping stations, tank farms, refineries, power plants, and port facilities."

To occupy such a large area of desert, and take over with minimum damage so many major industrial installations, would be exceedingly difficult, particularly if the invaders were faced with powerful defence forces. The operation could become a military planner's nightmare.

Gulf States may actually ask for US military assistance to help to protect oilfields. But the most difficult, and perhaps the most likely, assault task for a US rapid deployment force in the Gulf would be to seize oilfields and re-start deliberately-interrupted oil supplies. In such an operation, the speed at which combat troops could be put into action would be of the essence. But, according to Collins and Mark, airlifting the essential elements of America's only airborne division "half-way around the world with a basic load of ammunition and a five-day supply of rations and fuel would take, with prior preparation, ten days or more. The Army's only air assault division could then begin to deploy, with its organic equipment, completing that process during the next three weeks. A follow-up infantry division could close in its objective area but would take about the same time it would take a mechanised division to travel by sea." Such an operation would hardly be a surprise attack.

It would also be difficult to provide adequate aircover for the assault operations. The nearest available airfields are in Israel or Egypt and aircraft carriers would presumably have to be kept some distance away, perhaps in the Arabian Sea.

If the airlift and amphibious operations were successfully completed, the troops would have to be sustained by sea. To satisfy the needs of a three to five division occupation force for some months would stretch US shipping capabilities, possibly beyond their limit.

While the oil fields were being seized, their equipment could be damaged or destroyed by saboteurs and major oilfires started. Repairing very extensive damage would require extraordinary capabilities, perhaps more than the US could initially provide. For example, according to Collins and Mark: "In America 16 private companies and three Government agencies once committed 650 men, two fire barges, a derrick barge with 500-ton crane, and a shore-based control centre complete with communications, power sources, fuel supply, helipad, seaplane dock, and living quarters just to combat a single platform fire." Extensive repair of damaged oilfields would be exceedingly expensive, possibly running into thousands of millions of dollars, impose vast logistics problems in the transport of large pieces of equipment and spare parts to the oilfields, and take many months.

Even a military victory would not be worthwhile if a significant fraction of the major oilfields were destroyed in the process.

Soviet armed intervention during an invasion would almost certainly turn the military scales against the Americans. Soviet logistics problems would be significant, but considerably less than American ones. And the USSR has much influence, including military, in or near the area — in Afghanistan, Syria and Ethiopia, as well as Iraq and South Yemen. Specifically, the USSR has the use of military base facilities at Aden, South Yemen and Dahlak Island, Ethiopia.

Gulf oil supplies may be interrupted for a variety of reasons — including the use of the oil embargo as a political weapon in a dispute with the West, a local war, a domestic upheaval, the sabotage of oilfields or installations by terrorists or revolutionaries, or the malicious blocking of the Straits of Hormuz.

But any unilateral Western military action to secure Gulf oil supplies would be risky indeed. It may well escalate to a nuclear world war.

4

Factors of Social and Economic Development in the Gulf in the Eighties

by Mohamed al-Rumaihi

Introduction

In the early 1970's the Arabian Gulf region began to receive wider attention from analysts and strategists throughout the world. By the end of that decade, this region had become the primary focus of international strategic attention.

A number of internal and external factors contributed to the growth of the region's importance. Three of them are primary:

1. Rising oil prices and an increased demand for oil in Western industrial nations, the USA and Japan.

2. The defusing of the Arab-Israeli conflict on the Egyptian-Israeli front following the Egyptian president's visit to Jerusalem in 1977, followed by the signing of the Camp David agreements, and hence a shift in attention to the eastern front in the Arab-Israeli conflict.

3. The stirrings of revolution in Iran, then the revolution itself and its repercussions on the Gulf region in particular and the Middle East in general. This was then followed by the "Gulf War," i.e. the Iraq-Iran war.

These three principal factors and their ramifications have

made the Gulf region the focus of international concern, both Eastern and Western. It is clear in this regard that such issues as oil, energy, the Palestine problem and the question of liberation from indirect imperialist domination are all interdependent.

The centre of the East-West conflict can be said to have shifted to the Gulf because of the enormous strategic and economic importance that it has come to occupy and because of its direct connection with the three issues mentioned above.

But while the Gulf has acquired such economic importance and influence, no radical change has taken place in its social structure or political systems.[1] At a time when the social and political structures have changed in many surrounding countries, the oil states of the Gulf have maintained fixed social structures and traditional political systems. The ruling families of the Gulf States (the Gulf Cooperation Council) have not introduced any radical changes such as have taken place in states like Iraq, Iran, Egypt and many others in the area. Despite the growth of oil wealth at the beginning of the seventies, especially when oil prices rose steeply and a number of changes were introduced into the economy and services of these states, the social structures did not simultaneously change in any radical fashion.[2] But the new dynamics did produce a number of diverse quantitative changes among wide sectors of society. It may thus be argued that these changes may become qualitative changes affecting not only the internal socio-political structures but also the international balance of

---

[1] By "Gulf" is meant here the states that make up the Gulf Cooperation Council. This does not of course exclude Iraq or even Iran. But since the analytical factors in these two countries differ from those that apply to the countries in the Cooperation Council, our analysis here concentrates on this latter, although realism dictates that we refer occasionally to Iraq and Iran.

[2] It is necessary to point out here that an increase in oil prices does not mean a true increase in the revenue of these countries when one takes into account the international inflation rate in the world capitalist market.

power in the Gulf and Arab regions. Accordingly, the conflict which seems international is in reality an internal struggle among diverse local powers attracting the interest of foreign powers.

There are, for example, the middle class groups which oil wealth has made to appear in these societies. These are urban-educated groups part of whom have joined the administrative institutions, governmental or military. These groups veer towards modernization and socio-political development. In Saudi Arabia they are concentrated in the central (Najd) and Western (Hijaz) regions, and they exist in the cities of other Gulf states.

These groups are not organized. However, two main streams may be distinguished within them. The first is the religious-political stream, an extension of the Muslim Brotherhood or its branches. It is insurrectionary in outlook since the existing regimes have, in their view, transgressed against the teachings of Islam, and so rebellion against them is justified. Two years ago, some of them attempted to occupy Mecca. Others among them are reformist in mentality, calling for the application of peaceful pressure upon these regimes to make them return to the genuine teachings of Islam through the espousal of a number of laws, regulations and practices which this group considers to be consonant with these teachings.

The second stream among contemporary middle class groups in Gulf societies is the radical current, calling for socialism, liberation from the West and the establishment of social and political justice. In this stream too we find the reformists who espouse gradual change, and they are in the majority, as well as a minority of insurrectionaries who call for radical and direct change.

In more than one place in the Third World, and recently in Iran, it has become an established fact that real changes are those which are the product of interaction inside a given society, with foreign interests being a mere reaction to such interactions. There is of course a dialectical relationship between foreign interests and local interaction, but these last are a secondary variable. In the case of the Gulf, foreign interests should not be under-estimated since they employ local tools and exploit periods of transition on the current world scene.

From another perspective, it has been shown that the conservative political regimes of the Gulf have thus far succeeded in absorbing the consequences of internal and external changes and in responding to them by bringing about "quantitative" transformations in their political and social systems which, however, fall short of being "qualitative" transformations that affect the basic structure of these societies.

In the last thirty years, the Gulf region has felt the effect of three major revolutions in the region, which has seriously affected its internal cohesion. As a result, the regimes have veered towards granting political and economic concessions to the new and emergent forces that call for change inside their societies.

First came the Iraqi revolution of 1958, which brought in a new regime in place of a traditional royalty. Then came the Yemen revolution of 1962 and its repercussions, leading to a radical change in South Yemen. Then followed the Iranian revolution of February 1979 and the events that ensued. It is to be noted that, following every one of these radical changes, the Gulf region is affected by the reverberations of change, and so the regimes offer a number of concessions which meet internal demand on the one hand and maintain political balance on the other.

The three revolutions, the Iraqi, the Yemeni (both halves) and the Iranian, were no sooner in power than they were embroiled in major internal conflicts which mitigated the force of their initial impact on the rest of the Gulf region. The recent Iranian revolution is no exception. Having first offered a model which many groups in Gulf society hoped to emulate, it was then caught up in bloody conflicts which, like the earlier Iraqi and Yemeni revolutions, dampened the enthu-siasm of the masses in the Gulf for it.

Despite the concessions offered by the regimes of the Gulf in the wake of every radical change of this kind, the shock is soon absorbed and an accommodation is reached with the new state of affairs. Diverse and numerous factors have helped this process of accommodation, including:

1. Lavish oil wealth.

2. Relative sparsity of population and the presence of large numbers of non-local inhabitants.

3. Weakness of local political consciousness.

4. Lack of any radical transformation in traditional social structures.

If we wish to allude to only a few examples of the response of the regimes in the Gulf to changes in surrounding countries, we can point to the independence of Kuwait in the early sixties in the wake of the Iraqi revolution, as well as the political changes and the appearance of a new political leader-ship in Saudi Arabia (King Faisal ibn Abd al-Aziz) in the wake of the Yemeni-Egyptian-Saudi conflict. One might also point to the series of administrative and political measures under-taken by King Faisal in Saudi Arabia, the independence of the small Gulf states in the early seventies and the establishment of the Gulf Cooperation Council in the wake of the Iranian revolution and the war that ensued.[3] All these point to the accommodation by traditional regimes in the Gulf to new regional factors.

If the basic changes brought about by the three revolutions in the past thirty years have had a partial influence on the situation in the Gulf and have been absorbed in various ways, the changes that have occurred in the member states of the

---

[3] See Mohamed al-Rumaihi, "The Gulf Cooperation Council: New Deal in the Gulf"; paper submitted to the AAUG annual convention held in Houston, November, 1981.

Cooperation Council are also the product of the new economic and political situation, creating new social groups that have their own demands as regards living standards and politics.

The Gulf and the Palestinian Revolution

The major problem facing the Gulf regimes today, especially the larger ones, and one of which they are fully aware is, quite specifically, the Palestinian revolution. There are many reasons for this. To begin with, the Palestinian revolution does not constitute an immediate danger that these regimes can absorb or accommodate themselves to. Nor does it constitute a specific material danger. The real threat of the Palestinian revolution is the great moral danger that it represents to basic policies of concern to Gulf regimes, especially the major regime, i.e. Saudi Arabia. The question of the liberation of Jerusalem and its restoration as an Arab-Islamic city is directly related to the protection of the Islamic holy places, which is regarded by Saudi Arabia as a basic principle of its internal and external policy. Along with oil wealth, they constitute the two basic pillars of the regime. This explains the oft-repeated statement by the late King Faisal that he wanted to pray in Jerusalem before he died. Although this statement is no longer made in public, the issue itself remains a major challenge to the Saudi regime. Last year, this statement was replaced by the call for a *jihad,* and now comes Prince Fahd's recent initiative which has to do with an honorable peace with Israel.

In addition to this moral pillar, the continued existence of the Palestinian revolution and its armed presence in some Arab regions (e.g.Lebanon) makes it into an experimental field for all Arabs rejecting the status quo, especially those in the Gulf who sympathize with certain groups in the Palestinian revolution, despite their small numbers at present.

The war in Lebanon, as far as the Arabs are concerned, thus resembles the Spanish civil war when sympathizers in Europe joined one or the other warring party, turning Spain into a field for political experiments. The Lebanese experimental field can have an adverse effect on conservative regimes (and of course on other regimes, but less so). This fact was demonstrated when it became clear that many groups in the Iranian revolution against the Shah had worked for long periods, and had received training, in the camps of Palestinian groups in Jordan or Lebanon.

The Palestinian revolution possesses yet another dimension in the Gulf, namely the sympathy of the Gulf masses for the revolution. Despite the obstacles placed before such sympathy, which reaches the point of hostility on the level of individuals, the great majority of the masses are sympathetic, especially as regards liberation and the struggle against the Israelis. Accordingly, this sympathy dictates support for the Palestinians in many powerful quarters in the Gulf. The final dimension of the Palestinian revolution is, quite simply, the presence of large numbers of Palestinians in the Gulf region. These constitute, on the one hand, mass pressure. On the other hand, the fact that many of them are close to decision-making in the media, administrative, educational and even political fields puts them in a position of influence and persuasion.

The Gulf: Continuity or Change?

TRADITIONAL PRODUCTION

Oil revenues and modern economic sectors have been introduced into a traditional society where economic surplus was so limited as to inhibit a clear division of labour and thus the rise of social groups (not to say classes). The traditional modes of production in these societies were, principally, no more than three in number: pastoralism, limited agriculture and diving for pearls. Commercial exchange had a limited surplus. Although the modes of traditional production differed as between the hinterland and the coast, the tribe was nonetheless the nodal point of social structure in these societies.[4] A mode of production which depended on chance and on nature directly affected social relations.

A human community living in an environment which dominates it rather then vice versa, where natural resources are poor, which has only grass and a limited rainfall and is thus forced to wander in search of grass and water — such a community is unstable. It has to deal with a parsimonious nature in order to eke out a minimum level of subsistence. This is the environment which produced the Gulf Arab. He is a nomad, at once plundering and generous. If he possesses a surplus, he is noble and generous. If his level of subsistence falls, he turns to plunder to satisfy his desires.

Agriculture in that environment was confined to a few oases in the hinterland or on the coast. It is noticeable that the inhabitants like to give their living areas names that suggest greenery and fertility. For instance, Riyadh, the capital of Saudi Arabia, is plural of "rawd" which means a land green with diverse vegetation. Al-Gabal al-Akhdar ("The Green Mountain") in Oman is self-explanatory. Washm, a region in Najd, means plants beginning to sprout. Doha, the Qatari capital, means a large and well shaped tree. Despite all these names, agricultural production was meagre. They were in fact names denoting their opposites.

In this natural environment, the tribe was the focal point of social structure. For the tribe is not confined to the desert; we find it also in sedentary communities of the coast. The tribe was also the focal point of economic organization. Accordingly, the societies of the Gulf are a group of tribes, whether they are engaged in pastoralism and agriculture or even in fishing

---

[4] See Mohamed al-Rumaihi, "Synchronous Formation and Consequent Development: a Study in What is Essential, General and Common among Gulf Oil Countries;" paper presented at the conference entitled Intellectual Framework of Arab Social Action held under the auspices of the Institute of Planning, Kuwait, September 26-29, 1981.

and pearl diving. "Urban tribalism" has represented some stability;[5] large sectors of the city populations incline to claims of kinship with one tribe or another. Such claims may not be accurate, but they underline the importance of tribal relations in these societies.

THE MODERN ECONOMY

Oil entered these societies at different times following World War II, producing a total transformation of their economic structure. Most traditional modes of economic activity have in effect vanished. This includes agriculture, since land now makes way for continuous modern building and increased housing needs. The life of man in the desert and agricultural regions has shrunk, moving towards the new oil cities. And although there was no division of labour in the technical sense of the term in the traditional mode of production, and females were not isolated from male society because of the need for them in production (e.g. in tending the flocks and gathering the harvest) and in performing other available work, society in a modern producing economy is characterized by a new dialectic which has had both positive and negative effects on the social and political scene.

It is important to note that production in the pre-oil period used to depend on nature. Dependence on oil has come to parallel that earlier dependence on nature, in the sense that Gulf society did not experience a natural and gradual growth of productive forces. The discovery of oil was an accident, a by-product of a natural situation and of the need for oil in the Western capitalist market. It was world capitalism and western technology which carried out the process of oil extraction. Gulf societies thus came to depend solely on the financial

---

[5] For this definition, see Emile A. Nakhleh, *Bahrain* (Lexington, Massachussetts: Lexington Books, 1976), pp. 165-166.

benefits of oil which they have spent in diverse ways to establish an infra-structure and provide services for the inhabitants who have been alienated from production.

A clear breach has occurred between these societies and production. This breach is seen in the disparity between the oil economy and the distribution of oil income. This in turn explains the dialectical antithesis in these societies and the role of the state-tribe in this.

The dialectic of change and continuity is therefore present in these societies. At a time when the dominant tribe was becoming the ruling tribe and the Shaykh of the tribe becoming an Emir, a King or a Sultan, the traditional tribal structure remained unchanged to become an instrument of social control. The modern state which came into existence in the post-oil period made use of traditional social relations on the one hand and oil wealth on the other to preserve the status quo. This has been accomplished through various means including:

(a) The attempt to create a welfare state.

(b) The new demographic structure.

(c) Cultural and political changes.

(a) *The Welfare State*

As the oil income of the new Gulf states increased, so did their expenditure on social, health care and educational services and on building a broad infrastructure of roads, electric power stations, housing schemes and social assistance. One cannot of course understand this welfare state without understanding the political and social change which accompanies it as well as the attempt to build a state to replace traditional tribal relations. Oil wealth has introduced its own challenges. If this wealth is to be preserved, a modern state must be built, possessing modern institutions like an army, a police force and a civil service. This in turn requires education, roads, housing and so forth. Diverse social care services have thus begun to grow in these societies, but despite their considerable expansion, their social effects remain limited. Some have argued that these effects have been limited because these societies have only recently opted for this path. Housing, educational and health service schemes are still unable to meet the expanding needs of society. Education, in particular, has not produced a qualitative change in the attitude of society to itself or in its awareness of its future. Several scholars have observed that the state has entrenched traditional tribal relations despite the existence of various social care services and has also entrenched traditional values in order to preserve the status quo. It is here that the traditional polarity adopted between the "sword of repression" and the "course of justice" appears, i.e. in the tribe.[6] The total resettlement of the tribe and its dissolution would rob a regime based on tribal relations of its legitimacy. Therefore, in order to preserve it, the modern Gulf state enshrines the tribe socially and economically, but deprives it of its political authority. Entry into the army, police force and even some senior administrative posts must proceed from tribal or clan support. The Shaykh of a tribe still enjoys the respect of the regime, which satisfies his needs and the needs of his fellow tribesmen provided that his loyalty to the dominant clan remains firm.

The tribal relationship constitutes an obstacle in the process of transformation from a "tribal" to a "state" society. A revolutionary tract from Oman puts the problem as follows:

"They all (i.e. Gulf regimes) neither desire nor consciously tend to destroy the tribal structure. A member of a tribe, before developing either a nationalist or, in particular, a class consciousness, continues to feel that the tribe is his existence, his life, both private and public. He does not feel his influence

---

6 Waddah Sharar, *al-Ahl wal-Ghanima: muqawwimat al-siyasa fi al-Mamlaka al-'Arabiyya al-Sa'udiyya* ("The clan and the booty: the structure of politics in the kingdom of Saudi Arabia") (Beirut: Dar al-Tali'a, 1981), p. 76.

or his value in society except through his tribe and whatever influence or value it may have in society is therefore his own too."[7]

The welfare society has absorbed the tribe as is, making the necessary adjustments to the new set of loyalties. The revenue from oil has made it possible to maintain these loyalties through the new social services provided and the transformation of public wealth into private wealth through state schemes. Accordingly, many groups in this society which enjoy the benefits of the welfare state are motivated to offer their political allegiance, intermixed with tribal relations, to the dominant clan. This is the prevailing pattern in the period of transition.

(b) *The New Demographic Structure*

The Gulf oil societies have witnessed a demographic revolution not experienced hitherto. This revolution has been in two directions: an internal migration from the countryside and the desert to the cities, especially the capitals and the oil cities, and an external migration from Arab or foreign countries. Despite the lack of accurate population statistics in some countries, statistical estimates and general statistics point to an enormous jump in the number of inhabitants in the past thirty years.

Estimates of the population of Saudi Arabia have been divergent and contradictory to a large degree. The 1962/63 estimate was 3.3 million,[8] a figure regarded as inflated by some. The 1974/75 figure is 6.7 million, but more scientific

---

[7] "The Tribe: Whence and Whither," in *Dirasat Tis'a Yunyu* ("Ninth of June studies") for the Popular Front for the Liberation of Oman (Beirut: Dar al-Tali'a, 1981), p. 15.

[8] For these estimates, see J.S. Berkes and K.A. Sinclair, *Population and International Immigration in the Arab States* (Beirut: International Labour Organisation for ECWA, 1980), pp. 121 ff.

and accurate estimates point to a figure of 6.1 million for the mid-seventies, of whom 4.6 million are citizens (74.6%).[9] Statistical estimates indicate that the migrant labour force in Saudi Arabia had increased by 15.7% between the years 1966 and 1974/75.

While the population figures for Saudi Arabia are only approximate, the increase in population in other Gulf states is statistically documented and highly significant as regards the growth of population in the past thirty years. The population of Kuwait rose from 206, 473 in the first census of 1957 to 1,355,827 in the census of 1980, representing more than a six-fold increase. And while the increase in the number of native Kuwaitis was a result of natural increase and resettlement from the desert, the non-Kuwaiti population increased as a result of diverse factors, such as the growth of economic opportunities and unemployment in producing countries. The Kuwaitis constitute only 41.5% of the total population, the rest (58.5%) being non-Kuwaitis.

In Bahrein, where fairly accurate statistics have been available since 1941, the population was then 90,000. After forty years, the population rose to 358,857 in 1981, a four-fold increase. The available statistics for 1981 indicate that if Asiatic immigration continues at the same rate as that of the past decade, Bahreini citizens will become a minority in about 15 years, while the ratio of citizens to immigrants is at present (1981) 67.6% to 32.4% respectively.

In Qatar, the population estimate for 1950 was about 50,000. Estimates of the late seventies indicated that Qatar's population had reached 200,000, most of whom (74%) were non-Qatari. The first census in the UAE, in 1968, gave an estimate of 180,000, reaching in the 1980 census 1,150,155. Thus, in the space of twelve years, the numbers had increased

---

[9] Berkes and Sinclair, p. 136.

by more than six times. The ratio of local inhabitants to immigrants changed radically. These latter were 37% of the total population in 1968 and became about 80% in 1980.

If we view the problem from a different perspective, viz. the contribution of the local labour force, we find that the ratio of immigrant labour becomes the majority in the local labour market, reaching a total of 69.7% of the total labour force in the countries under study (Kuwait, Qatar, the UAE, Bahrain and Saudi Arabia – see Table 1).

There are no accurate statistics available for these countries as regards the contribution of Arab and non-Arab labour forces. But the studies that exist point to two important facts. First, there are increasing numbers of Asiatic immigrants to the Gulf States, even to countries which had traditionally, and until the mid-seventies, maintained a high rate of Arab immigration, such as Saudi Arabia and Kuwait. The other countries (excluding Oman) are tending to bring in a considerable Asiatic labour force. In Bahrein, for instance, nine out of ten applications for labour permits in 1975 were submitted by Asiatics.[10]

Secondly, the Arab immigrants, unlike the Asiatics, maintain a more or less balanced structure in sex and age whereas the Asiatic immigrants are predominantly young males. Immigration to the Gulf states in the sixties and seventies was predominantly Arab, a result of Omani immigration to the northern Gulf region, of Yemenis to Saudi Arabia and of a flood of Palestinians, Jordanians and Egyptians. This labour force was able in part to meet the needs of the local labour market. But once development had started in Oman, on the coast and in the hinterland, and the pattern of labour required began to change, the importing of a labour force in the mid-seventies shifted to a new source, Asia: Korea, Thailand and the Philippines, as well as India, Pakistan and Bangladesh.

---

[10] Berkes and Sinclair, p. 221.

Arab labour and the role of the Palestinians: The labour market is still in need of Arabs, especially in the fields of government service, education, health services and the mass media. This makes the Arabs relatively influential because of their proximity to the civil service, education and the media. Therefore, Arab issues are ever-present in the media and in education in particular, and these have a direct effect on the local population. It is not, of course, possible to arrive at some unequivocal generalization regarding the relations between the Arab expatriates and the locals. Any unilateral assessment is liable to be erroneous. There are, for example, studies which argue that there is "a deep and unbridgeable gulf between locals and expatriates. Social relations in general are almost non-existent except those within the context of the work itself. The local tends to be wary of the expatriate and this wariness is practically confined to one issue: the difference in customs and traditions."[11]

The above conclusion clearly mixes together Arab and non-Arab expatriates, for it is well known that there are many common denominators in Arab customs and traditions. Other studies maintain that "the presence of foreigners (in Kuwait) has changed many local customs and traditions — Kuwaiti society, for instance, has borrowed many Indian customs."[12] One might add here that this is true of Palestinian, Egyptian and other customs.

It is certain that the impact of Arab immigrants is greater than that of non-Arabs. Certain cultural factors are common, such as language, religion and a general sentiment of Arabism, in addition to propinquity in places of work and in some residential areas. This is in contrast to Asiatic immigrants of the past five years, who are isolated in special labour camps.

[11] See Faysal al-Salim, "Expatriate Labour in the Arab Gulf States: Preliminary Observations on the General Situation," unpublished study.

[12] Mentioned in a study by Faysal al-Salim, Maria al-Salim and Tawfiq Farah entitled "Expatriate Labor in Kuwait."

Relations between the Arab immigrants and the resident population are complex and not amenable to simplification. They amount to a dichotomy of attraction and replusion, love and hatred, and this for both objective and subjective reasons.[13] But groups who are politically aware and some quarters in the political establishment of the Gulf appreciate the importance of Arab expatriate labour, and call for expanding it, whereas they view the Asiatic labour force with apprehension for political and security reasons.

The popular and official viewpoints are in agreement, however, as regards support for Arab causes, especially the question of Palestine. The Palestinians in the Gulf constitute, no doubt, an important reserve force for the Palestinian Revolution. Western crisis-management studies in particular point to the "danger" of the Palestinians in the Gulf. Following the Iranian revolution and the intimate relationship established immediately with the Palestinians, the Western mass media spoke frequently of the PLO's domination of the Gulf and hence of oil.[14]

This relationship, and before it the large Palestinian presence in the Gulf, was used to intimidate or blackmail the Arab Gulf states. Studies devoted to the status of the Palestinians in the Gulf show that despite their negative and repressed feelings due to their being denied certain political privileges, they nevertheless do not pose any direct threat to the status quo in the Gulf because of the freedom they enjoy to organize themselves vis-à-vis the outside world, and their relative economic comfort.[15]

[13] For a detailed study of this question, see Mohamed al-Rumaihi, "A Nationalist Gulf Viewpoint Regarding the Social and Political Effects of Expatriate Labour", al-Mustaqbal al-'Arabi, No. 23 (January, 1981), pp. 68-79.

[14] John K. Cooley, "Iran, the Palestinians and the Gulf," Foreign Affairs, No. 57 (Summer 1979), pp. 1017-1034.

[15] Asad Abd al-Rahman, "The Palestinians in Kuwait: Their Political Significance", The United States, Arabia and the Gulf (Georgetown University: Center for Contemporary Arab Studies in Arab-American Relations), pp. 14-17.

The Palestinians in the Gulf are primarily concerned with the question of the liberation of their homeland to the point where they are ready to abandon certain social traditions for the sake of the struggle, while, as a group, they are passing through a transitional stage, the result of uprooting and expulsion.[16]

But the question still stands: Are all the Palestinians in the Gulf actively engaged in working for Palestinian national goals? It is to be noted that there is a small, active and organized minority, whereas the Palestinian masses in the Gulf are unorganized even though they sympathize with the PLO. There is also a Palestinian middle class which is perfectly satisfied with its material status and shuns any Palestinian political activity if it conflicts with current policies.

(c) *Cultural and Political Changes*

Among the most potent agents of change in Gulf oil societies are cultural and political changes. Through ever-increasing expenditure on education at all levels, larger groups of citizens are receiving general and higher education. Despite the disparity at the early stages of government education as between males and females, the term "silent cultural revolution" may be cautiously applied to what is happening today in the field of education. The modern states of the Gulf have come to need educated people to fill administrative posts in the government and military posts in the police and army. So, alongside government education, there is also non-government education which takes place in many fields of training. This education, in spite of the reservations one may have regarding

---

[16] In a study by Dr. Basim Sirhan entitled *Family and Kinship Among Palestinians in Kuwait* (Kuwait: Arab Planning Institute, 1977), pp. 23-24, the author found that while 97% of the sample he studied agreed that the adult Palestinian woman should take part in the Palestinian struggle, only 45% of that sample agreed that she could participate in political activity.

its quality, does, however, quantitatively affect the social structure, creating new aspirations among wide sectors of society with peasant or pastoral backgrounds. It also affects political and nationalist consciousness.

In addition, some societies have adopted modern constitutions and relatively modern regimes of government.

Modern constitutions have been proclaimed in Kuwait, Qatar, Bahrein and the UAE. Only Oman and Saudi Arabia, despite modernization of the government service, remain without a modern constitution. Kuwait has gone beyond the adoption of a modern constitution, adopting also an electoral parliamentary system of popular representation. The new consciousness, and the growth of new social groups which had not existed before in these societies, such as workers, employees and soldiers, when combined with education, turns these groups into pressure groups on the economic and political level. This pressure has crystallized into local opposition groups such as the Oman Liberation Front, the Popular Front, the two Bahrein Liberation Fronts and other opposition groups in Kuwait and Saudi Arabia. Only in Kuwait does opposition assume an admissible and quasi-official form, while the other opposition groups in the remaining Gulf states are underground organizations. When one examines the literature produced by these organizations and groups, one finds them to vary between religious and leftist. But common to them all is criticism of the existing state of affairs and a call for reforms, some of which are radical, in the government structure and administration of these societies. As education expands, an ever larger number of citizens is likely to read this literature and sympathize with it.

Dynamics of Change in Gulf Society

The dynamics of change operating inside Gulf societies are many and various. Some are a product of the impact of new economic conditions on a traditional society, others of the impact of events in the surrounding region. In Saudi Arabia, dominated by Najdi culture, i.e. the culture of the region to which the dominant clan belongs, there are at least three different cultural areas. There is, first of all Najd, where political and economic power is concentrated. But there is also Hijaz, 'Asir and al-Ahsa, where the inhabitants are subject to a number of economic and political pressures. The man from Hijaz, al-Ahsa and 'Asir is deprived of many of the benefits which oil wealth has bestowed upon privileged groups in Saudi society. Problems such as the distribution of wealth and services, a complex and aging bureaucratic routine, deprivation of any form of political participation, the dominance of traditional norms such as the deprivation of women and their socio-economic isolation, when combined on the other hand with the opening of these societies to advanced societies in the West and East, makes it almost impossible for the present state of affairs to continue without any change. It is to be noted that the Saudi regime grants certain unwritten concessions in times of crisis, as happened for instance after the dethrone-ment of King Saud bin 'Abd al-'Aziz in the early sixties or the assassination of King Faisal in the mid-seventies, or the occupation of the Grand Mosque in Mecca in the fall of 1979. After each crisis, the Saudi regime renews its promise to establish a "Consultative Council" or a "regional adminis-tration" in the various regions but promptly ignores these promises once the crisis has passed.

Oman suffers from a number of internal problems chief among which is the inequitable distribution of wealth, with a tiny group in society receiving most of the benefits to the detriment of the majority. Corruption is rife in the bureau-cracy, a malady that also afflicts the Gulf oil states in varying degrees. The mal-distribution of wealth and the lack of any medium or long-term outlook on the future have become the subject of severe criticism by technocrats and intellectuals. In a direct criticism of public schemes and of their administration in Gulf States, one such study declares: "The present facts about public schemes in the Gulf indicate a lack of several prerequisites and preliminary studies, which are indispensable if these schemes are to function efficiently. Malfunctioning is the result of inefficient supervision and a faulty organizational and administrative structure, combined with the negative impact of the surrounding social environment in which these schemes operate."[17]

The prerequisites for stability are in conflict with the status quo and with current policies. These societies are divided into local and expatriate, and subdivided into sects, tribes and groups, some of which are extremely rich and others extremely poor. Their development plans are short-term and do not conform to a long-term development scheme. Furthermore, some are tied to the new forces of imperialism. This contradiction in the prerequisites for independence renders them liable to radical and unexpected transformation.

The foreign and especially imperialist powers attempt to exploit the fragile status quo for their own ends. Sometimes they threaten with the Rapid Deployment Force. At others, they apply pressure to maintain certain oil production levels and prices and refer ominously to a supposed expected Soviet expansion. Thus these powers combat any drive towards independence or neutrality that the Gulf countries may contemplate. The dymanics of change have in the eighties approached the stage of transformation from quantitative to qualitative change, and this will put the region on a new historic and social track.

---

[17] Ali Khalifa al-Kuwari, *The Role of Public Schemes in Economic Development: An Introduction to the Study of the Efficiency of Public Schemes in the Oil-Producing Countries of the Arabian Peninsula* (Kuwait: The National Council for Culture, Arts and Letters) (*'Alam al-Ma'rifa* series, No. 42, 1981), p. 195.

Conclusion

The conclusion that many geo-political studies of the Gulf arrive at is that the West is concerned with the Gulf for three reasons: principally, oil, then geographical location, and then the conservative character of the political regimes.[18] These are three concentric circles. The Soviet Union is also interested in the Gulf for three main reasons: to isolate Europe from the USA, to increase its power in the Gulf, and to circumvent China.[19] Between these two grand strategies, various Arab sides manoeuvre tactically towards political objectives, serving either regional or international interests. There are numerous indications that the regional parties in the Middle East manoeuvre within this grand strategy. Oman, for instance, recognizes China and accepts Chinese diplomatic envoys, but is hostile to the Soviet Union because of its "atheism"! Again, Israel and Saudi Arabia, the major regime in the Gulf, are both allies of the USA. The link between the Palestine question and the Gulf stems from the fact that both Israel and Saudi Arabia work within the "American axis." They are connected by strategy but have divergent regional policies. This divergence was illustrated when Israel attacked the Iraqi nuclear reactor in June 1981 and announced its readiness to shoot down the AWACS since Saudi Arabia is a confrontation state. The governments of the Gulf feel that they might become direct targets for Israel but at the same time are neither able nor willing (except for Kuwait) to establish balanced relations with the Eastern bloc. And thus the oil and Gulf arenas are

---

[18] For further details regarding this topic, see Mahjub 'Umar, "Gulf Security and Its Relationship to Arab National Security in the Light of the Arab-Israeli Conflict", *al-Mustaqbal al-'Arabi,* No. 30 (August, 1981), pp. 23-39.

[19] This Soviet strategy is not one that is openly proclaimed by the Soviets but rather the result of western analyses of Soviet objectives; see 'Umar *op. cit.,* p. 26. The declared Soviet policy objectives are the seven points announced by President Brezhnev during his Indian visit in December, 1980. They call, in sum, for neutrality of the Gulf region and the absence of all foreign troops therefrom.

linked together with the Palestine question in a manner that is unprecedented since the creation of the Zionist entity.

The regional options in the Gulf are fairly limited. At a time when Kuwait is seeking to fortify its neutrality as regards the two super-powers and announces more than once that Israel is the real threat to the Gulf, while the Soviet threat is illusory and impalpable, other Gulf countries have adopted a clear stand against any relations with the Eastern bloc and its diverse currents: Eastern Europe, the Soviet Union and China. Still others opt for relations with China, e.g. Oman. Therefore we find that the Gulf, especially Saudi Arabia, is actively pursuing a settlement of the problem (one example is Prince Fahd's recent initiative) that would be acceptable to both the Palestinians and Israel in order to solve or freeze this regional contradiction within the "American axis" without resorting to a clash with Israel which may either disturb that axis further, or do away with the Palestine question, thus destabilizing the regimes internally.

If the second half of the seventies witnessed a shift in the international focus of politics from the banks of the Suez Canal and Sinai to the Gulf, the assassination of President Sadat in October 1981 may shift the focus back to the first arena. The peoples of the Gulf cannot but proclaim their full support for the Palestinian problem. They were unable to go along publicly with the Sadat policy in the four year period between his visit to Jerusalem and his assassination. After his departure they will assuredly be unable to stand by and watch what might happen in the region especially if the new Egyptian administration were to adopt a complete or partial reversal of Sadat's previous line. Factors of economic and social change will blow their winds through the Gulf, filling the sails of its population and moving them away from a direct and organic relationship with the US, Israel's principal and strategic ally. Nor can the US be expected to adopt a moderate or acceptable attitude.

Accordingly, we find that whenever the Gulf region is the locus of political pressure *for* the Palestine problem it is also a means of pressure *on* the Palestinians to accept a settlement. Hence the implicit acceptance of Israel is included as one of Prince Fahd's proposals, which speaks of the right of all states in the region to live in peace. The initiative thus achieves two objectives: warding off the direct Israeli threat, and not granting the masses a legitimate reason to topple the regime in case the regime decides to abandon the issue. The Iran-Iraq war has added a number of possibilities, some of which have become probabilities and others have become expectations. What is virtually certain is that this war has weakened two basic sides in the Gulf. This is especially true of Iraq, which, had it preserved its forces and its political stance, both of which had increased in the late seventies, would have played a role of primary importance in the Gulf especially after the Iranian revolution. The war, however, has weakened both sides making it difficult to face any foreign or American intervention, and this in turn intensifies the existing vacuum. In addition, the possibility that the war might escalate and spread to other areas in the Gulf exposes the Gulf region to incalculable risks and thus affects the course and direction of the Palestine question.

What has been termed the Middle East problem is no longer the question of Palestine's liberation from Zionism but has grown much more extensive. It is really the problem of Arab liberation from colonialist and economic neo-imperialism. The key to a qualitative transformation in this liberation lies in the use of Arab oil wealth in the Gulf and elsewhere for the service of Arab causes in a more effective manner, in view of the experiences of the past decade.

In the coming stage it is certain that the new Gulf Cooperation Council will play a notable role in Arab affairs. It is known that there are two main currents inside the Council. The first is led by Kuwait, which calls for adoption of liberal policies internally and neutral policies externally. The second is led by Oman and calls for total alignment with the West and repressive internal policies. New developments, however, are likely to make the Kuwaiti position increasingly attractive.

Despite the indirect importance of the Palestine question as regards the political scene in the Gulf in the eighties, it is likely that the Palestinians residing in the Gulf will not have a direct role to play in socio-political transformation. Most of the social groups of the Palestinian community, seek, above all, to preserve their source of livelihood, and are therefore not prepared to be engaged as a party in any internal political conflict.

But the possibility remains that the expatriates in general may participate in socio-political change or join up with local forces to effect such a change. Probably, however, the effect will be felt in the form of pressure to improve the living conditions of the expatriates in the region as a whole and the eighties may witness strikes and other problems having to do with wages, working conditions, residency requirements and so forth. Several studies have already appeared regarding the inferior status of expatriates in the Gulf, both Arab and non-Arab. A number of international reports have also alluded to this problem. If these countries persist in ignoring the issue without either setting minimum living standards on the one hand or limiting the influx of expatriates on the other, this may become one of the problems to be faced by these societies in the eighties.

II
THE INTERNATIONAL ACTORS

5

Palestine and the Gulf:
A European Perspective

by Michel Tatu

Nowhere more than in Western Europe have the perceptions and positions about the Arab-Israeli conflict and other Middle East issues changed so much in the last fifteen years. France and Great Britain, the two countries which, together with Israel, attacked Egypt in 1956, maintaining for years thereafter an adamantly pro-Israeli stand, are now in the forefront of the trend towards pressuring Israel to withdraw from the territories occupied in 1967, and urging self-determination for the Palestinians and a recognition of the PLO. These two countries have been followed progressively by other EEC countries — somewhat reluctantly at the beginning by the Benelux countries and West Germany, the latter keeping a generally low profile on this issue because of past guilt for the World War Two holocaust and more predominantly European interests.

Among all the European countries, De Gaulle's France was the first to distance itself from Israel at the time of the Six-Day War (in fact, a few days before the outbreak of open hostilities), and years before the oil factor played any significant role in West European calculations. This position, which at the time was not well accepted by French public opinion and coming as it did after years of intensive cooperation with Israel, was intended to restore good relations with the Arab countries in the wake of the Algerian war, and was, in fact, motivated by a clearer awareness of Israeli strength vis-à-vis the Arab armies. The grounds for this policy were laid by a June 2 1967 statement of the French government — three days before the Israeli attack — warning that "any state which uses arms first, wherever it be, will not benefit from France's appro-bation, and even less from her support." As was subsequently reported by witnesses, De Gaulle warned Israel's foreign minister, Abba Eban, that although Israel would start the fight and win it, her success would bring the Soviets into the area to an extent that even Soviet leaders would find uncongenial and would help to create a "Palestinian problem."

This attitude persisted during all the years of the Fifth Republic, even though Giscard d'Estaing in 1974 and Mitter-rand in 1981 began their mandate by trying to improve their relations with Israel and creating a better image in Israeli eyes. The election of a Socialist president in France is too recent to permit any definite conclusions, but it seems that the change will be limited. Although Mitterrand intends to exploit the traditionally better Israeli connections of the Socialist Party, and announced a trip to Jerusalem for 1982 (the first by a French president to Israel), the initial moves of the new French diplomacy and of Foreign Minister Claude Cheysson (backed by the traditionally pro-Arab Quai d'Orsay) show the same old trend towards improving ties with Arab countries, including the PLO connection. The Arafat-Cheysson meeting in Beirut at the end of August, 1981, and the French admission that the PLO is a representative — but not the sole one — of the Palestinian people are good examples of that trend, and French diplomacy was quick to move after Sadat's assassination to state, though the remark was highly criticized as a slip of the tongue, that the death of the Egyptian President might be an occasion for a new gathering of the Arab world.

What has changed in the last few months is the European perception of the Camp David agreements, again, at least in part, under the influence of the change in France. Giscard d'Estaing's attitude towards the "peace process" was rather ambiguous, as it was towards East-West relations and other issues. In order to maintain the previous good relations of France with the Arab world, including "radical" countries like Syria and Iraq, the pre-May 1981 French government abstained from praising officially the Camp David agreements and the Israeli-Egypt peace treaty, though on the other hand it did not criticize them. By insisting on an overall settlement including a "guarantee" by other big powers – including France – Giscard seemed to prefer a multilateral peace process of the Geneva conference type.

Mitterrand already had another view of the Camp David agreements when he was in opposition. Among all political parties in France, the Socialist Party was the only one to approve the Carter deal. Even though Mitterrand and his comrades admitted that the Egyptian-Israeli peace treaty could not in itself bring general peace to the Middle East, the treaty was, nevertheless, considered an important step to peace and it had to be supported. For the new French president, it is nonsense to wait until the PLO, Syria, the USSR, Israel and the western powers sit around a table for talks and to negotiate peace agreements. Nevertheless, in the last period and especially since Sadat's assassination, the trend has been to say that the "peace process" inherited from Camp David has exhausted its possibilities and that a new approach is needed.

As far as the general view of the Palestine problem is concerned, there has been great continuity in the line of the various French governments over the last twenty years, and a regular progress towards recogntion of Palestinian rights. After initially stressing the "national rights" of the Palestinians, under Pompidou, France went further with Giscard by voting in the UN in favor of a resolution recognizing the representativity of the PLO, and by authorizing the Palestinian organization to open an office in Paris. At the same time, Giscard started to recognize publicly the right of the Palestinian people to "une patrie." Though this notion sounds stronger in French than the English "homeland," the move could be considered as a step towards the position held by Carter, who admitted at the same time the need for a "homeland." In the last period, and that includes under Mitterrand, Paris went further by talking publicly about "state structures" for the Palestinian people, then more directly about a "state," in the framework of "self-determination."

The other EEC states, with the possible exception of Britain (particularly after the return to power of the traditionally more Arab-oriented conservatives), were much slower in their evolution, though they eventually rallied around the French position. We had to wait until 1970 to see the European Community accept a statement calling for the withdrawal of Israel from all territories occupied in 1967, but it was mainly after the 1973 war that the change took place. Though France was mostly criticized in Israel and elsewhere for taking a pro-Arab stand only because of the oil problem and for "mercantile" motivations, it must be noticed that it was the 1973 war and the oil embargo which brought about the change in the Western European position, pushing other governments to a stand adopted long ago in Paris. Firstly, EEC governments realized their heavy dependence on Arab oil, which accounts for 80% of their imports. Secondly, they discovered that they might be involved in an unwanted war, if only because US forces have to use European territory if they want to supply any fighting party in the Middle-East. A German protest against the use of FRG facilities to help Israel in 1973 demonstrated the sensitivity of this issue and the perceived need of the Europeans to distance themselves from the US and from traditionally pro-Israeli positions.

Years later, this need was expressed very explicitly by Sir

Frederic Bennett, Chairman of the General Affairs Committee of the Western European Union, in a report on "The Situation in the Gulf and European Security." He said:

> It is not in the interest of Europe to seem to be too closely identified in this area with the American political scheme. This does not mean, naturally, that the European countries must dissociate themselves from the United States ... Nevertheless, as far as the United States is involved in policies which do not contribute to a just and peaceful solution of the conflicts which are taking place there, nor to deterring the Soviet intervention, it is up to the Europeans to promote such policies, if possible in consultation with their American allies, but without coercion.[1]

This new approach culminates on June 13, 1980 with the adoption of the EEC Venice summit declaration on the Middle East. The statement, which just mentions in passing the "agreements signed by Israel and Egypt in March 1979," without praising them or even calling them a "peace treaty," calls for a "comprehensive solution" of the conflict, which "requires the involvement and support of all the parties concerned... and the PLO, which will have to be associated with the negotiations." It refuses "any unilateral initiative designed to change the status of Jerusalem" and stresses the need for Israel "to put an end to the territorial occupation which it has maintained since the conflict of 1967."

The timing of this declaration is significant, since the Carter administration had warned against any European "initiative," and was trying to rally the Europeans to the support of the autonomy talks underway between Egypt and Israel. The Israeli reaction was particularly strong, speaking of a "Munich-like capitulation to totalitarian blackmail."

In fact, a year later, with the new Mitterrand approach to Camp David this declaration seemed to have been quietly shelved. The European move to take part in the Sinai peace force is a clear recognition 'of the Camp David process and

---

[1] WEU 27th Ordinary Session, Document 871, addendum, June 17, 1981.

supports the American position, even though it is clearly intended to help Israel go ahead with the decision to withdraw fully from Sinai, despite Sadat's death. It remains to be seen if Europe will try to be involved in the autonomy talks or at least to recognize them as a necessary step to peace. But in any case, the principles enunciated in the Venice statement are still clearly those which the European governments will follow in any further negotiations, whatever the framework.[2]

Europe and the Gulf

The process of establishing a distance from US positions is at work as far as the situation in the Gulf is concerned, but in a more contradictory manner and with a much more limited effect. On the one side, as we have seen in the context of the Arab-Israeli conflict, the European governments clearly have a more sophisticated approach to the regional problems involved, and they tend to apprehend better the local causes of conflicts and the internal evolution of the societies, including the Islamic revival. Unlike the Americans, they do not exaggerate the East-West dimension of local tensions and are highly sceptical about the Reagan administration's idea of a "strategic consensus" among various nations of the Middle East on the common basis of an anti-Soviet attitude. In their view, any such consensus is unlikely — short of overt Soviet agression —

---

[2] This is not altered by the blunder of Claude Cheysson, French Minister for Foreign Affairs, during his trip to Israel in December 1981, when he hinted that the Venice Declaration was "wrong" and that the Europeans are not going to take any other "initiative." This statement, which was made to Israel radio, was ambiguous in itself and was in any case considered a blunder by its author. Nevertheless, while the new French government has distanced itself from the Venice Declaration as a policy enacted by its predecessor, its stance on the substance of the Arab-Israeli conflict, including the constitution of a Palestinian state and recognition of the PLO as "one of the representative components" of the Palestinian people, goes further towards the traditional Arab position than that of the previous government. That is why many Arab reactions to this blunder seem to have been excessive.

as long as Israel opposes the aspirations of the Arabs and even provokes them with her settlements in the occupied territories, attacks on Lebanon or such operations as the bombing of the Baghdad reactor. That is why a settlement of the Arab-Israeli conflict must have priority in their view.

But, on the other side, European interests are much closer to those of the United States as far as oil is concerned. In fact, Europe's interest is much higher, since she is far more dependent than the US on the Gulf exports, which means a shared concern with Washington about the strategic implications of any development there. In addition, other factors complicate the European situation:

1. Despite its dependence, Europe has very few means or resources to ensure on her own the security of her oil imports. With the exception of some French forces in Djibouti or further South in the Indian Ocean, and of some British ships in the area in case of trouble, Europe has to rely on the good will of the Gulf nations or on the US forces in the area. Some people argue that this is inevitable, and that there is no way to protect sea lanes in modern times, either in the Indian Ocean or anywhere else. But the European governments should be more cautious. Even if they press the US to take, as far as possible, a non-provocative posture, even if they perfectly understand the desire of Arab nations to stay away from any big power confrontation or presence, they do not oppose the current American programme of building a Rapid Deployment Force: the aim must be in their view to deter not only Soviet intervention, but any extension of local hostilities which might threaten the freedom of navigation and the flow of oil.

2. Europe is strategically involved, too, in any conflict in the Gulf area, which is in fact a vital part of the Southern approach, or "Southern flank" of the NATO area. Albert Wohlstetter, the famous American strategist, points out that the main military base on which the US administration seems to count for facing an insurgency, the Diego Garcia base, is

further from the Upper Gulf area than Dublin, the Irish capital. In his view, the only practical way of approaching the area, in order to counter, say, a Soviet move against Iran in the direction of the Gulf, is through Turkey, which is a European country, and also a full-fledged NATO member. In other words, it will be impossible for Europe to remain aloof from any contingency in the Gulf area, whatever its cause — provoked or unprovoked by the US — and even without the oil problem.

3. Finally, any American involvement in the Gulf will put a new burden on NATO: both geographically, as we have seen, because the US forces will have to use their logistic facilities in Europe to a much higher degree than in 1973, and also as far as the resources are concerned — already the US administration has asked the European members of NATO to be ready to "fill the gap" in military deployments in Europe should Washington need to divert forces from Europe to the Gulf area, and if they do not want to remain an "empty shell" facing the Warsaw pact forces in Central Europe.

All these factors explain why the European governments cannot remain inactive nor feel uncommitted faced with any significant trouble in the area, even though their role can be only secondary. This situation has been illustrated in September-October 1980, at the outbreak of the Iraqi-Iranian war. In a matter of days, we witnessed a strong, though non-official, agreement among most Western powers, including Europe and the US, to keep to a few principles of action:

• To have some military demonstrations in the Indian Ocean, with the US in the key role but with a substantial participation of the Europeans, notably the French and the British, and with coordination at the technical level. For example, France brought into the area some mine-sweepers which the US did not have on the spot, in case such ships would be needed to clear the Gulf of mines;

• To make strong statements announcing that any encroachment against the freedom of navigation in the Gulf would hurt the "vital interests" of the Western nations. This declaratory policy, together with the military measures mentioned above, may have played a role in preventing the extension of the war. Clearly, Iraq was deterred from using friendly territories along the Gulf for extending its military operations against Iran, and Iran in turn decided not to make good a threat which had been aired in the early days of the war, to interfere with the movements of ships in the Gulf.

This example shows how sensitive those issues are, and how the attitude of the European countries may change if interests of importance to them are involved. The same governments which had been most friendly to the Arab nations at various phases of the Arab-Israeli conflict were apparently ready to use force in the area should their oil imports be seriously threatened. There is no reason to believe that the pattern might be different in the future.

Altogether, what seems to be a duality of position — close to the Arab position as far as Israel is concerned, close to the U S in regard to the Gulf issues — is going to persist for a long time to come. One can even expect a deepening of the European-Israeli tension, at least as long as the Begin government is in power. Even a government with the best initial intentions towards Israel, as Mitterrand's government was, very quickly had to face crises in its relations with Begin, first with the attack on the French-made Iraqi reactor, then with the annexation of the Golan just a few days after Cheysson's visit to Israel and a few weeks before the projected Mitterrand trip. That trip has since been postponed, at least until the final Sinai withdrawal is accomplished. In fact, it is quite possible that it will never materialize, either because the Sinai commitment will not be kept, or, more simply, because French officials are aware of the risk of exposing Mitterand to unpleasant attacks on the part of Begin.

But we have to see the limits of this frustration. First, the situation might change if the Israeli Labour Party returns to power. Its close connections with many Socialist parties in Europe, its better image in world public opinion, would certainly introduce a sort of honeymoon in relations, especially with Mitterrand's party. Secondly, no or almost no government in Europe – with the possible exception of Papandreou's Greece – will support any solution or position which does not recognize the right of Israel to exist within "recognised and guaranteed boundaries," together with its withdrawal from the West Bank and Gaza. For this reason, the relationship with the PLO will be hampered as long as this organization does not recognize Israel and/or change its Charter. Improvements are certainly possible, especially if terrorist actions continue to be denounced by PLO leaders. But it is unlikely that the organization will be recognized as "the sole" representative, short of general elections and/or if it accepts formally Israel's existence.

This explains too the somewhat ambiguous attitudes of European states towards the Camp David agreements. Those agreements, and the Egyptian-Israeli treaty, were met with reservation and some criticism, mainly because they divided the Arab world and harmed the interests of some Arab governments with good connections in Europe, such as Syria and Jordan, and not because they installed peace between Israel and Egypt. On the contrary, this peace is exactly the kind of peace which most European governments see as suitable for other Arab states, namely, formal recognition, total withdrawal from, and demilitarization of, the territories occupied in 1967. Furthermore, although many countries, beginning with France, would like to see Egypt getting closer to the other Arab states, most European capitals will base their future policy on the "fait accompli" of the Camp David agreements, not on their denunciation.

As far as the Gulf is concerned, no change is to be anticipated, but the sense of common interests with the US on the need to preserve the flow of oil does not mean an identification of policies. As long as most governments in the area remain "moderate," there will be no real problem with them or with the US, and one could even speak of a "division of labor" between the US and Europe, with the Americans taking care of the military hardware, and the Europeans of civilian investments. This could take place if a strong competition did not oppose businessmen from both sides of the Atlantic, including in the area of military sales. In Saudi Arabia this competition is open, while in other countries, like Iraq, which have severed relations with the US, France has taken the lead.

In fact, the feeling of security which the Europeans may have with regard to the Gulf relies on two elements: stability in the area and friendly relations with the "moderate" local governments, on one hand and a deterrent US military presence not too far away, on the other. When one of those elements fails, as in Iran after 1979, the picture is disturbed, and divergent policies may appear. In general, the Europeans showed themselves more moderate than the Americans when confronted with the crises both in Iran and in Afghanistan. But this is a part of a more general situation, the effects of which may be detected nowadays around Poland. If we except emotional reactions, the Europeans not only emphasize much less than the Americans the military means of "crisis management," they are much more careful, too, in using economic sanctions and political retaliation. And this applies to any area of the world.

6

The Atlantic Alliance and the Middle East in the Early 1950's and Today: Retrospect and Prospect

by Marwan Buheiry

1. Introduction

In sharp contrast to the political and colonial interests of Britain, France, Tsarist Russia, or Italy, the interest of America in the Middle East before the First World War focused in the main on commercial and missionary activity, including education. However, this picture was to change gradually. Following the Balfour Declaration and the Mandate System, which the United States supported, an additional factor developed: the growth of political Zionism in Palestine and its repercussions on the American domestic scene. Furthermore in the late thirties, the Middle Eastern oil dimension and the entrance of American oil companies into the Arab world assumed strategic importance and inextricable linkage with politics and defence.[1]

During the Second World War the strategic importance of the Middle East was fully recognized by policy-makers and public opinion in America. The region at large was shown to be a crucial centre of land, sea, and air communications, as

---

[1] Marwan Buheiry, "From Truman to Kissinger: US Policy in the Middle East," *al-Mustaqbal al-'Arabi* (Beirut), July 1981, p. 73 (in Arabic).

well as an indispensable reservoir of petroleum which helped the allies' war effort. It is also significant that despite their wartime alliance against the Axis powers, the United States and the Soviet Union clashed on the question of Iran even while the war was in progress: the Soviets supported separatist movements among the Kurds and Azerbaijanis, and, in 1944, "even attacked the presence in Iran of the American troops who were bringing lend-lease supplies to Russia."[2] This episode confirms the perception of Admiral A.T. Mahan who drew attention to the Middle East and the Gulf as a permanent arena of strategic confrontation between rival powers as early as 1902.[3] Whatever the definition, the Middle East was and remains above all a strategic, rather than a geographic, concept.

After 1945, as the Cold War and the containment of the Soviet Union became the dominant concern of the Western allies, the strategic importance of the Middle East reached new heights. Henceforth it was argued that Soviet penetration of the region would outflank the Atlantic alliance, causing a decisive rupture in the world balance. A second perception was that Soviet control over Middle East oil resources would dislocate the economy of the Western world.[4]

[2] George Lenczowski, *United States Interests in the Middle East* (Washington: American Enterprise Institute, 1968), p. 13.

[3] Alfred Mahan, "The Persian Gulf and International Relations," *National Review* (London), September 1902.

[4] John Campbell, *Defense of the Middle East: Problems of American Policy* (New York: Harper, 1960), pp. 4-5. A third argument heard perhaps less often than the other two was that "the triumph of Communism in the heart of the Islamic world could be the prelude to its triumph throughout Asia, Africa and Europe." *Ibid.* An influential example of a "grand design" policy paper is the NSC – 68, the product of Dean Acheson in 1950, which in his words stated the conflicting aims and purposes of the two superpowers: "The priority given by the Soviet rulers to the Kremlin design, world domination, contrasted with the American aim, an environment in which free societies could exist and flourish." This major policy paper recommended "specific measures for a large and immediate improvement of military forces and weapons, and the economic and morale factors which underlay our own and our allies' ability to influence the conduct of other societies." Dean Acheson, *Present at the Creation* (New York: Norton, 1969), pp. 375-6.

In the late forties and early fifties, during the process of formalizing the Atlantic alliance as NATO, questions of linkage with the Middle East and the enlargement of the NATO area of responsibility were raised and several options debated. Thereafter, interest in this thorny matter fluctuated according to the level of tension in the world. Today, it is evident that the expansion of the Alliance's zone of operation is once more the subject of intense deliberation and concern: the logic of a new Cold War is being imposed on the Middle East, while NATO appears intent on bringing the area into association with it by extending the perimeter of action beyond the Tropic of Cancer (the traditional limit of NATO deployment as specified in the Organization's Charter) and by formal and informal arrangements with some of the region's states.

The purpose of this study is to examine the dynamics and implications of this fateful trend, both in its first manifestations in the early 1950's and today, with major emphasis placed on the United States and Britain.

2. The Alliance and the Middle East in the Early 1950's

In the confrontationist atmosphere of the Cold War, the Administration of President Truman established the main lines of America's Middle East policy. To some extent these were inherited from Imperial Britain or developed in response to domestic pressures, particularly in the case of Palestine. Another influence flowed from the nature and scope of America's wartime strategy exemplified by the sharing with Britain of the Persian Gulf Command, the supply channel to the Soviet Union through Iran, and the construction of an air base at Dhahran during the final year of the war. There was also the factor of oil.[5]

---

5 On the complicated question of America's wartime oil policy, there was a great deal of concern on the part of the Office of Mobilization about the

A cornerstone of America's policy was the global containment of the Soviet Union, which in effect meant keeping it out of the Middle East and the Arab world, as well as other regions. Dominated as it was by Cold War and Globalist outlooks, the main lines of US policy hardly took account of Arab hopes and fears: Arab nationalism and the drive for Arab unity, decolonization, full sovereignty, and non-alignment were generally seen in terms of conflict with or obstruction of American and allied global aims and objectives. All this was reinforced by the traditional penchant in favour of Israel.

When Britain gave notice in early 1947 that it was no longer able to fulfil its economic and military commitments to Greece and Turkey, the Truman Administration (particularly Harriman, Acheson, Marshall, Forrestal and, of course, the President himself) stepped in with the Truman Doctrine: perhaps the first evidence of the application of containment in the Middle East, with clear implications for its extension anywhere in the world. Furthermore, the doctrine opened the way to other major moves on the bipolar and Cold War chequerboard: The Marshall Plan of 1947, the North Atlantic Treaty of April 1948, and the North Atlantic Treaty Organization of August 1949 (although the last two also evolved from the 1947 Anglo-French Treaty of Dunkirk and the Brussels Pact of 1948). Yet another step was the Point Four proposal of 1949 which extended the principle of economic development and recovery to the less developed areas of the world.

---

depletion of America's domestic oil reserves caused by the requirements of war. An abortive plan for the government to nationalize American foreign oil holdings in support of the war effort was even considered. The thorny questions of the competition between foreign and domestic oil and of the public versus private ownership of the oil industry tended to be adjudicated by considerations of national security. One ought not to forget also the crucial importance of Middle Eastern oil in the European recovery programme. Robert Stookey, *America and the Arab States* (New York: J. Wiley, 1975), pp. 69-70.

NATO's original membership of twelve included the United States, Canada, Great Britain, Iceland, Norway, Denmark, France, Belgium, Luxembourg, Holland, Portugal, and Italy. Sweden was pressured to join but refused to. Later on Greece, Turkey, and West Germany were brought into the alliance, raising the membership to fifteen. From the very start there were reservations about the Treaty both in America and in Europe. Voices were heard in Congress against stationing American forces in Europe. The mutuality of obligations set out in the key operative articles 3 and 5 were judged to be too precise and restrictive. Also, in the words of a group of Brookings Institution analysts writing in the mid-fifties, "public feeling became restive at the implication that United States policy was abandoning the United Nations, was organizing a military coalition against the Soviet Union, and was moving toward developing military means to achieve its objectives."[6]

In Europe too the northern states were not altogether happy about the widening scope of commitments. To cite one example, reflecting on the problem of additional membership in NATO, Dean Acheson remarked:

> A press leak in May (1951) that Britain, France and the United States were consulting together about invitations to Greece and Turkey alarmed and annoyed the other allies. The 'North Atlantic' had been stretched in 1949 to include Italy; now we were trying to take in the Eastern Mediterranean, a snake pit of troubles. How could Northern European statesmen convince their people that attacks in the Levant should be regarded as attacks on Scandinavia or the Low Countries? In carrying the debate for the invitations, I pointed out the absence of any feasible alternative. A year before, recognizing the importance of Greece and Turkey as an eastern flank of European defense, the Nato Council had decided to associate the two countries through a defence agency, but it had

---

[6] William Reitzel, Morton Kaplan, and Constance Coblenz, *United States Foreign Policy 1945-1955* (Washington: The Brookings Institution, 1956), p. 127.

not worked. They wanted full membership, which from our point of view had the advantage of mutuality of obligations."[7]

As to the Middle East, the leading partners in the Alliance (America, Britain and France) perceived the region as one of vital strategic importance in relation to the Soviet Union, and, on occasion, in relation to each other. France and Britain were colonial powers with special interests in the Eastern Mediterranean and a long tradition of rivalry. In this respect, Britain's perception of French rivalry and fears may be gauged by a Permanent Under-Secretary's Committee paper on the Middle East (April 30, 1949). The French attitude toward the region was seen as "a combination of fear that the area may be given undue attention to the detriment of security arrangements in Western Europe; of desire to retain or partially recover France's interests (largely cultural) and prestige, especially in the Levant States; and of concern for continued or increased supplies of Middle East oil." The Committee's paper acknowledged French interest in Palestine's Holy Places, "largely in response to Catholic opinion."[8] As to the recent origin and consequences of this rivalry, the paper perceived it in familiar terms:

> The French blame British policy in 1942 and after for the loss of their position in the Levant States, and they regard with the highest suspicion any positive move by the United Kingdom to co-operate with Syria or the Lebanon for security purposes. They are inclined to attribute to His Majesty's Government Machiavellian schemes to counter French influence and to absorb the Levant States into a British-controlled Greater Syria. In order to combat these imaginary schemes, they are all too ready to intrigue against us and we must accept that France's policy is likely to be one of mistrust and covert opposition to us. There have been recent instances of this on the occasion of M. Bidault's visit to the Levant States, and over Persian oil.[9]

---

[7] Acheson, *Present at the Creation,* p. 570.

[8] *Foreign Office* (FO) 371/75067, PUSC (19) on Middle East, 30 April 1949.

[9] *Ibid.*

While recognizing that such feelings of mistrust were present to a greater extent in Frenchmen in the Middle East than in the government in Paris, the Committee also felt that France was "preoccupied with the risk of the growth of Arab nationalism in North Africa, and consequently opposed to manifestations of Arab national unity in the Middle East, and in particular a revival of the Arab League or the realization of plans for Greater Syria or the Union of the Fertile Crescent."[10]

However, Anglo-French relations did improve with the joint US-British-French statement on the Middle East of 25 May 1950 (the Tripartite Declaration). Yet here again, the Foreign Office appeared less than enthusiastic about France's association, preferring to bring France in at the last moment (in fact almost as a fait accompli).[11] And there was some opposition by British diplomats in the Middle East. Sir Ronald Campbell's opinion from Cairo, as late as 30 April 1950, was that the declaration would "be stronger if confined to the United Kingdom and the United States since France is unfortunately regarded here as weak and also self-seeking."[12]

In addition to the Anglo-French rivalry, account had to be taken of the fact that not everyone in the world was willing to abide by the bipolar logic: a third bloc, voicing the politics of neutralism and non-alignment, was manifesting its presence at the United Nations.

Nonetheless the mood in the United States suggested a different order of priorities. A year before announcing his doctrine, Truman had stated:

> The Near and Middle East comprise an area which presents grave problems. This area contains vast natural resources of enormous

---

10 *Ibid.*

11 FO 371/81910; E1023/91; 8 May 1950: "Possibility of Statement by Americans and Ourselves and Perhaps the French About the Middle East."

12 FO 371/81907; E1023/15: Campbell to FO.

value. It lies across the most convenient routes of land, air, and water communication between the west and east. It is consequently an area of great strategic importance. In this area there are a number of friendly sovereign states, members of the United Nations. They are not strong enough individually or collectively to withstand armed aggression on the part of any great power. It is easy to see, therefore, how the Near and Middle East might become an arena of intense rivalry between outside powers, and how such rivalry might suddenly erupt in armed conflict.[13]

Viewed in the context of global containment and NATO, there is a strong implication that commitments could be extended beyond the core area of the North Atlantic and the Western Hemisphere in general.

(a) AMERICAN AND BRITISH PERCEPTIONS OF NATO'S EXTENSION: 1949-1950

In March 1949 Secretary of State Dean Acheson set the general tone for the debate. "During the drafting of the North Atlantic Pact," he declared at a press conference, "we were aware of the possibility that our formal expression of serious interest in the security of countries in the North Atlantic area might be misinterpreted as implying a lessening of our interest in the security of countries in other areas, particularly the near and Middle East." After stressing the special importance of Turkey, Greece, and Iran, he went on to say: "In the compact world of today, the security of the United States cannot be defined in terms of boundaries and frontiers."[14] At this point, it may be of interest to recall that the National Security Council considered that the United States had "greater long-range strategic interests in the military establishments of Turkey than in those of Greece."[15]

[13] Reitzel, et al, *United States Foreign Policy 1945-1955*, p. 210.
[14] Quoted in *Foreign Relations of the United States* (hereafter *FRUS*), 1949, Vol. VI, p. 44.
[15] *FRUS*, 1949, Vol. 6, p. 40 (NSC report 42/1 of March 22, 1949 to President Truman).

On the question of extension, a long memorandum prepared by Gordon P. Merriam of the State Department's Policy
Planning Staff (dated June 13, 1949 and marked Top Secret)
is a reflection of the official position at the time. It began with
a statement of "The Problem: To determine whether the
North Atlantic Treaty should be extended to include Middle
Eastern countries, and the possibility of creating one or more
additional Article 51 treaties embracing the Middle East...
considered for the purposes of this discussion (as) Greece,
Turkey, Syria, Lebanon, Israel, Jordan, Egypt, the Sudan,
Eritrea, Ethiopia, Saudi Arabia, Iraq, Iran, Afghanistan,
Pakistan and India."[16] The memo acknowledged that American security requirements were "closely interwoven with
those of Great Britain."[17]

Merriam concurred that it would be unwise, because of the
limitations of US resources and the potential provocation to
the Soviet Union, "(a) To send US Forces to Greece, even as
token forces; (b) To construct medium bomber and fighter
fields in Turkey with a view to use by US Forces; (c) To stock
existing Turkish airfields with aviation gasoline to be held for
use by US Force." On the other hand it was considered
desirable "to construct a suitable air-field in the Suez area
which could be used by US bombers."[18]

Turning to the Arab countries, Merriam observed that all
had "indicated at one time or another a desire to enter into a
military alliance or other military arrangements with the US or
with both the US and the UK.. (yet) with the exception of
Saudi Arabia, none of the Arab governments could enter into
an alliance with the US at this time due to the deterioration of
relations resulting from the Palestine question."[19] The early

[16] *FRUS,* 1949, Vol. VI, p. 31.
[17] *Ibid.,* p. 32.
[18] *Ibid.*
[19] *Ibid.* p. 133.

reference to the impact of the Palestinian question is to be noted. As will be shown below, this factor figured prominently in the calculations of such American and British foreign affairs policy-makers as Ernest Bevin, George McGhee, and Loy Henderson.

As to the steps open to the United States, Merriam listed six that could be taken singly or simultaneously (and as options they appear to retain relevance for policy even today):

(a) Continuing along present lines, i.e. by unilateral diplomatic, economic and military support as determined by us on the basis of *ad hoc* need and availabilities, but refraining from any mutual commitment except as provided by the UN Charter, with such assistance and cooperation as other like-minded nations, particularly by UK, can and will provide.

(b) Extension of the North Atlantic Treaty to include certain selected countries in the area.

(c) Creation of a regional pact, pure and simple.

(d) Creation of a regional pact linked to the strongest members of the North Atlantic Treaty system.

(e) Creation of a regional pact having some kind of association, or possibility of association, with the North Atlantic Treaty.

(f) Creation of a new UN procedure.[20]

The first step offered the "advantage of simplicity" but also the disadvantages inherent in an *"ad hoc,* country by country basis" which would undermine what Merriam called the "area approach" — the preferred course given the circumstances. But the prerequisite for the "area approach," which he saw as being the "friendship, trust and cooperation" of the Arab countries, was lacking. Hence he felt that the "acquisition or construction of adequate facilities" in Arab countries would be "extremely difficult if not impossible so long as the US maintained a policy of favoritism in regard to Israel."[21] Merriam argued that a relationship of friendship and trust with

---

[20] *Ibid.*, pp. 33 and 34.
[21] *Ibid.*

the Arabs had once existed but that it had "suffered severe though not irreparable damage." As to the implications:

> Until the damage has been repaired, (the US) task of supporting the integrity of the three northern countries of Greece, Turkey and Iran will be that of holding up an arch which lacks foundations. Furthermore, the relations between the various countries of the area must be on a sound basis. The Palestine question has caused the contrary effect.[22]

The second option, extension of NATO to include selected countries (primarily Greece and Turkey), was rejected as an immediate possibility for two reasons. Firstly, with the inclusion of Norway and Italy, the area of commitment had grown considerably. Secondly, the inclusion of Greece would "throw the question of aid to Greek guerrillas into the NAP framework and risk magnifying the question into a crude and primary power issue."[23]   Besides, the extension in the direction of the Middle East would be vulnerable if Germany became a security risk.

The third option (creation of a regional pact, pure and simple) offered no solution, again because of regional discord created by the Palestine question, and also because "the area lacked a power center on the basis of which a pact could be built."[24]   The fourth option, linking a regional pact with strong NAP (North Atlantic Pact) members such as the US and the UK, placed too heavy a burden on the two Atlantic allies. Besides, as Merriam put it, "the Arab countries, while having a pervading fear of the USSR, have a closer and more immediate problem in Israel."[25]   Finally, there was a basic difference between the US and the UK:

> The US has supported and favored Israel, and endeavored at the same time to remain on friendly terms with the Arab states. The

22 *Ibid.*
23 *Ibid.*
24 *Ibid.*,p. 35.
25 *Ibid.*

UK, on the contrary, places Arab relations ahead of relations with
Israel, and has temporarily departed from this policy only when
necessary in the interest of Anglo-American relations.[26]

For much the same reasons, the fifth option — a regional pact
linked in some form with the NAP — was not immediately viable, although it did offer positive prospects "if the Middle East
(could) be sufficiently pulled together."[27] It could help to
resolve some of the area's chronic tensions and possessed more
flexibility in its linkage structure than other options. In
addition, individual requests might be formulated with more
moderation because of group consideration.

The last option was developing existing UN machinery not
subject to veto "to contribute to general international security
including the security of the Middle East."[28] The idea here
proposed was to give more muscle to the General Assembly so
that there would "be a judgment of the international community on the facts of any situation in which armed attack is
alleged and the Security Council fails to take adequate measures."[29] Merriam felt that the proposal was immediately
practicable and could make "a significant political contribution to security as a deterrent, particularly in regions outside
the Western Hemisphere and the North Atlantic area."[30]

This in short was Merriam's argument and list of options.
How representative his views and options were of the conventional wisdom in Washington and London is not easily
answered. But they do offer a useful framework for the
subject under study. How true was Merriam's contention that
American security requirements were "closely interwoven"
with those of Britain? Was Britain's definition of the Middle

---

[26] *Ibid.*, p. 36.
[27] *Ibid.* p. 37.
[28] *Ibid.*
[29] *Ibid.* p. 38.
[30] *Ibid.* p. 39.

East substantially similar? Was Merriam's hesitancy regarding further extensions and entanglements shared by American representatives on the spot in the Middle East? One might also ask the question as to whether Merriam's view of the centrality of the Palestine question was shared by others.

(b) THE CENTRALITY OF THE PALESTINE QUESTION

Following high level talks in 1947 which drew the principal guidelines for Anglo-American policy towards the Middle East, the two Atlantic partners continued to hold their periodic and closely coordinated reviews of questions related to defence of the region, arms transfers, economic aid, oil policy, the desirability of regional security pacts, base facilities, and the Palestine question. Differences of perception and policy were never absent. For instance at the 1947 talks, the Palestine question was deliberately kept out of the discussions in order to facilitate progress on other issues.[31] Later, during the George McGhee-Michael Wright negotiations of November 1949, the British record reveals vigorous discussions on the Palestine issue, with American opposition to the British plan to incorporate Arab Palestine into Jordan shifting from a question of principle to one of timing.[32] Britain and the United States were drawing closer, but differences remained. In an important paper dated April 1949 the Permanent Under-Secretary's Committee (PUSC) in the Foreign Office argued:

> We want the whole of the Middle East, including Israel, to be friendly towards us. If, however, we were to secure the friendship of Israel at the expense of the friendship of the Arab countries, we

[31] Paul Jabber, *Nor By War Alone* (Berkeley: University of California Press, 1981), p. 70.
[32] *Foreign Office* (FO) 371/78056; E14770/1026/65. Record of discussion between Mr. Michael Wright and members of the State Department, November 14, 1949 (Discussion on a Palestine Settlement).

should lose economically and strategically more than we should gain. Our object must be, therefore, to endeavour to promote friendly relations with Israel, but not to the point of losing the friendship of the Arab world. Strategically, facilities in Israel would be no substitute for facilities in Egypt and other Arab countries.[33]

A month later a document entitled "Policy Towards Israel" bearing Ernest Bevin's signature expressed the same concern and priority: "If for any reason we are faced with the position of having to choose between Israel and the Arabs our overriding interest must be to do our utmost to preserve our position in the Arab countries."[34] The other bone of contention was oil. A Foreign Office minute on "Conversations with the Americans About the Middle East" dated 19 December, 1949 recorded: "Issues such as Palestine and Middle East oil (are) capable of leading to such a degree of friction and tension with the United States as to endanger the general policy embodied in the Atlantic pact and the European Recovery Programme."[35] The Foreign Office was expressing the hope that, by 1951, 82% of Britain's oil would be drawn from the Middle East.[36] The stakes were enormous.

The Policy Planning Staff of the State Department believed that US support for the partition of Palestine could adversely affect the development of Middle Eastern petroleum, thus presenting "a serious threat to the overall success of the Marshall Plan" for the recovery of Europe.[37] The National Security Council (NSC) was even more emphatic on this point, linking Palestine with US strategic interests and security directly. As A.D. Miller, author of *Search For Security: Saudi*

---

[33] FO 371/75067 PUSC (19) on Middle East, April 30, 1949.

[34] FO 371/75054; E 6145/1026/65 "Policy Towards Israel," signed Ernest Bevin, May 20, 1949.

[35] FO 371/78056; E 15252/1026/65 by Michael Wright, December 19, 1949.

[36] FO 371/78067; PUSC (19), April 30, 1949.

[37] A.D. Miller, *Search For Security: Saudi Arabian Oil and American Foreign Policy 1939-1945* (Chapel Hill: University of North Carolina Press, 1980), p. 192.

Arabian Oil and American Foreign Policy 1939-1949, put it: the NSC argued "that unrestricted access to Middle Eastern oil was essential to the economy of the United States and to the economic recovery of Europe under the ERP (Economic Recovery Program)."[38] Similar views were also shared by Loy Henderson, head of the State Department's Office of Near Eastern and African Affairs (NEA) and by the Joint Chiefs of Staff (JCS).

Henderson pointed to the American stake in Middle Eastern oil and to the lurking danger in late 1947:

> We shall need Arab friendship if we are to retain our petroleum position in the Arab world. During the next few years we are planning to obtain huge quantities of oil from Iraq, Bahrein, Kuwait, and Saudi Arabia, not only for our use but for the reconstruction of Europe. Furthermore we are intending to transport oil from Persia, Iraq, and Saudi Arabia across a number of Arab countries by pipelines to the Mediterranean ports. Already, partly as a result of our policies regarding Palestine the attitude of Saudi Arabia towards the United States has changed sharply...[39]

In this respect Tapline and its 300,000 barrels a day capacity was seen as an indispensable component of Europe's economic recovery, and therefore of the Alliance's security. As for the military planners, the Joint Chiefs of Staff warned: "The most serious of all possible consequences from a military point of view is that implementation of a decision to partition Palestine would gravely prejudice access by the US to (Middle East) oil."[40]

Finally, the centrality of the Palestine question was reflected in an important report to the House Committee on Foreign Affairs by Assistant Secretary of State George McGhee in February 1950:

> Let me speak very frankly on this question. The political loss of

---

[38] *Ibid.*, p. 193.
[39] *Ibid.*, pp. 186-187.
[40] *Ibid.*

this area to the Soviet Union would be a major disaster comparable to its loss during war... The Near East may be critical to our national interests in time of war, but it is vital to us in time of peace.

Against this background, our solicitude for the Palestine refugees, partly based on humanitarian considerations, has additional justification. As long as the refugee problem remains unresolved, the delicate equilibrium affected by the armistices is endangered. As long as this problem remains unresolved, attainment of a political settlement in Palestine is delayed, and a major source of friction between Israel and the Arab states is perpetuated to the detriment of peace in the entire Near East. Finally, as long as this problem remains unresolved, the refugees themselves will continue to serve as a natural focal point for exploitation by Communist and disruptive elements which neither we nor the Near Eastern governments can ignore. In this critical area we can ill afford to stand by in the face of any major security threat. The presence of three-quarters of a million idle, destitute people – a number greater than the combined strength of all the standing armies of the Near East – whose discontent increases with the passage of time, is the greatest threat to the security of the area which now exists.[41]

(c) WHERE IS THE MIDDLE EAST: THE INNER AND
    OUTER RINGS

Writing in 1903 (and acknowledging that Alfred Mahan invented the term Middle East as a strategic concept) Valentine Chirol, foreign editor of the *Times,* defined it as encompassing "those regions in Asia which extend to the borders of India or command the approaches to India, and which are consequently bound up with the problems of Indian political as well military defence."[42] Chirol also perceived the Middle Eastern question as the "outcome of that constant projection of European forces – moral, commercial and military – into

[41] Quoted in FO 371/81907; E 1023/8-11.
[42] Valentine Chirol, *The Middle Eastern Question or Some Political Problems of Indian Defence* (London: John Murray, 1903), p. 5.

Asia which is slowly but steadily transforming all the conditions that enabled (Britain) to achieve... a position of
unparalleled ascendancy in the Asiatic continent."[43] The
central problem as he saw at the turn of the century was how
to preserve this position of unrivalled hegemony acquired in
the past through the Royal Navy's control of the seas, under
new conditions in which land-power, exemplified by Tsarist
Russia's thrust in Central Asia, was growing at an alarming
rate.[44]

There has never really been a consensus on where the
Middle East is, nor an accepted core for it. In the mid-fifties,
John Foster Dulles defined it in Congress as the "area lying
between and including Libya on the West and Pakistan on the
East and Turkey on the North and the Arabian Peninsula to
the South," plus the Sudan and Ethiopia.[45] As mentioned
earlier in this paper, our contention is that it is better
understood as a shifting strategic concept than as "immutable
geography."

Nonetheless the two Atlantic allies did not widely differ on
the question of definitions. Ernest Bevin defined it in one
document as "the area stretching from Corfu to Kabul which
is next in strategic importance after Europe to our interests as
a whole."[46] The reference to Afghanistan is of some interest.
The document bears the following note: "There are traditional
links between Afghanistan, Persia, and Turkey, and from the
Soviet point of view if not from ours Afghanistan is strategically important to Middle East defence. Inclusion of Afghan-

---

[43] *Ibid.*

[44] *Ibid.*

[45] Roderic Davison, "Where Is the Middle East? ," in Richard Nolte, ed., *The Modern Middle East* (New York: Atherton Press, 1963), p. 14. Davison sees the term as "a projection of European, particularly British, thinking." p. 18. Equally valuable is Nikkie Keddie, "Is there a Middle East," *International Journal of Middle Eastern Studies,* Vol. IV, 1973, p. 257.

[46] FO 371/75079; E 5020/1074/65; Ernest Bevin.

istan in a Middle Eastern Pact would therefore be logical."[47]

But if agreement existed as to definition, there was a fundamental divergence of views regarding the relative importance of the outer and inner rings. And in this respect the asessment of B.A.B. Burrows, a British diplomat reporting from Washington in September 1950, is especially perceptive and deserves lengthy quotation:

> I am assuming that it is still very much our wish to have the Americans strategically committed in the Middle East, even though at the present time there is a higher priority for giving practical effect to the general commitment they are undertaking to put more troops into Europe. I feel that one of the factors which influences the divergent views on Middle East strategical priority held by us and the Americans is that their thoughts always start from the outer ring of Greece, Turkey and Persia, whereas ours start from Cairo and radiate outwards. The Americans think like this partly because Greece, Turkey and Persia border on Russian or satellite territory, and therefore the first attack on the Middle East must come through them, and the first impact of such an attack on American opinion will be related to these countries and not to the Arab world. This way of thinking has become crystallised and confirmed because Greece, Turkey and Persia are treated together in both Congressional and State Department practice for purposes of military assistance, and because the State Department put Greece, Turkey and Persia together in a single office under the Near Eastern, South Asian and African Affairs Bureau. These factors are reinforced by a perhaps sub-conscious reluctance on the part of the State Department to consider commitments in the Arab world, owing to memories of the emotional pressure exercised by Jewish groups here and by more national misgivings about the local and economic conditions in most of the Arab states"[48]

On the question of Merriam's hesitancy regarding extension of the Atlantic Alliance being shared by American representatives in the Middle East, the records of the Istanbul (November 1949) and Cairo (March 1950) Conferences of

---

[47] *Ibid.*
[48] FO 371/81967; E 1195/3/G, Burrows to Wright; September 14, 1950.

American diplomats indicate downright opposition to any further commitments. At Istanbul the Conference recommended that the United States "should not attempt to negotiate multilateral or bilateral security pacts with the Near Eastern States, at least until such time as it is prepared to commit military forces required to carry out the guarantees given."[49] The Cairo Conference "confirmed the continued validity of the (Istanbul) position."[50] But despite the very real caution discussed above, and the danger that the Atlantic alliance might find itself involved in the region's conflicts, including the Arab-Israeli or inter-Arab conflicts, the Cold War perspective of Secretary of State Dean Acheson dominated the scene. In February 1950 he had asserted that "the only way to deal with the Soviet Union... is to create situations of strength."[51] In this respect it was pointed out shortly thereafter that the Middle East was "a region that seemed to call preeminently for creating a 'situation of strength'... (for it) seemed almost to invite a Soviet push that would split the free world along its North-South axis, deny it the abundant oil resources of Iran, Iraq, and the Arabian peninsula, and open a path for the extension of Soviet influence westward across Africa and eastward into Pakistan and India."[52]

In early 1949 Ernest Bevin had remarked: "Once the Atlantic Pact is concluded... we shall then be free to give more attention to the area stretching from Corfu to Kabul."[53] The abortive proposals for the Middle East Command (MEC), the Middle East Defence Organisation (MEDO), as well as various blueprints for Mediterranean pacts, the Baghdad Pact, and

---

[49] *FRUS*, 1949, Vol. VI, p. 169.

[50] *FRUS*, 1950, Vol. V, p. 3.

[51] Jabber, *Not By War Alone*, p. 73.

[52] *Ibid.*, quoting Richard Stebbins, et al., *The United States in World Affairs, 1950* (New York: Harper, 1951), p. 307.

[53] FO 371/75079; E 5020/1074/65; Ernest Bevin.

CENTO, flowed from the logic of both Dean Acheson and Ernest Bevin. In virtually every instance, formal linkage with the North Atlantic Alliance, particularly Merriam's options (d) and (e), was established, and the spectrum of responsibilities as well as the area of deployment and operations expanded, without much concern for the aspirations of the peoples of the Middle East, especially the Arabs. In this type of grand design, particularly in view of the zero-sum game atmosphere of the cold war, the regional population tended to recede from the concerns of policy-makers, giving way to the "realism" of eyeball-to-eyeball confrontation between "rimland and heart-land."

(d) THE ARAB RESPONSE

It is a fact that the official Arab response to the debate on the extension of NATO and the setting up of Western-sponsored Middle East Pacts modelled on the Atlantic Pact was varied. But on the level of public opinion it was one of angry opposition. To cite one or two examples: In April 1950 Ma'ruf Dawalibi denounced the policy of Western pacts and called for a treaty of friendship with Russia, which Soviet diplomat Daniel Solod quickly took up by offering Syria a treaty of friendship, and credits for the purchase of Soviet and Czech armaments. There was also the mainstream Arab nationalist answer to all such pacts, as expressed in early 1952 by George Habash, who was then a fifth-year medical student at the American University of Beirut (AUB). In the course of a lecture at West Hall (AUB) sponsored by the influential AUB Arab nationalist student association *al-'Urwa al-Wuthqa,* Habash argued that during World Wars I and II, the Arabs had adopted a policy of cooperation with the Allies. He asked what this policy brought other than occupation, partition, and disaster upon disaster. Besides, the pacts were clearly de-signed to perpetuate the condition of semi-sovereignty and to inhibit the Arabs from changing their internal status quo.[54]

The MEC and MEDO proposals provide interesting cases in point. They meant, in effect, the setting in place of joint defence pacts with NATO linkage. In many Arab states — Iraq, Jordan and Egypt — Britain maintained a powerful influence bolstered by an extensive network of land, sea and air bases centred on the Suez Canal base complex. It is out of considerations such as the Truman doctrine of containment and the continuing British military presence that the concept of the Middle East Command (MEC) was born. The United States and Britain asked France and Turkey to join them as sponsors of the proposal. Egypt held the key by virtue of the Suez Canal position and its leadership of the Arab League. The idea was that if Egypt accepted the MEC, other Arab states would follow suit.[55] It is significant that the MEC proposals were presented to Egypt by the governments of the United States, Britain, France and Turkey on October 13, 1951 (and rejected by Egypt two days later) while the principles underlying this controversial defence pact were published by NATO a month later.[56] At the same time, invitations to participate in the MEC were addressed to Australia, New Zealand, and South Africa. The principal points in the proposal required Egypt to furnish the MEC with "such strategic defence and other facilities on her soil as are indispensable for the organisation in peacetime of the defence of the Middle East..." [and] undertake to grant forces of the Allied Middle East Command all necessary facilities and assistance in the event of war, imminent menace of war, or apprehended international emergency including the use of Egyptian ports, airfields, and

---

[54] George Habash, "al-Difaʿ al-Mushtarak", *Manshurat Jamʿiyyat al-ʿUrwa al-Wuthqa*, (Beirut: AUB, 1952)

[55] Campbell, *Defence of the Middle East*, p. 42.

[56] Stookey, *America and the Arab States*, p. 133.

means of communication."[57] In return, Britain would abrogate the Anglo-Egyptian treaty of 1936 and withdraw military forces not earmarked for the MEC.

It was clear to Arab opinion that the MEC was merely a device to perpetuate a somewhat disguised imperial domination of the region. The government of Nahhas Pasha replied by abrogating, unilaterally, the Anglo-Egyptian Defence Treaty of 1936 and the Anglo-Egyptian Condominium of 1899 over the Sudan. The evacuation of the Canal Zone was also demanded. Yet there was no let up on the part of the senior partners of the Alliance. Analyzing this episode, Halford Hoskins wrote:

> ...in an announcement by the Department of State on October 24, 1951... the United States intended to establish a Middle East defense command despite Egypt's refusal to join. Plans were being worked out for the cooperation in this task of the United States, Britain, France, Turkey, New Zealand, Australia, and the Union of South Africa. Once plans had been completed, invitations to membership might be extended to the Arab states and Israel. Meanwhile, the announcement implied, the Suez Canal would continue to be used as a base of operations.[58]

Again there was no progress, and the MEC project was abandoned in favor of MEDO, sponsored by the same countries, and which Hoskins characterized as "consisting essentially of a committee of generals to plan the defenses of the area, (and to be) concerned also with the issues making for instability": i.e. the Arab-Israeli conflict, Iran under Mossadeq, and Egypt in revolution.[59]

Labyrinthine and often disingenuous explanations have been provided for the failure of the MEC and MEDO projects.

---

[57] Text in Ralph Magnus, ed., *Documents on the Middle East,* (Washington, Enterprise Institute, 1969), p. 76.

[58] Halford Hoskins, *The Middle East: Problem Area in World Politics* (New York: Macmillan, 1954), pp. 282-283.

[59] *Ibid.,* p. 284.

The true explanation is, however, much simpler. For the Arabs, these initiatives generally spelled a return to, or a maintenance of, dependent status; besides, the immediate object of Arab apprehension was Israeli expansionism. One consequence of their failure was that western interest shifted to the Northern Tier or Outer Ring, where there was a more pronounced willingness to come under the Alliance's umbrella, and where the Central Treaty Organization (CENTO) was ultimately established.

3. The Atlantic Alliance and the Middle East Today

There is growing evidence today of a renewed interest in extending NATO's perimeter beyond the Tropic of Cancer and in enlarging the scope and membership of the Alliance, especially by informal means. This evidence is to be found in the official pronouncements of many Western political figures, military commanders, and parliamentary bodies as well as in the position papers of authoritative experts and in the publications of leading Western research institutes. Although such material is fundamentally different in nature from the unpublished primary documents which underpinned the earlier sections, it reveals elements of continuity in several themes from the post-war period until the 1980's.

(a) VIEWS FROM BRITAIN

Clear signs that a more forceful British strategic posture was in the making began to emerge in the press in 1979. In September of that year the weekly *Economist* called for a vigorous programme of Western "counter-arming" to rectify a vulnerable situation which, it felt, would grow strategically worse in the following two or three years. Three especially grave vulnerabilities were singled out: in the US, in Europe, and in "areas important to the West in other parts of the world."[60]

[60] *Economist,* September 8, 1979, pp. 15-17.

First, argued the *Economist,* by 1982 Russia's missile force could destroy enough American land-based, submarine, and air-launched missiles in a surprise attack on the United States to make it impossible for the surviving American nuclear arsenal to destroy Russia's still unused warheads. Second, Europe also was placed in an increasingly vulnerable situation because of the massive deployment of Soviet SS 20 missiles and Backfire bombers. Third, areas important to the West in other parts of the world were likewise in an exposed position. Russia's decade of rearmament had equipped it with sufficient aircraft and ships to deploy troops anywhere in the globe. The well-informed weekly observed: "Once the Russians and their allies have established non-nuclear superiority in a given area, they can put it to use under the protection of their new nuclear power. It is they, not the West, who will be holding the nuclear umbrella..."[61]

In answer, the *Economist* proposed for the West an ambitious programme of counter-arming that would "set out to do four specific things: (1.) as soon as possible, to make some of America's land-based missiles invulnerable, by making them mobile; (2.) to give America's nuclear force the ability to hit more of Russia's missile silos, so as to reduce the damage Russia can do to America; (3.) to restore the balance of shorter-range nuclear weapons in Europe; (4.) to strengthen the West's conventional forces, so that they have a better chance of holding off Russia's without resorting to the threat of going nuclear."[62]

This was in September 1979. With the Soviet intervention in Afghanistan in December, British fears together with Western fears in general, reached a high point. As Gregory Treverton of London's International Institute of Strategic Studies put it: "Most past so-called crises in the Alliance have been

[61] *Ibid.*
[62] *Ibid.*

pre-eminently about fashioning new Alliance political arrangements to reassure ourselves. In contrast, this crisis is about
confronting an adversary, about the stakes, about perceptions
and capabilities of Europe and America. It cuts to the
bone."[63] There was a growing feeling of insecurity. Whereas in
1977 only 14 per cent of Europeans felt they might be
involved in a war in the next ten years, a 1980 poll indicated
that 35 per cent felt this way.[64]

It is perhaps not surprising that Britain developed and
released plans to press ahead with the development of intervention units and strike forces, as the next two examples will
show. The *International Herald Tribune* in a special report on
the new strategy of NATO wrote in July 1980:

> Britain has earmarked Marine Commandos for intervention out-
> side NATO. Margaret Thatcher's government also favours re-
> creating an assault paratroop battalion trained to jump in enemy-
> held terrain, and the Royal Air Force has started lengthening the
> fuselages of their C-130 Hercules — the transport used by Israel in
> the Entebbe raid.
>
> Welcoming the new European capability, a US official said:
> 'There are scenarios France or Britain could handle alone, avoiding
> any superpower involvement.'[65]

Britain's 1980 Defence White Paper stated: "The Services
should also be able to operate effectively outside the NATO
area without diminishing our central commitment to the
alliance."[66] Such recent Command Papers as *Defence in the
1980's* and *Statement on the Defence Estimates for 1981* are
much more explicit in their emphasis on action over a wider
area than the traditional NATO perimeter. This ambition to
establish such strike forces capable of intervention — for

---

[63] Joseph Fitchett, "Nato Seeks New Strategy," *IHT*, July 18, 1980, p. 1.
[64] *Ibid.*
[65] *Ibid.*
[66] David Fairhall, "Assault Battalion Idea is Poppycock," *The Guardian Weekly*,
July 6, 1980, p. 4.

example in the Gulf and Indian Ocean – has led to a debate as to the nature of the force. One school of thought sees it in terms of a parachute battalion, possessing its own stockpiles of equipment, and requiring the services of RAF Hercules transport aircraft.

This capability is envisaged in modest terms, with tasks ranging from gaining rapid control of an airfield, to providing assistance to friendly governments "threatened by rebellion," to acting in support of US operations in the Gulf.[67] But the cost involved could run to tens of millions of pounds, which would have to be reallocated from within the existing defense budget.

On the other hand, another school represented by Field Marshal Lord Carver, a former Chief of Defence Staff, has dismissed such ideas of seeking to reassert Britain's "imperial past on this small scale as military poppycock." He did not think it wise "to extend NATO's area of responsibility east of Suez or south of the Tropic of Cancer."[68] And with respect to unilateral intervention, he noted a growing trend in the Western world "to threaten military force without any credible means of implementation, or conception of the risks and costs involved." The only effective military power Britain could deploy quickly anywhere in the Middle East, in his view, was air power, and in this context if Britain was really determined to make a contribution, "the best move could be to reactivate the RAF base at Akrotiri, in Cyprus, for strike, reconnaissance and transport operations."[69]

Which school of thought will win in the eighties? Britain will probably resort to the proverbial compromise and end up combining a parachute assault force with the Akrotiri option. The stress in any case will most likely be on the contribution

[67] *Ibid.*
[68] *Ibid.*
[69] *Ibid.*

that can be made within a larger American-dominated frame-work, if some recent official positions are any indication.

In March 1981, Prime Minister Thatcher expressed un-restrained enthusiasm for a joint NATO Rapid Deployment Force, although her Common Market partners appeared far less enthusiastic about such prospects, particularly her pledge to President Reagan which began with the words: "There is an urgent need for a new defence policy beyond the North Atlantic."[70]

In this respect, a close look at *Defence in the 1980's* prepared by the British Minister of Defence, is instructive, particularly paragraphs 401, 402, 408, and 409 where the following arguments are developed:

(a) In common with NATO allies, we also have wider interests outside the NATO area ... We depend on the developing world for many raw materials. The security of our trade routes is therefore of vital importance to our economy...[71]

(b) The West must make it clear to the Soviet Union and its allies that it is capable of protecting essential interests by military means should the need arise. That task should not be left to the United States alone. Of our European partners, France has major defence commitments in Africa and elsewhere, and retains per-manent forces in the Indian and Pacific Oceans. Vessels of the Federal German, Italian and Dutch navies undertake occasional deployments beyond the NATO area. Belgium provides training assistance to Zaire. All such activities help to protect Western interests worldwide.[72]

(c) The government believes that the Services should also be able to operate effectively outside the NATO area... British forces will therefore continue to deploy and exercise outside the NATO area from time to time.... From April this year (1980) one parachute battalion will always be available to provide a parachute capability at seven days notice.[73]

[70] *Guardian*, March 3, 1981.
[71] *Defence in the 1980's* (London: H.M. Stationery Office, April 1980), Vol. 1, Command Paper p. 7826-1, p. 39.
[72] *Ibid.*, p. 41.
[73] *Ibid.*

This capability was upgraded in John Nott's *Statement on the Defence Estimates 1981* (Chapter Four: Wider Defence Interests) in terms of dropping "an entire battalion group if necessary within 15 minutes."[74] The *Statement* also spoke of a three-fold task for the Services: "assistance, deployment (including periodic exercises) and intervention"; and referred to a Royal Navy Task Group Deployment (RNTGD) comprising two destroyers, three frigates, and the three Royal Fleet Auxiliaries with which "the United Kingdom was able to respond promptly [with] a naval presence in the Gulf of Oman" at the outset of the Iraq-Iran war of 1980.[75]

(b) THE PERCEPTION OF WESTERN SECURITY
   BY FOUR WESTERN INSTITUTES

The trend towards greater NATO involvement in the Middle East extends beyond the US and Great Britain. In this context the cooperation of four influential Western institutes in preparing the report: *"Western Security: What has Changed: What Should Be Done?"* was an unprecedented event. The report carried the signatures of Karl Kaiser, Director of the German Foreign Policy Institute, Winston Lord, President of the Council on Foreign Relations (US), Thierry de Montbrial, Director of the Institut Français des Relations Internationales (IFRI), and David Watt, Director of the Royal Institute of International Affairs (London). As the report saw it, Western security can no longer be limited to events and threats occurring in the NATO region alone, because of: (a) "increased tensions between East and West and enhanced Soviet military threats both in Europe and in Third World Regions," (b) the fact that "the West will also be facing an increasingly unstable and volatile Third World upon which it will depend

---

[74] Statement on the Defence Estimates 1981 (London: H.M. Stationery Office, April 1981), Command Paper 8212-1, p. 32.
[75] *Ibid.*, p. 30.

more and more for its economic survival (this is particularly true of the Persian Gulf region)", and (c) the fact that "the period ahead will also be one of prolonged economic crisis worldwide."[76]

Neither was it possible "to isolate European security from crises arising in other regions vital for the West." The report's central theses stated "that the days of the old Atlantic system, based on US predominance and its corollary European reluctance, to take wider responsibilities, are over."[77] It added that the Arab-Israel conflict of 1973, oil dependence, and the Soviet intervention in Afghanistan have contributed to produce "a new arena of the East-West conflict outside the traditional NATO area and imposed it on the existing regional conflicts."[78] The report recommended a Western naval task force able to keep open the straits of Hormuz, and approved of the RDF. It also recognized that the failure to resolve the Palestinian problem is a permanent cause of instability.

Furthermore, the Report injected a note of realism regarding the formal expansion of NATO: "We do not propose," said the directors, "that NATO undertakes major institutional innovations, concerning political and security developments in the Third World. To enlarge formally its geographical responsibility would require fundamental amendment of the Treaty and ratification in fifteen parliaments. Such change would be highly contentious."[79] What they urged instead was a "thicker web of consultations" by adding to the NATO forum the seven-nation summit of leaders of the advanced industrialized countries which began in Rambouillet in 1975. This seven-nation summit should also expand its concerns to political and

---

[76] Karl Kaiser et al., Western Security: What Has Changed? What Should Be Done? (New York: 1981), p. 7.

[77] Ibid., p. 17.

[78] Ibid., p. 23.

[79] Ibid., p. 44.

military issues. In addition, a mechanism called the Principal Nations Approach with a core group composed of the US, Britain, France, Germany, and Japan should be established at once to deal with "developments in the Gulf and South West Asia" on a continuing "Watch" basis.[80]

(c) THE VIEW OF THE NATO ASSEMBLIES, MILITARY COMMANDERS, AND LOBBIES

There is mounting evidence of this trend towards the expansion of Alliance interests south- and east-wards in the deliberations of NATO and its associated bodies. At the 26th Annual Session (November, 1980) of the North Atlantic Assembly (which provides a forum for 150 Alliance parliamentarians representing the fifteen member countries), were four observers from the Spanish Cortes, and, for the first time, eight members of the Japanese Diet. The overriding theme of the session was the situation in the Gulf and its implications for Western security. Despite a critique of the RDF by Colonel Alford, Deputy Director of the International Institute of Strategic Studies, characterizing this enterprise as a *King Lear Syndrome* ("I will do such things — what they are yet I know not — but they shall be the terror of the earth") the Assembly voted a resolution on the Gulf urging member countries "to deal effectively with conflicts in other areas where the NATO Treaty cannot be applied."[81]

Also in the same year, J.M. Luns, Secretary-General of NATO, made a speech at the Royal Institute for International Relations in Brussels entitled "NATO in the Present World Situation" in which he concluded: "I am not suggesting that any attempt be made to amend the North Atlantic Treaty. What I am suggesting is that it will not suffice in the future for

[80] *Ibid.*, p. 46.
[81] *NATO Review*, February 1981, p. 23.

the Alliance to confine its attentions to the territorial limits embodied in that Treaty if it is to duplicate its past success in protecting the vital interests of its member states."[82]

Similarly, the final communiques of the NATO Council, meeting in Ministerial Session in Rome in May 1981, devoted considerable attention to the Gulf area, and how to cope with emergency situations outside the Alliance's traditional boundaries. In particular, article 5 of the Defence Planning Committee's final communique recognized that "situations outside NATO's boundaries may... threaten the vital interest of the West and therefore have implications for the security of members of the Alliance." It called for consultations when members of the Alliance "are considering out-of-area deployment of forces." The communiqué also recognized that "common objectives identified in such consultations may require members of the Alliance to facilitate out-of-area deployments in support of the vital interests of all."[83]

Writing in the June 1981 issue of the *NATO Review,* General Bernard Rogers, Supreme Allied Commander Europe (SACEUR), argued that the strategic environment of the 1980's contained an "added challenge outside the boundaries of NATO" which had had to be met as well. An adequate response, in his view, involved the following steps:

> The first step is to acknowledge that, to meet these challenges, member nations must provide additional forces and resources, not simply redistribute already inadequate ones. The second is to recognize that only a few member nations have the military capability to protect common vital interests in external regions. Thus, these few Allies must rely on the remainder to take up the slack within NATO for any forces committed outside its area. Specifically, our force planning must address candidly the challenges posed by the possible commitment of the US Rapid

[82] J.M. Luns, "NATO in the Present World Situation," *Studia Diplomatica* (XXXIII, 6), 1980, p. 646.

[83] *NATO Review,* June 1981, p. 30.

Deployment Force (RDF) to an outlying area which would reduce the number of US forces 'and resources available to reinforce Europe.[84]

Such views are shared by Admiral Harry D. Train, Supreme Allied Commander Atlantic, who argued that from the very first days of the Alliance "an informal agreed interpretation" of consultations as specified in article 4 of the Treaty applied to threats in any part of the world. "Simply stated," said Train, "there is no NATO border. Time – not distance – must determine NATO's sphere of geopolitical interest."[85] As to the restriction contained in article 6 defining the Tropic of Cancer as boundary, it applied, in his view, to a casus belli, and was never meant to "prevent collective planning, maneuvers, or operations south of the Tropic of Cancer."[86]

In a lecture at the Royal Institute of International Relations (November 1980) on the subject of "NATO's Maritime Increased Challenges"(sic), Admiral Train stressed the growing power of the Soviet Navy and its projection capabilities which necessitated that NATO "look beyond national and Atlantic interests and embrace a fundamental philosophy of world-wide maritime commitment."[87] The United States and NATO were commited "to a policy of maritime superiority" to ensure control over vital sea lines of communications and choke points, such as the Strait of Hormuz, "during periods of crisis or general war."[88] He believed "this basic premise of maritime power [to be] one of the most challenging aspects of geopolitics," that a war between NATO and the Warsaw Pact was "more likely to start in a remote region such as the Mideast or

[84] General Bernard Rogers, "Increasing Threats to NATO's Security Call for Sustained Response," NATO Review, June 1981, p. 5.

[85] Admiral Harry D. Train, "NATO's Maritime Increased Challenges," Studia Diplomatica (XXXIII, 6), 1980, p. 651.

[86] Ibid.

[87] Ibid., p. 654.

[88] Ibid., p. 658-659.

Persian Gulf," and that during this decade of the dangerous eighties, "the regional inferiority of NATO must be offset by confronting the Warsaw Pact, and especially the Soviets, with a global strategy."[89]

This major perception of crises originating beyond NATO's traditional sphere of military responsibilities also found expression in an article by Sir John Killick (Britain's Permanent Representative to NATO from 1975 to 1979) entitled "Is NATO Relevant to the 1980's? ," and is shared by Air Chief Marshal Sir Alasdair Steedman, a former British Military Representative of NATO. In Killick's view, the chief threats "presented themselves outside the area of the North Atlantic Treaty... (and) the Alliance recognized in the Ottawa Declaration that developments outside the Alliance area could have implications for the interests of the Allies." While acknowledging that a "political consensus does not now exist in favour of the expansion of the responsibilities of the Alliance as such," Killick nevertheless urged that:

> ...extra-Alliance situations must therefore remain the responsibility of those member countries, acting individually or in consortium, who are willing and able to take action – political, economic or even military.... The Allies concerned will not be acting under a NATO label, but NATO must continue to provide the forum for the monitoring and exchange of information about extra-Alliance developments and their implications...[90]

In similar vein, Air Chief Marshal Steedman, in arguing that "NATO is much more than a military alliance; it is a political military alliance," has also concluded that the boundaries of NATO and the "inhibitions which this has imposed upon a number of the members who tend to sit upon those boundaries looking inwards at the day to day minutiae of their own

---

[89] *Ibid.* See also Harry D. Train, "Preserving the Atlantic Alliance," *Proceedings of the US Naval Institute,* January 1981, pp. 24-28.

[90] Sir John Killick, "Is NATO Relevant to the 1980's", *The World Today,* January 1980, p. 7.

country" constitue a very real problem. Drawing support from Lord Hill-Norton's book *No Soft Options,* Marshal Steedman added: "There is no question that there is a real need to look outside because that is now where the biggest threat is."[91]

We bring to an end this review of NATO's renewed interest in expanding its perimeter beyond the Tropic of Cancer by examining the perceptions and recommendations of various NATO "lobbies": the Atlantic Council of the United States, the Institute for the Study of Conflict (London), and the Foreign Affairs Research Institute (London).

Nearly three years ago, the Atlantic Council of the United States and the Japanese Research Institute for Peace and Security (RIPS) began an unprecedented joint project on common security concerns. The joint working group, under U. Alexis Johnson and George R. Packard (Dean of the John Hopkins School of Advanced International Studies, SAIS), published a summary of their assessment and recommendations in the *NATO Review* (February and May, 1981) under the title "The Common Security Interests of Japan, the United States, and its NATO Allies." As it saw it, NATO and Japan's dependence on Middle Eastern oil would remain critical for the foreseeable future. Consequently, a substantial military force should be "positioned in the area before access is denied, either by Soviet military power or by local political upheavals."[92] The United States was seen as "the only country capable of taking the lead in this operation." But there were also important roles for other North Atlantic Treaty nations and Japan:

> France, the Federal Republic of Germany, the United Kingdom and Canada should provide appropriate military assets to the Middle East-Persian Gulf area to enhance allied capability and to

---

[91] Air Chief Marshal Sir Alasdair Steedman, "Problems of Coalition War," *RUSI,* September 1981, pp. 11 and 13.

[92] *NATO Review,* February 1981, p. 12.

demonstrate allied solidarity; other NATÓ Europe nations and Japan should apply their own civil assets, including airlift and sealift, to support this allied presence in the Middle East-Persian Gulf area. Countries with past operational experience in the Middle East region could provide valuable intelligence and training support for forces in, or being deployed to, the area.[93]

Another group of the Atlantic Council, the Special Working Group on the Middle East, published its report *Oil and Turmoil: Western Choices in the Middle East,* in September 1979, three months before the Soviet intervention in Afghanistan. In contrast to the above mentioned working group on US, Japan, and NATO, and reflecting the atmosphere of detente that prevailed even in late 1979, this special Middle East group's recommendations were much more moderate. Convened in the aftermath of the Iranian revolution and the collapse of the Shah's regime, its membership of thirty experts included many former ambassadors to Arab countries, and their recommendations tended to mirror the State Department's conventional balance of approaches to the region, focusing on five major areas of policy: "availability of oil, Arab-Israeli settlement, strengthening of Turkey, a stronger military posture, and political relations."[94]

While opposing any revival of CENTO, or the building of "a new alliance linking Middle East states with the West," or finding a "new policeman of the Gulf to replace Iran", the report nevertheless urged a "strengthening of the US military posture through the increase of US naval power in the Indian Ocean supplemented by forces of allied navies," in response to what was perceived as a growing Soviet military threat.[95]

[93] *Ibid.*, April 1981, p. 14.
[94] John Campbell, Andrew Goodpaster, and Brent Scowcroft, *Oil and Turmoil: Western Choices in the Middle East* (Boulder, Colorado: Westview Press, September 1979), pp. 9-11.
[95] *Ibid.*, pp. 33-35.

On the question of Palestine, acknowledged by the working group as "remain(ing) at the heart of the Arab-Israeli conflict," the report concluded: "we do not see any solution possible unless the negotiators take up the hard questions of Palestinian self-determination together with those relating to borders and security arrangements, aiming at an eventual total package that can reconcile Palestinian rights to self-government with Israel's right to security."[96] However, the report thought that this was not "the moment to bring the PLO into active negotiations," but that this "should not rule out informal contacts between the United States and the PLO with the purpose of ascertaining the latter's views and modifying them."[97] Indeed, elsewhere in the report, the implications to the Western Alliance of the failure to resolve the issue of Palestinian self-determination were forcefully stated:

> The question of Palestinian self-determination in the West Bank and the Gaza Strip is crucial to the process of negotiation and to the prospects of a political settlement. Unresolved, it will continue to drive wedges between the US and a number of states in the Middle East whose cooperation it needs, Saudi Arabia in particular. America's European and Japanese allies, for whose vital interest in Middle East oil the cooperation of the producing states is essential, also have strong reasons to see the Palestinian question resolved. Thus, lack of progress on this question threatens not only the Israeli-Egyptian peace treaty but other essential American interests, including the cohesion of the Western Alliance.[98]

Compared to the Institute For the Study of Conflict's special paper written by Admiral of the Fleet (ret.), Lord Hill-Norton (which was also published in September 1979), the Atlantic Council's report is mild. Lord Hill-Norton estimated that Soviet behaviour in Angola, Afghanistan, and the region of the Horn of Africa necessitated a vigorous response by

[96] *Ibid.*, pp. 36-37.
[97] *Ibid.*,
[98] *Ibid.*, p. 19.

NATO and its associates through the immediate establishment of an allied "constabulary force on the seas," the abandoning of the restrictive Tropic of Cancer limit, the enlargement of NATO (because of the demise of SEATO and CENTO) to include Japan, ASEAN, and others, and, on the level of strategic planning, a "shift from the land-air confrontation in Europe to the steadily increasing risks... on and over and under the world's oceans." Waxing nostalgic while contemplating this dramatic swerve "from the narrow confines of the European theatre to the great oceans of the world," the Admiral asked: "Who better to take the lead than the United Kingdom, whose *Pax Britannica* was the longest and greatest maritime success story in the history of the world? "[99]

In the same category, one would also find proposals by the Foreign Affairs Research Institute (London) – a consistent advocate of the unrestrained expansion of NATO. It has promoted the case for expansion in its own conferences: Winchester in 1976, Brighton in 1978, and Leeds Castle, Kent in 1980 with such papers as "Reclaiming the Initiative From the Soviet Heartland, the Case For a Tri-Oceanic Alliance of the Imperiled Rimlands"; "A Strategy For the Coming Resource War"; "Will the United States Formulate and Implement a Grand Strategy For Global Freedom"; "The One Open High-

---

[99] Admiral Lord Hill-Norton, "World Shipping at Risk: The Looming Threat to the Lifelines," *Conflict Studies*, No. 111, September 1979, pp. 9 and 14. There is a perception in NATO that Soviet naval doctrine has been increasingly emphasizing the interruption of sea lines of communications (SLOC): what Maurizio Cremasco of the *Istituto Affari Internazionali* (Rome) has called a "return to concepts expounded by Marshall Sokolovski in the 1962 edition of his famous book *Military Strategy.*" Thus, whereas the mission of "disrupting the enemy's ocean and sea communications" was listed by Admiral Gorshkov in 1971 as the lowest priority of the Soviet Navy, the same task was moved in 1976 from last to third place in his article in the *Soviet Military Encyclopedia* and in his book *The Sea Power of the State.* See Maurizio Cremasco, "The Mediterranean, the Atlantic and the Indian Ocean: A Difficult Strategic Equation," *Lo Spettatore Internazionale*, (XV, 1), January-March, 1980 p. 8.

way"; and a call by Dr. Jun Tsunoda, Director of the Japanese Centre For Strategic Studies, for the construction of "a Super-NATO... equipped with a system of regular summit and ministerial conferences with a small but efficient permanent secretariat."[100]

4. Concluding Remarks

We have now assembled a body of evidence of differing kinds relating to NATO and the Middle East in two distinct periods. The following observations concerning continuity and change can be made in conclusion.

(a) With respect to the Middle East, there is a remarkable permanence of certain basic geographic realities and strategic concepts. Ernest Bevin's definition of the Middle East as stretching from Corfu to Kabul holds substantially true today, with perhaps one important difference: the expansion southward to include at least half of the Indian Ocean, with anchor points at the French island of Reunion and the Anglo-American base at Diego Garcia.

(b) For the years 1948 to 1951, it would appear from the Foreign Office archives that the moving force behind the expansion of commitments into the "inner ring" was Britain; and the Americans were being persuaded to join in defence arrangements there by the British. In the "outer ring," however, the roles were reversed; and Britain, initially, opposed the entrance of Turkey into NATO. Today, there appears to be a blurring of the distinction between outer and inner rings, particularly in the views of Secretary of State Haig. This is to some extent a reflection of renewed cold war atmosphere. From a report to the US Senate Committee on Foreign Relations, "Perspectives on NATO's Southern Flank," pre-

---

[100] *Towards a Grand Strategy of Global Freedom* (London: Foreign Affairs Publishing Co., 1981), pp. 9, 34,51,58, and 106.

pared by a fact-finding mission of Senators who visited the region, it would appear that Oman, Turkey, Greece and Italy, are considered to be crucial in any examination of "problems facing American foreign policy on the southern flank of Nato and in the securing of oil flowing to the West from the Persian Gulf."[101]

Also on the question of the inversion of roles, today the pressure for additional involvement of NATO in the Middle Eastern region such as the calls for the reinforcement of support facilities in Europe, the setting up of joint naval task forces, and the creation of a Multinational Force, is being exerted largely by the United States. In this respect, the Multinational Force, as indeed the Rapid Deployment Force and Allied Deployment Force (suggested by Jonathan Alford, a Director of the International Institute for Strategic Studies, London), may be seen as informal expansions of NATO. The fact that four European members of NATO have concerted to act together in the Middle East outside the framework of the United Nations is a grave precedent in terms of troop commitment and responsibility.[102]

(c) On the question of support for Israel, the difference between the British and American positions which dates from the late forties remains an element of remarkable continuity. Thus, Gordon Merriam's contention, referred to earlier, still holds true: "The US has supported and favored Israel, and endeavoured at the same time to remain on friendly terms with the Arab states [while] the UK, on the contrary, places Arab relations ahead of relations with Israel, and has temporarily departed from this policy only when necessary in the interest of Anglo-American relations."[103] Another element of

---

[101] US Senate, Committee on Foreign Relations, *Perspectives on NATO's Southern Flank* (Washington: 1980) p. iii.

[102] Jonathan Alford, "Les Occidentaux et la Sécurité du Golfe," *Politique Etrangère*, No. 3, September 1981, p. 681.

[103] *FRUS*, 1949, Vol. VI, p. 36.

continuity is the persistent attempt to bring Arab states to join Israel in a Western-sponsored alliance (or "strategic consensus") against the Soviet Union, undeterred by a long record of failure since the late forties (MEC, MEDO, the Baghdad Pact, and CENTO), and seemingly oblivious of Arab public opinion's profound attachment to non-alignment.

The change from the late forties is that Israel has been promoted to the rank of a "strategic asset" possessing F-15's and F-16's, a nuclear option, and what has been described as the most rapid of all rapid deployment forces. The danger posed to the Arab states, including those of the Arabian Peninsula, is obvious.

(d) It is a truism that NATO has become the victim of its own relative success in protecting the economic recovery of Europe in the late forties and in providing an adequate defence shield thereafter. There has been, of course, much controversy and friction within the Alliance, while beyond the traditional NATO perimeter, interests and policies have diverged more sharply still. In this respect, the Middle East has been a focal point of major conflicts of interest: Algerian decolonization, the Suez War of 1956, the Arab-Israeli War of 1973, the ensuing energy crisis, and the Venice Declaration. From both sides of the Atlantic, the bulk of writings and analysis speak of an unprecedented disarray of the Alliance. There are sharp divisions over such matters as volatile interest rates, trade wars, grain supplies to the Soviet Union, the Siberian gas pipeline to Western Europe, the North-South dialogue, sanctions against the socialist bloc, Cruise missiles, Central America, and Europe's Arab and Palestinian policy. To this must be added America's fears of European "Finlandization" and Europe's corresponding fear of "decoupling."

Security in the West has traditionally been perceived in military terms. Today, however, it is clear that in the West, the concern for economic security is taking precedence. The United States is being perceived more often as a bitter rival than as an ally in this context. In the fifties, the Middle East was an important factor in the economic recovery of Europe. Today, the sheer survival of the European economy is perceived as being at stake and as depending largely on Third World energy resources, raw materials, markets, and investments, all in open competition with the United States. This does not mean that the unravelling of the Alliance is a real danger, particularly its Anglo-American core. The Trident connection is equivalent to the cementing experience of the Polaris. However, the reluctance of the Allies to follow America's lead and order of priorities, and the ensuing annoyance with what are perceived in Washington as recalcitrant Allies, will continue to trouble the Alliance in this decade. The principal challenge for the Arab states will consist of maintaining non-alignment on the one hand, and countering Israel's hegemonic objectives on the other.

As regards the prospect of NATO extension, the significance of the growing strategic weight of Europe (both economic and military) within the Alliance is an open question, as is the impact of this weight on Arab options for the 1980's.

7

The Gulf and Palestine in Soviet Policy

by Rashid Khalidi

1. Introduction

History, of course, never repeats itself. If it appears to, we should be wary of taking such appearances at face value. Yet there is an attractiveness to some historical parallels which lies in the light they can shed on the present, irrespective of whether the two situations invoked are truly comparable.

If we look back to the end of the age of Britain's imperial grandeur, before the First World War, we find that among the last "frontiers" of its territorial expansion were the very regions which are the subject of our seminar. In the Gulf, the British Indian Empire slowly encroached on Ottoman power, and in Palestine and the other Ottoman provinces to the East of Egypt, the foundations were being laid for Britain to take control during and after the War.[1]

What is of relevance to us in all this is the fact that in justifying and explaining Britain's expansion in the Gulf, as well as other neighbouring regions, the danger from Moscow

---

[1] For details of the latter process, see R. Khalidi, *British Policy Towards Syria and Palestine 1906-1914* (London: Ithaca, 1980).

was the main pretext invoked by such imperial viceroys as Lord Curzon, as well as by the press in London[2].

Then, as now, a Russian drive for "warm water ports" was described as necessitating a decisive response, whether in the form of the tour of the Gulf by Lord Curzon accompanied by a powerful naval squadron in 1903[3], or the visit of US Secretary of State Haig accompanied by the stationing of AWACS in the region in 1981. Then, as now, there was disagreement as to the intentions of the power to the North, and then, as now, it was a perhaps exaggerated estimation of capabilities which was chosen as the basis on which to judge that power's probable future moves.

Although we are today dealing with a power of a nature fundamentally different from that of Tsarist Russia (unlikely though it may seem, there are some who would dispute even that) there is probably as much confusion about that power's intentions in the Gulf and around it today as there was in Curzon's day. While it will certainly not be possible in this paper to dispel all this confusion, at least a few points of relevance can be made and a certain amount of misinformation and disinformation countered.

Part of our problem is that in the Middle East generally, and in the Gulf in particular, we are dealing with a region which American strategists describe as vital to United States' interests, whether strategic or economic, while simultaneously

[2] See, e.g., J.A.S. Grenville, *Lord Salisbury and Foreign Policy: The Close of the 19th Century* (London: Univ. of London, 1964), p. 298.

[3] For details of this naval tour and more on Curzon's perception of the "Russian menace," see the official biography by Lord Ronaldshay, *The Life of Lord Curzon* (London, 1928) Vol. II, pp. 45-53; 99-102; 311-312. In 1903 a statement by the then Foreign Secretary, Lord Lansdowne, to the House of Lords, that Britain would regard the establishment of any other power on the Gulf as "a very grave menace to British interests" was met with thunderous applause, and was followed the next day by a démarche from the Russian ambassador, who assured Lansdowne that his country had no intention of establishing a base on the Gulf. Hansards, *Lords*, Vol. IV, p. 121 (1903), p. 1348; and Ronaldshay, *op. cit.*, II, 312.

denying the legitimacy of interests other powers might have there. This was incidentally the case with imperial Britain decades ago, and it is all the more so today in the wake of the revelation of the industrial world's apparently precarious dependence on oil after the 1973 war.

We have, moreover, to deal with a number of very red herrings, such as the great "Soviet need for Middle East oil" scare of the past few years, which muddy the waters and make rational discourse virtually impossible.

What can be done, nevertheless, is the following: first, we will attempt to place Soviet policy towards the Gulf region in its international and its regional context, at the same time enumerating Soviet interests in the area; secondly, certain particularly pernicious myths about this subject will be briefly discussed; and finally, the recent evolution of Soviet Gulf policy will be traced, concluding with particular emphasis on the linkage between the Gulf and neighbouring regions. Here we will examine specifically the extent to which the problem of the Gulf region and the broader Middle East crisis are seen from Moscow as being intertwined.

2. Soviet Interests in the Gulf in the International and Regional Context

Because the Soviet Union was, and, it can be argued, still is, the second nuclear super-power, it is necessary to assess its policy in some spheres in the light of that of its rival. And it is always necessary to attempt to ascertain the Soviet leadership's *perception* of the policy of its rival in making a serious attempt to trace Soviet policy. As the author attempted to show in an earlier paper[4], the Soviet perception of the overall

---

[4] *The Soviet Union and the Middle East in the 1980's* (Beirut: Institute for Palestine Studies, 1980), IPS Paper No. 7. See also the author's "L'URSS et le Moyen Orient: Mythes et réalités" in *Revue d'études Palestiniennes,* No. 3, Spring 1982, parts I and II.

strategic balance between the two super-powers differs markedly from that of many Western observers, and this perception influences greatly Soviet Middle East policy — in some senses it is its primary determinant.

THE STRATEGIC INTEREST

What makes the above generalities (some of which can just as well be applied to either super-power) particularly relevant is the fact that the Middle East is seen by the Soviet Union as one of the decisive arenas in which the strategic competition between it and the United States is currently being carried on[5]. Over the past year, a number of new Soviet statements have reaffirmed this idea and amplified it.

It is a common theme in recent Soviet writings that the United States is attempting to achieve a dominant, indeed hegemonic position in the Indian Ocean, the Gulf, and the neighbouring regions. In the words of a senior Soviet military officer writing in the armed forces newspaper, *Krasnaya Zvezda,* US policy in the region is aimed at establishing a military presence "comparatively close to the USSR's southern borders. In the opinion of overseas strategists, US naval forces in the Arabian Sea and bases in adjacent states would ensure Washington a dominant position in all of South-West Asia."[6]

A *Pravda* article entitled "Operation Persian Gulf" declares that "in turning their sights on the Persian Gulf region, the imperialist strategists are pursuing far-reaching objectives. What is involved here is an attempt to establish an American diktat over a strategically important part of the globe."[7] An

[5] Cf. in this regard *The Soviet Union and the Middle East,* pp. 7-24.

[6] Col. M. Ponomaryov, "Who is taking Advantage of the Conflict? " (the reference is to the Iraq-Iran war), October 26, 1980, cited in *Current Digest of the Soviet Press (CDSP)* (Ohio State University) XXXII, 44, pp. 2-3.

[7] Commentary by Y. Glukhov, November 3, 1980, cited in *CDSP,* XXXII, 44, pp. 3-4.

article in *Izvestia* in November 1980 speaks of US attempts to obtain "direct military control, military domination" over the Gulf,[8] while another *Pravda* commentary on the Gulf both emphasizes the growing importance of the region as a focus of rivalry with the United States, and suggests a significant reason for the Soviet leadership's concern at this development. "In perhaps no other part of our planet," writes Pavel Demchenko in the Party's official organ, "has tension grown so fast and reached such a sharp pitch." The author blames the United States for this, and goes on to add: "The overseas strategists don't conceal the fact that their military goal is the creation in the Persian Gulf of a 'third (in addition to Western Europe and the Far East) centre of military power outside the United States' covered by an 'atomic umbrella'." He concludes: "In short, large-scale militaristic manoeuvres are being carried out near the Soviet borders, and there is a danger that nuclear weapons will proliferate further and the zone of confrontation will expand."[9]

A Soviet diplomat speaking to Michael Kaufman of the *New York Times* was even more explicit in explaining the Soviet concerns which he claimed necessitated his country's naval presence in the Indian Ocean: "Our presence in the Indian Ocean is also a matter of national defence. Your missiles from subs in this ocean can reach any part of the USSR."[10] What all of this means is clear. Soviet strategists find themselves faced in the vast region to the south of their

[8] Cited in *Soviet News (SN)*, published by the Soviet Embassy in London, No. 605, p. 347.

[9] "The Persian Gulf Can be a Zone of Peace," January 3, 1981, cited in *CDSP* XXXIII, 1, p. 1.

[10] "Ports and Oil Spur Naval Build-ups by U.S. and Soviet," *New York Times (NYT)*, April 20, 1981, pp. A1, A12. For a balanced view of Soviet security interests in the Gulf, see R.D. McLaurin, "Soviet Policy in the Persian Gulf" in M. Mughisuddin, ed., *Conflict and Cooperation in the Persian Gulf*, (New York: Praeger, 1977), pp. 116-139.

borders not just with a regional competition with the United States, acute though that has become over the past few years. They perceive that with its growing naval presence in the Indian Ocean, the Gulf and other adjacent seas, and its expanding network of bases in the same region, the United States is capable of directing a strategic threat at the Soviet heartland, partly via Trident submarines and partly via carrier-based nuclear systems. Thus, just as in Europe, where the potential deployment of new NATO theatre nuclear forces presents the Soviets with the prospect of a new and un-favourable factor in the central strategic balance with the US, something no number of SS-20's aimed at Western Europe can counter, so in the Middle East and Indian Ocean regions the new US military deployments can only be matched, if at all, *in situ.* But the forces the Soviets oppose them with regionally, just as in Europe, have no effect whatever on the central equation of nuclear deterrence between the two super-powers.

It might be argued that the American Trident submarine deployment so far apparently does not include the permanent stationing of these vessels in the Indian Ocean, and that the US military presence in the region is being built up in response to Soviet moves in Afghanistan, the Horn of Africa and else-where. But in the Soviet view each of these arguments is flawed. In the case of the latter, as the author had de-monstrated before,[11] the Soviet leadership is apparently convinced that the United States' strategic concentration on the Gulf region and the Indian Ocean in fact *preceded* the Afghanistan intervention, the Iran-Iraq war, the hostages crisis, the Iranian revolution and other events often referred to as having provoked this build-up. As far as the former argument is concerned, Soviet strategists are just as prone as their American counter-parts to focus on what their opponent *could*

[11] R. Khalidi, *The Soviet Union and the Middle East,* pp. 13-24.

do, rather than on his likely behaviour. In the words of Yuri Velikanov, the Soviet diplomat quoted in Kaufman's article in the *New York Times,* "In this world you must deal with capabilities, not probabilities."[12] And it is the strategic capabilities represented by the Trident, the B-52's based at Diego Garcia, which in 1981 took part in exercises in Egypt, and the carrier-borne nuclear strike aircraft stationed in the Indian Ocean and Mediterranean that undoubtedly preoccupy Soviet strategists when they turn their gaze to this region.

THE REGIONAL INTEREST

But the strategic balance is only part of the picture which must be considered by a super-power, particularly in a vital area bordering its own frontiers. The Soviet Union also has an obvious interest in matching US efforts on a regional level, whether this involves support of client and allied states against their local rivals backed by the Americans, or establishing a direct local presence in the form of Mediterranean and Indian Ocean squadrons. Thus, in addition to their "strategic" role, Soviet military and naval forces in the region have a function which is related to the competition with the United States for the favour of local powers. Here economic, political, propaganda and diplomatic means of exerting influence play a vital role alongside that of military power in advancing Soviet interests.

It is not solely the intensity of the struggle with the United States for regional influence, or the proximity of the Soviet borders or similar geo-strategic factors, which cause the USSR to invest so much energy and such extensive foreign policy resources in this region. There is in addition a factor which can be defined either as prestige or in terms of past investments, and which reflects the fact that the Arab countries represent

[12] "Ports and Oil Spur Naval Build-ups," *NYT,* p. A. 12.

the Third World area where the post-Stalin Soviet leadership scored its first notable foreign policy successes. In the years which followed this mid-fifties breakthrough, the USSR expended massive amounts of economic and military aid and considerable prestige in the Arab states, notably Egypt.[13] The "loss" of Egypt during the Sadat years and the deep Soviet involvement which continues in Syria and several other Arab states are both important in explaining current Soviet policy, for they constitute, in different ways, an important past commitment which has to be maintained in the present, if only to justify the original decisions involved. We are talking, moreover, of a commitment of considerable magnitude, for of all Soviet military and economic aid to the less developed countries during the period 1954-75, the Middle East region as broadly defined received over 70%.[14] The Middle East's proportion of military aid was even higher. It is impossible to assess precisely the importance of these past investments, and of the Soviet prestige thereby involved, in the eyes of the Soviet leadership when they weigh current and future policy alternatives. It would be foolish, however, to assume that such intangibles play no role at all, and that it is only hard and fast strategic, political and economic realities which count in defining great power interests.

[13] In his paper "Economic Aspects of Soviet Involvement in the Middle East," in Y. Ro'i ed., *The Limits to Power: Soviet Policy in the Middle East* (London: Croom Helm, 1979), pp. 67-93. G. Ofer estimates that the Middle East as broadly defined received about 10 billion roubles in Soviet military and economic aid from 1954 until 1975 (Table, p. 70). Egypt received almost 30% of Soviet military aid and nearly 20% of economic aid over the same period (Tables, pp. 76-7 and 79). Roger Pajak, in "Soviet Arms Transfers as an Instrument of Influence," *Survival*, XXXIII, 4, July-August 1981, pp. 165-179, gives somewhat different figures: $25.8 billion in arms deliveries to the Middle East and North Africa from 1955-1979, or about 13% of deliveries to non-communist countries.

[14] Ofer., *op. cit.*, p. 72.

THE ECONOMIC INTEREST: THE "SOVIET NEED FOR MIDDLE EAST OIL" MYTH

This brings us to a last Soviet interest in the Middle East, one which because of its controversial nature is particularly hard to assess. This is the potential economic interest of the Middle East to the USSR, particularly insofar as oil is concerned. We are dealing here with a topic which has been the subject of considerably more heat than light in recent years, and at the same time one regarding which each observer's particular bias has great importance.

There are those who assume that the USSR's foreign policy is based at least in part on short term and/or economically defined gains; that it is "exploitative" in the sense applied by Marxist critics to US relations with the developing countries; and thus that if the Soviet Union has shown such a great interest in the Middle East over the past three decades, the motive must lie in economic factors, particularly oil. In its more sober forms, this is an argument which has at least a kernel of truth in it, for the Soviet Union is not and has never claimed to be a cornucopia for the less-developed countries, willing to extend endless quantities of aid from altruistic motives, and with no hope of obtaining something in return. On the contrary, Soviet sources usually describe economic relations with developing countries as being of *mutual* benefit, clearly implying that the USSR expects at least some recompense for its efforts in this sphere.[15] Of course, much of this recompense is political, in the form of the increased influence of the USSR in the recipient countries, and some-

---

[15] Thus, for example, Kosygin declared at a January 1977 Moscow lunch for Saddam Hussein, then Vice-President of the Iraqi Revolutionary Command Council, that in its economic relations with other states, the USSR was not "engaged in some sort of charitable activity; but these relations rested on a basis of mutual interests and national economic requirements." *USSR and the Third World,* Vol. VII, Nos. 1-2, p. 23.

times comes in the form of direct or indirect strategic advantage. But at least some of it is economic, and as recent research has shown, Soviet foreign policy-makers have of late been showing a greater interest than before in maximizing this economic return, whether in the form of repayment of debts, increased two-way trade, or obtaining oil from the Middle Eastern oil-producing states.[16]

All this is logical, for it certainly makes sense for a power with something to offer in the military sphere like the USSR, when dealing with powers with large oil or gas reserves and equally large oil revenues, like Libya, Iraq, Algeria or Kuwait, to expect to obtain something in return for its arms. And however much oil the USSR may have or may be able to produce (assuming that the earlier CIA predictions of a Soviet oil shortfall are as unfounded as other assessments and the CIA's own latest figures seem to show[17]), it has such extensive energy needs and foreign energy commitments that one can assume that it can always use more of a good thing.

But to say all this is not to accept the more extreme forms of the economic thesis outlined above. During the period, only recently ended, when the imaginations of some were dangerously over-stimulated by the CIA's predictions and other similar alarmist reports, we were expected to believe that the Soviet Union, desperate for oil, was motivated in its Middle

[16] e.g., Ofer, *op. cit.,* and the postscript, pp. 368-369; Y. Ro'i, "Soviet Economic Presence in Egypt," *The Jerusalem Quarterly,* No. 3 (1977), pp. 104-23; for a sensible summary see K. Dawisha, *Soviet Foreign Policy Towards Egypt* (London: Macmillan, 1979), pp. 161-15. See also R. Pajak, *op. cit.,* as this interest in an economic return relates to arms sales.

[17] For the latest episode in the saga of the CIA's fluctuating predictions regarding Soviet oil needs, see B. Gwertzman, "CIA Believes Russia Can Meet Oil Needs Through Mid-1980's," in *International Herald Tribune (IHT),* May 20, 1981, p. 2. As the title indicates, the article describes the CIA's retraction of its earlier alarmist predictions. For a US Defense Intelligence Agency assessment see "Soviet Energy Outlook Seen Highly Favourable by a New US *Report,*" *IHT,* September 3, 1981.

East policy by the acute need to take control of the region's oil resources. In fact, it required quite a feat of the imagination to envision the world's biggest oil producer risking the near-certainty of nuclear confrontation with the West to obtain more of this commodity. In the first place, there was always ample evidence for those who cared to look for it, that the Soviet leadership was fully aware of their country's energy needs, and completely intent on meeting them without recourse to foreign sources of supply.[18] Secondly, and perhaps more importantly, there was the fact, which any serious student of Soviet policy should have been able to perceive, that far from depending on external sources of strategic raw materials, the USSR has always in the past attempted, generally successfully, to establish and maintain a situation of self-sufficiency in this regard.[19] Here we return to a point made earlier. For while it is reasonable to assume that the Soviet Union expects at least some return, where possible, in its external economic relations with the Third World, there is little if any evidence for the assumption that, like some other countries, it expects a continuous and considerable profit in its

[18] For an earlier discussion of the question by the author, see R. Khalidi, *The USSR and the Middle East* pp. 20-21, especially note 40. See also the analysis in the author's "L'URSS et le Moyen Orient", part IV. For a few examples of more recent Soviet material on this subject, see A. Guber, "Soviet Oil Production Will Grow – Despite the CIA's Forecasts," a Novosti commentary cited in *SN,* No. 6057, p. 43; an interview with Vladimir Filanovsky, Head of the Oil and Gas Industry Department at the USSR State Planning Commission, in *Moscow News,* No. 7 (February, 15, 1981), p. 1; and a comprehensive article on future Soviet energy prospects by A. Aleksandrov, President of the USSR Academy of Sciences, in *Izvestia,* February 21, 1981, cited in *CDSP,* XXXIII, 9, pp. 1-4. At the end of 1981, the USSR had met its annual planning target for oil production, and exceeded that for gas: *IHT,* January 25, 1982, pp. 1-2.

[19] In the words of Dawisha, *op. cit.,* p. 163, "beginning with the first five-year plan, the Soviet government has pursued a policy of economic autarky." For a judicious discussion of Soviet energy prospects, see L. Dienes and T. Shabad, *The Soviet Energy System: Resource Use and Policies* (Washington D.C.: Winton, 1979).

economic relations with the developing countries. Thus, for a number of reasons, we are inclined to agree with the opinion expressed by a student of Soviet economic relations with the region: "I find it very hard to believe that the Soviet Union will at any point allow itself to become dependent on external sources of such an essential material as oil."[20]

In sum therefore, we can add an economic interest, albeit one very narrowly defined, to those we have already enumerated above as motivating Soviet policy in the Middle East, namely strategic considerations, the local requirements of the super-power rivalry, and the weight of Soviet prestige and other resources already invested there over the past three decades. Our discussion of the oil question has shown us that however important this commodity may be, the need for it is apparently not one of the primary determinants of Soviet regional policy. We will now attempt to outline Soviet Gulf policy as it has developed recently, concluding with the Soviet perception of the linkage between the Gulf and the Arab-Israeli dispute.

3. The Soviet Union and the Gulf

As it has grown in perceived importance in recent years, so has some observers' definition of the Gulf region seemed to expand to include a broader and broader geographic region. And at the same time, a conflict over the very name of this body of water has arisen, with both "Persian" and "Arab" advanced as the only proper title for it. Inasmuch as the name *al-Khalij al-farisi* was good enough for the classical Arab geographers and historians,[21] it is something of a mystery why

---

[20] G. Ofer, *op. cit.,* p. 88. McLaurin, *op. cit.,* p. 135, is even more harsh in dealing with a related myth: "Those who fear that the Soviet intention in the Gulf is to cut off Western oil cannot have undertaken a systematic analysis of Soviet resources, policy, and over-all objectives."

[21] At times the term used was *bahr faris.* See, *inter alia,* al-Tabari, *Annales,* ed.

Arab nationalist fervour now dictates another name, but the very dispute is symptomatic of the growing significance of this region. For our purposes, it will be defined to include the Arab countries of the Gulf's southern littoral. Arbitrarily enough, this definition excludes Iran, the major Gulf power, for the reason that its relations with the USSR are defined by its position on that country's southern frontiers, rather than solely or mainly by its being on the Gulf. Iraq is excluded because it is not primarily a Gulf (but rather a Mashriq) power. The Yemens, the Horn of Africa and the Red Sea will not be included, although they are adjacent to the Gulf and certain very elastic definitions seem to include some or all of them when the Gulf is spoken of. We will, however, have frequent occasion to refer to the Indian Ocean, which for the Soviet Union is intimately connected with the Gulf.

Not surprisingly, in view of the point noted at the outset of the preceding section, concerted Soviet interest in the Gulf, and frequent reference to it in official statements, seem to have begun after the massive upswing in US attention to it, coinciding with the fall of the Shah. In the wake of the storm of American comment in early 1980, both official and in the press, which linked the Soviet intervention in Afghanistan to a Soviet intention to threaten Western oil supplies coming from the Gulf, the Soviet leadership attempted to reassure the West. This came in the authoritative form of a speech in February 1980 by Soviet President Brezhnev, who described Western fears for the security of the sea lanes through which Middle Eastern oil passed as "partly understandable."[22] What

M.J. de Goeje (Leiden: Brill, 1879-1901), Vol. I, p. 817, and Vol. III, p. 841, where it is called by this name; and al-Mas'udi, *Muruj al-Dhahab*, ed. Ch. Pellat (Beirut, 1966), paragraph 255, where it is described as *al-Khalij al-farisi*, or the Persian Gulf.

[22] For an earlier discussion of this episode, see R. Khalidi, *The Soviet Union and the Middle East*, p. 21, and especially note 41. The Brezhnev speech is in *CDSP*, XXXII, 8, pp. 1-4 and in *SN*, No. 6011, pp. 65, 68-70. Soviet scholarly and media interest in the Gulf has also increased recently. See, e.g. Academician Gregory

Brezhnev was in effect suggesting was some form of international guarantee for the security of oil transport, as was made clear in an article written for Tass by a senior Soviet party official soon afterwards, which amplified and clarified the proposal of the Soviet leader.[23] Not surprisingly in the wake of the Afghanistan crisis, the US and its allies failed to respond to this Soviet initiative. It may be doubted whether in any circumstances they would have been willing to allow the USSR to have any role whatsoever in ensuring the security of oil shipments, because of the implicit recognition this would have constituted of the USSR's power and standing in a region where the West considered itself paramount.

As we shall see, the USSR eventually changed tack after its attempt to appeal directly to the West failed to elicit any response, and following the continued increase of expressions of concern for the security of the Gulf region in the US and Europe, combined with overt preparations for intervention there involving the establishment both of new bases in the region and of the Rapid Deployment Force. The new Soviet approach involved appealing to the states of the Gulf and the broader Middle East region, with the aim of placing them on their guard against the United States, thereby if possible moving them closer to Moscow. At the same time, a diplomatic offensive was launched, involving both publicly-announced Soviet initiatives directed at the West and the states of the region, and efforts to develop bilateral relations with the latter.

Bondarievski, *al-Khalij al-'Arabi* (Moscow, 1981), who also notes parallels between the era of Lord Curzon and the present day: pp. 126-132, 180-3.

23 The commentary was by N. Portugalov of the CPSU Central Committee International Information Department on 29 February, 1980, and is discussed in depth by D. Vernet in *Le Monde*, March 2-3, 1980, pp. 1-2, in an article entitled "Moscou suggère aux Européens d'exiger une 'guarantie internationale' pour la sécurité des transports pétroliers."

Since this offensive involved moves on a number of levels, it will be impossible here to do more than chronicle and briefly describe some of the most important of them. And although in some sense Brezhnev's February 1980 speech in the midst of the Afghan imbroglio was the starting point, it was not until the outbreak of the Iraq-Iran war in September of the same year that the question became a constant focus of attention for Soviet policy-makers. Thus, on the occasion of the first visit by an Arab leader to Moscow after the outbreak of the war, that of Syrian President Asad in early October, Brezhnev included in his speech of welcome pointed references to the Gulf situation, which were to be constantly repeated thereafter. After delivering a warning to the United States not to intervene in the conflict, and pledging Soviet non-interference, the Soviet leader went on:

> The Persian Gulf, just as any other region of the world, is a sphere of vital interests of the states situated there, and not of some other states. And no one has the right to meddle from outside in their affairs, to appear in the role of their guardians or self-styled 'custodians of order.'[24]

The Soviet-Syrian joint communique released at the end of the Asad visit, which was highlighted by the signing of a Treaty of Friendship and Cooperation, also referred to the Gulf. It declared that both sides condemned "the increased attempts by the United States to interfere in the internal affairs" of the states of the Gulf and Red Sea regions, which they claimed were aimed at forcing them to "relinquish their inalienable right to use their national wealth at their discretion." The communique also described the establishment of US bases in the region as a serious threat to the security and independence of the states of the region, stated the opposition of both sides to the creation of blocs and military alliances there, and affirmed that freedom of navigation in the Gulf

---

[24] *Pravda,* October 9, 1980, cited in *CDSP,* XXXII, No. 41, pp. 5-6.

must be observed.[25]

The fact that the latter point was intended to defend the USSR against charges that it threatened the Gulf countries as well as the oil supply lines to the US and Western Europe, was confirmed by a Novosti commentary a few weeks later. This explicitly stated that, far from having any hostile intentions with respect to the countries of the Near and Middle East, "the Soviet Union has never had any intention of 'breaking through' to the warm seas." It went on to declare that, as distinct from the US, the USSR "has never laid claim to the wealth of other nations and has never included them in the sphere of its 'vital interests.' "[26] A message by Brezhnev to the conference held in Nicosia at the end of October in solidarity with the struggle of the peoples of the Persian Gulf repeated many of the same themes, and stressed the link between Western policy in the Gulf and on the Palestine issue, a point to which we will return below. Brezhnev further affirmed that both the Persian Gulf and the Indian Ocean should be turned into "zones of peace."[27]

The Soviet position was summed up authoritatively by Brezhnev in a speech before the Indian Parliament in December 1980, in which he scoffed at the "world-wide hullabaloo about a 'Soviet threat' either to Pakistan or to the Persian Gulf countries, or God knows whom, although they are well aware that no such threat exists whatsoever." He went on:

> On the invented pretext of the protection of their 'vital interests', powers situated many thousands of kilometres from the region have concentrated a military armada there and are intensively building up armaments, expanding the network of their military

[25] *Pravda*, October 11, 1980, cited in *Moscow News*, No. 43, (October 26, 1980), (supplement), pp. 6-7.

[26] E. Cheporov, "The USSR Stands for Non-interference in the Iraq-Iran War," cited in *SN*, No. 6042, p. 326.

[27] Cited in *SN*, No. 6044, p. 339.

bases, and subjecting to pressure and threats the small countries which do not follow in their wake. Attempts are being made to justify such actions by talk of the 'Soviet threat' to this region's oil wealth. It goes without saying that this is a sheer fabrication, and its authors are well aware of that. The USSR does not intend to encroach either on Middle East oil or its supply route.

Having said that, Brezhnev immediately afterwards confirmed that the USSR had an interest in the question, asserting: "It is certainly not all the same to us what is taking place in an area so close to our frontiers." He then proceeded to state that what the USSR wanted was a "normal, calm situation" to be created in the region, which he proposed be brought about via agreement between all the concerned parties on a number of principles. These included non-establishment of military bases in the Gulf and adjacent islands, non-deployment of nuclear weapons there, refraining from use or threat of the use of force, and from interference in the internal affairs of states of the Gulf area, respect of their sovereign right to dispose of their natural resources, and refraining from obstructing the sea lanes linking the region with the rest of the world.[28]

Clearly, Western agreement to such a set of principles, innocuous though most of them were (and some, such as the first point, which would have affected the US and the UK more than the USSR, were by no means innocuous) would have implied admitting the USSR to the ranks of the powers with an interest in this region, and therefore with a right to a voice in its affairs. Clearly, this was not something the US and its allies were prepared to admit, and this proposal, like that made in February, was treated as no more than propaganda by the West.

The Indian position can best be seen from the text of the joint communique released after the visit, in which the

---

[28] Cited in *SN*, No. 6050, pp. 385 and 392.

Arab-Israeli dispute, the problem of the Gulf and the Afghan question were all lumped together under the rubric of "hot-beds of tension in South-West Asia." Thus, although the text did stress that both sides in effect accepted most of the principles enunciated by the Soviet leader in his speech, it linked them also to Afghanistan, laying stress on the non-aligned status, sovereignty and independence of the states of the region, and the inadmissability of "outside interference" in their internal affairs.[29] Brezhnev's Indian hosts thereby deprived him of the satisfaction of seeing these principles accepted regarding the Gulf alone, although their application to Afghanistan, since it was open to several different interpretations, was obviously not unacceptable to the Soviet side.

The next occasion on which the USSR expressed its position on the Gulf was from the podium of the 26th Congress of the Soviet Communist Party on February 23, 1981, where the Party's General Secretary delivered the report of the Central Committee. Here Brezhnev further developed the proposals he made a year earlier and in New Delhi, explicitly calling for an international agreement regarding the Gulf whereby "the sovereign rights of the countries there and the security of maritime and other communications connecting the region with the rest of the world can be guaranteed." This proposal was preceded by a sarcastic swipe at the US, with Brezhnev declaring that "it is absurd to think that the oil interests of the West can be 'defended' by turning that region into a powder keg."[30]

Perhaps the most significant element in this formulation of the Soviet stand was the emphasis on the rights of the countries in the region. For whereas the proposals and the propaganda until this point seem to have been at least partly

[29] The text can be found in *SN,* No. 6050, pp. 390-91.
[30] Published in full in *Moscow News,* No. 9 (March 1, 1981), supplement; the passages discussed are on pp. 4-5.

directed at the West by Soviet policy-makers, from here on, the countries of the region were the main focus, and reassuring them became the primary Soviet concern.

The fruits of this approach were quickly apparent during the succession of visits by Arab leaders to Moscow during a two month period from April to June, visits which were the occasion for a series of favourable statements about the Soviet proposals regarding the Gulf. Most important, perhaps, in all this was the fact that in addition to representatives of states aligned to a greater or lesser degree with the USSR, such as Presidents Qadhafi and Ben Jedid of Libya and Algeria, and PLO Political Department Head Faruq al-Qaddumi, the visitors also included leaders of conservative states such as the Kuwaiti Foreign Minister, Shaykh Sabah al-Ahmed al-Sabah and King Hussein of Jordan. These meetings in Moscow, moreover, were followed in September by the visit of the Amir of Kuwait, Shaykh Jabir al-Ahmed al-Sabah, to four Eastern European countries, among them Hungary and Bulgaria, both close to the USSR.[31] In October, North Yemeni President Ali Abdullah Sabah and PLO Executive Committee Chairman Yasser Arafat also visited Moscow.

The most important of these bilateral contacts as far as we are concerned was probably the Kuwaiti Minister's visit to Moscow, which took place in April 1981, and was followed by a joint communique which constituted a minor victory for Soviet diplomacy. For although its wording included the phrase "exchange of opinions" regarding the Gulf, a sure sign that there was less than perfect agreement, the text indicates that the Soviet proposals did not fall on deaf ears. It stated that the talks on the Gulf:

---

[31] The dates of the Moscow visits were as follows: Sabah al-Ahmed, April 23-25; Qadhafi, April 27-29; Hussein, May 26-29; Ben Jedid, June 8-10; and al-Qaddumi, 28-30 June. Jabir al-Ahmed visited Bulgaria, Rumania, Hungary and Yugoslavia on September 10-12, 12-14, 14-16, and 16-19 respectively.

... showed the closeness of the two sides' views with respect to ways of ensuring peace and security in that region. The two sides voiced support for the right of the Persian Gulf countries to safeguard the security of that region themselves, without outside interference, and to freely dispose of their natural resources. They stated that they oppose the creation of foreign military bases and the deployment of nuclear weapons in that region and all forms of outside interference in the internal affairs of the states there.[32]

Nevertheless, a close examination of this communique in comparison with earlier Soviet statements indicates that the Soviet position was not accepted in its entirety by the Kuwaiti side. And when it is recalled that earlier Soviet comment on efforts by the Gulf states, through the Gulf Cooperation Council, to "safeguard the security of that region themselves" was unfavourable,[33] it is clear that a change in the Soviet stand was being made in deference to the views of the Kuwaiti government and those of the other Gulf states. This new line was, incidentally, maintained, and public Soviet references to the Gulf Council thereafter were more nuanced and restrained.[34]

Among the factors which enhance the interest and importance of the Moscow visit of Sabah al-Ahmed were the statements and press reports which emerged before and during

[32] *Pravda,* April 26, 1981; *CDSP,* XXXIII, No. 17, p. 13.

[33] At a Beirut press conference, reported in *al-Safir,* March 18, 1981, p. 12, given by Dr. Evgeny Primakov, Director of the Institute of Oriental Studies of the USSR Academy of Sciences and Dr. Igor Belyayev, correspondent of *Literaturnaya Gazeta,* the former declared that "the form of the Gulf Security Council causes us concern in some of its aspects. However, it will not lead to any results, and we will wait and see." He also commented unfavourably on attempts to equate the US and Soviet naval presences in the Indian Ocean.

[34] See, for example, a Tass commentary, published in *al-Nahar* on May 29, 1981, which condemns US attempts, through Oman, to "give a military character to the peaceful cooperation between states of the Gulf." The implication – that the Gulf Council is acceptable as long as it does not become a military pact aligned with the West, as the Omanis had been urging – is clear. See also the article by Belyayev, "The Middle East-Time to Decide" in *Literaturnaya Gazeta,* cited in *CDSP,* XXXIII, No. 21, pp. 11-13, which is discussed below in section 4, for the change in the tone of Soviet comments on the Gulf.

it, which indicated clearly that Kuwait was speaking in the name of all the Gulf states in the Soviet capital. This was the gist of an AP report citing Kuwaiti Government sources who refused to be named. The Kuwaiti minister himself was quoted by the same agency during his stay in Moscow as saying that the Gulf Cooperation Council had wanted him to visit the USSR, and that he intended to demonstrate to his hosts (as he apparently did successfully) that the Council was not directed against any power. Sabah al-Ahmed is quoted in the same report as saying: "This visit was desired by all the states of the region."[35] In view of the clear and longstanding interest of the Soviet Union in developing its relations with the leading power in the Council, Saudi Arabia, such words must have been welcome indeed, although they only marked a step in that direction.

The visit of the Libyan leader to Moscow only a few days afterwards was the occasion for a much more extensive identity of views on the Gulf. Brezhnev and his colleagues in the Soviet leadership had by this point apparently given up hope of a Western response to their proposals, as is evidenced by the Soviet President's expression, at a dinner for Qadhafi, of doubts that the US and its allies are seriously concerned for the safety of oil transport, since "they won't even discuss international agreements that would reliably ensure that security."[36] In the joint communique issued after the visit, both

[35] The reports are datelined Kuwait and Moscow, and were published in *al-Safir* on April 22 and 24 respectively.

[36] *Pravda*, April, 28, 1981, cited in *CDSP*, XXXIII, No. 17, pp 10-11. Qadhafi's speech in response called for "the neutrality of the Gulf and its exclusion from the sphere of international conflicts," according to the same source. A *New York Times* report from Moscow by Serge Schmemann on April 30, 1981, p. A 4, makes much of differences between the *Pravda* text of the speech and another distributed by the Libyan embassy in Moscow. Neither with regard to the Gulf nor over Afghanistan does there appear to be any major omission by *Pravda*, although it failed to report the Libyan leader's call for a "decisive posture" of support for the Steadfastness Front and for "more energetic efforts" to back it.

sides strongly condemned the policy of the US "and other imperialist powers" in the Gulf, their establishment of bases in the neighbouring regions, and the formation of military and political blocs in that part of the world (the latter perhaps a veiled reference to the Gulf Cooperation Council?). Security and tranquillity in the Gulf, the communique stated, depended on "guarantees of the sovereign rights of the littoral states and the security of the sea lanes and other lines of communication linking it to the rest of the world."[37]

The focus on the states of the region which had emerged in Soviet official statements by this point was apparent in a commentary entitled "Prospects for a settlement in the Middle East" written by the influential Head of the Central Committee's International Information Department, Leonid Zamyatin, in May 1981, which discussed both the Arab-Israeli dispute — at that point at a stage of acute crisis over Lebanon — and the Gulf issue. Zamyatin laid particular stress on points likely to be of concern to the states of the area, such as the charge that the US Rapid Deployment Force would fulfil a "police function" with regard to those Arab states the US might decide were within the "zone of its vital interests." He continued: "All of this can lead to the seizure of the oil fields of one Arab country or another if it decides, for certain considerations, to reduce oil production or discontinue it temporarily." Zamyatin reassured the states of the Gulf that the Soviet Gulf proposal did not mean an exclusive Soviet-American dialogue, but was rather predicated on security consultations "first of all between countries in the area."

The Soviet party official, however, added an assertion directed not so much at the Gulf states as at the West: "We hold the view that freedom of navigation in the area is vital not only to the US, and not so much to the US, whose territory lies in the other hemisphere, as to the Asian and

<hr />

[37] *Pravda*, April 30, 1981, cited in *CDSP*, XXXIII, No. 17, pp. 11-13.

African countries as well as the USSR."[38] This remark must be seen in the context of the point made by the *New York Times* article on the Indian Ocean cited earlier, which stressed the importance of the area to the USSR for fishing and maritime transport, and noted that "traffic between Vladivostok and Black Sea ports has increased and has formed one of the country's most important naval highways."[39]

A Novosti interview with the Commander-in-Chief of the Warsaw Pact forces at about the same time throws further light on the Soviet perception of the strategic importance of the Gulf-Indian Ocean area. Commenting on the recent discussion by the NATO Council of the extension of the Alliance's "sphere of activity" to the Near and Middle East, Marshal Victor Kulikov stated:

> If we look at the map, we shall notice that this 'sphere of activity' stretches along the borders of the Soviet Union and other Socialist countries. In other words, the NATO leaders are trying in every way to restore the chain of blocs which has been broken as a result of the collapse of SEATO and CENTO. These blocs, as you know, were directed against the countries of the Socialist community.[40]

If this process were to be thwarted by the Soviet Union, the key states were the so-called Arab 'moderates', notably the Arab Gulf states, whose adhesion to or abstention from the "chain of blocs" in Kulikov's words — the "strategic consensus" in those of Haig and other US policy-makers — would spell success or failure for American policy in the post-Iran, post-Afghanisatan and post Camp David era. The visit of Jordan's King Hussein to Moscow at the end of May 1981 was therefore of particular importance to his hosts, and seems to have come up to their expectations.

The extremely tense situation in Lebanon, where Israel and

---

[38] Cited in *SN*, No. 6070, pp. 158-9.
[39] Michael Kaufman, April 20, 1981, pp. A1, A12 NYT.
[40] Cited in *SN*, No. 6070, pp. 156-7.

Syria seemed on the brink of a major conflict, occupied the attention of both sides during the visit, and was the main subject of speeches and the joint communique issued afterwards. But the Gulf was mentioned, and here again, the Soviet side could take some comfort in the results. Brezhnev, in his dinner speech for the Jordanian monarch, again contrasted the policies of the US and the USSR:

> This power, it seems, regards the natural wealth of the Middle East as if it were in the bowels of Texas or California. The other power, meanwhile, the Soviet Union, has no such claims whatsoever. We do not think that we have any right to the natural resources of the Middle East countries. We do not see ourselves as the self-styled guardians of these countries.[41]

In response, Hussein confined himself to stating Jordan's support for Gulf "self-defence with Arab assistance," and her opposition to foreign interference and hegemony.[42] The joint communique issued afterwards was nearly identical in its wording on the Gulf with that issued after the visit of Sabah al-Ahmed. The only differences were minor: there was no mention of an "exchange of opinions," only of an "examination of the situation" in the Gulf region, and otherwise the wording was very slighty modified.[43] The overall impression is that, as with the Kuwaitis, the Soviet side succeeded in convincing its guests of the value of their Gulf proposals, although it should be noted that in neither communique is there specific mention of the principles accepted by both sides as constituting a Soviet proposal or initiative, or of explicit Kuwaiti or Jordanian approval of any such initiative.

There was a further reference to the Gulf in the joint communique issued less than two weeks later after the visit to Moscow of the next Arab leader, Chadhli Ben Jedid. While in

---

41 *Pravda*, May 27, 1981, cited in *CDSP*, XXXIII, No. 21, pp. 9-10.
42 *Ibid.*
43 *Pravda*, May 30, 1981, cited in *CDSP*, XXXIII, No. 21, pp. 10-11.

most points similar to the passages on the same subject in the Kuwaiti-Soviet and Jordanian-Soviet documents, there are some differences. One is the reference to the two sides having "exchanged opinions" on the Gulf, while another proclaims them as not only against the establishment of new foreign military bases, but also for the dismantling of the existing ones, a point not mentioned in the two earlier communiques.[44]

The last prominent Arab visitor to Moscow during this busy two months of Arab-Soviet diplomacy was Faruq al-Qaddumi, who was reported as having, on behalf of the PLO leadership, "praised the constructive initiatives of the Soviet Union". This was a reference to, among other things, the Soviet Gulf initiative, since the other major Soviet initiative related to the Middle East, that for a reconvening of the Geneva conference with the participation of the PLO, is specifically referred to in detail in the preceding paragraph of this Soviet report of the meeting.[45] Moreover, at a Moscow press conference on June 30th, al-Qaddumi reiterated that "the PLO fully approves the new peaceful initiatives set forth in President Brezhnev's report to the 26th Congress of the Communist Party of the Soviet Union."[46]

The Soviet leadership was undoubtedly pleased by this spectrum of Arab statements of support for a considerable part of its proposals on the Gulf. And yet, for all their value, statements are only words, and do not necessarily reflect intentions, policies and, most important of all, realities on the ground. There, the refusal of the US and its allies to respond to the Soviet initiative prevented its translation into a regional

---

[44] Cited in *SN*, No. 6075, pp. 196-7.

[45] *SN*, No. 6078, p. 222. A report in the Palestine News Agency (WAFA) English Bulletin, No. 136/81, June 30, 1981, p. 2, makes no mention of either matter.

[46] WAFA English Bulletin, No. 137/81, July 1, 1981, pp. 2-3.

settlement in which the USSR would play a major and recognized part. Failing this ideal outcome, to be judged a partial success the initiative would have to elicit not only a positive response in theory from the Gulf states and their fellow-Arabs — which it did in large measure — but also a development of bilateral relations. In the last analysis, this depended almost entirely on the Gulf states themselves, all the more so because the Soviet intervention in Afghanistan had alienated a number of Muslim governments, notably that of Saudi Arabia. The failure to arrive at a settlement of the crisis over that country deprived the USSR of the ability to meet the diplomatic demand of this most important of Gulf states, thus severely limiting its manoeuverability.

In view of these circumstances, it is all the more remarkable that the USSR met with such a positive response from Kuwait. This small Gulf state, closely linked to Saudi Arabia, and yet with a more adventurous and far-ranging foreign policy, not only sent its Foreign Minister to Moscow, where, as we have seen, he seems to have reached a large measure of agreement with his hosts. In September its ruler went on a week-long tour of four Eastern European countries, the first of its kind, which in addition to expressions of agreement on the status of the Gulf,[47] seems to have been the precursor of a series of

---

[47] The Kuwaiti-Rumanian, -Hungarian and -Yugoslav joint communiques are published in *al-Siyasa* (Kuwait), September 15, 17 and 20, 1981 respectively, in every case on p. 3. There are interesting differences between the former two (as well as the Kuwaiti-Bulgarian communique) and the latter. For whereas the former are very similar in wording to the Kuwaiti-Soviet communique of the preceding April, the Kuwaiti-Yugoslav text states that "the Kuwaiti side explained to the Yugoslav side the aims and objectives of the Gulf Cooperation Council. The Yugoslav side expressed full support for these aims and for the determination of the Council members to reinforce their security, independence and joint cooperation." They also stated that the fleets of the "great powers" in the Indian Ocean were a "threat to world peace and security" and called for their withdrawal. The Belgrade document, which is a frank expression of both sides' views, illustrates clearly the limits to the common ground between the Soviets and Kuwaitis.

economic deals, involving the supply of oil, and in the case of Yugoslavia, the extension of a $250 million soft loan to help out with that country's balance of payments problems.[48] In view of the Soviet Union's need to wean its Eastern European customers of their dependence on Soviet oil, these developments could only be welcomed in Moscow.

But it was on the political level that any decisive moves would have to take place, and here the Kuwaitis played a leading role. Already in August, the United Arab Emirates had begun negotiations with a Soviet envoy for the establishment of relations, although without result. According to an AP report datelined Kuwait:

> High-level officials meeting in Abu Dhabi failed to agree on establishing diplomatic relations between the Soviet Union and the UAE, but the Soviet Union would be allowed to open offices in Abu Dhabi for trade relations and the national airline Aeroflot...

The same report, quoting the Kuwaiti press, said the UAE negotiators described an exchange of diplomatic ties as "premature" to their Soviet interlocutor, Anatoli Filov of the Foreign Ministry Middle East Section.[49]

In the wake of the Amir of Kuwait's Eastern European tour, senior Kuwaiti officials repeatedly stated that their country would recommend that the states of the Gulf Cooperation Council establish relations with Moscow, with the aim of establishing a balance between East and West and reinforcing Arab non-alignment. This was picked up by a number of Gulf papers, including *al-Ittihad* in Abu Dhabi, *al-Wahda* in Abu Dhabi, and *al-Bayan* in Dubai, as well as the entire Kuwaiti press, all of which strongly seconded the Kuwaiti

---

[48] *Le Monde,* September 24, 1981, p. 6: "Koweit: L'Emirat recommande aux Etats du Golfe d'établir des relations diplomatiques avec Moscou" *L'Orient-Le Jour,* September 21, 1981, p. 6.

[49] *IHT,* August 31, 1981, p. 6: "Emirates Talks on Tie to Russia Said to Fail."

proposal.[50] Ultimately, of course, everything would depend on the response of the states of the Gulf Council, which included Bahrein and Oman, the sites of US and British military and naval bases, as well as Saudi Arabia, which is closely bound to the US in numerous spheres. The same press reports which quoted the Amir of Kuwait, his ministers and other officials as calling for links with the USSR also added that the question would be placed on the agenda of the November 1981 conference of the Gulf Council.[51] The key Council power, Saudi Arabia, has many reasons for reluctance on this question, and may well put a brake on any further such developments. But at least one press report, in *Le Monde,* indicated, regarding Kuwait's East European policy, that "in the estimation of numerous observers, in spite of certain divergences, this diplomacy has now received the blessing of Riyadh as a counterweight to American influence."[52] It remains to be seen how far Riyadh will be willing to go in this direction, a question which will not be determined solely by

[50] *al-Ba'th,* September 23, 1981, p. 1, "Suhuf al-Khalij tu'ayyid iqamat 'alaqat ma'al-ittihad al-sufyati."

[51] *al-Safir,* September 21, 1981, p. 12. In the event, the Council did not discuss relations with Moscow, although Soviet statements on Saudi Arabia, and Saudi statements on the USSR, continued to appear. Their focus was the Fahd plan and the AWACS deal. On the former the Soviets were cautiously positive, and on the latter cautiously critical. See, respectively *al-Safir,* 20 November 1981, p. 1, and 2 November, 1981, p. 13. The latter is a Novosti comment on AWACS written exclusively for *al-Safir.*

[52] *Le Monde,* September 24, 1981, p. 6. Kuwaiti-Soviet relations continued to develop even as this paper was being written. *al-Safir* on October 20, 1981, p. 1, quoted a Kuwaiti News Agency report that the Minister for Cabinet Affairs and Kuwait Government spokesman, 'Abd al-'Aziz Hussein, had arrived in Moscow the preceding day on a visit "to exchange views on bi-lateral relations between the two countries." On his departure, he declared to the Kuwaiti News Agency (*al-Safir,* October 24, 1981, p. 12) that the USSR and Kuwait "agree that the Security of the Gulf is the responsibilty of its citizens alone, without foreign interference," as well as on PLO representation of the Palestinians, and the need for a Palestinian state to be established. His talks, he said, were "very fruitful."

factors relating to the Gulf. The decisive factors in this regard will include developments in Saudi-American relations in the Middle East crisis, and in the situation in Afghanistan, as well as in the perceptions of the Saudi elite.

4. The Soviet Union and the Connection Between the Gulf and the Palestine Question

We have already reviewed a number of the factors which make the Gulf important to the USSR. If we now attempt to assess briefly the Soviet attitude towards the Palestine question, we can discern the connections between the two issues in Soviet policy.

The Palestine question and the Arab-Israeli dispute, which in a certain sense were the entry point for the USSR to the Arab world in the mid-50's, remain important to Soviet policy to this day for at least three compelling reasons.

(a) In the first place, the continued failure to resolve the Palestine question, which is universally perceived in the Arab world to be the fault of Israel, is the most powerful barrier to the reinforcement and enhancement of ties between the Arabs and the US, which is universally perceived to stand directly behind Israel. This applies both to the so-called "radicals" in the Arab world, which in virtually every case have extensive and growing economic links with the US, but are prevented from developing their political relations because of this issue; and to the "moderates", whose close relations with Washington are constantly disrupted for the same reason.

There is no question that this is a matter of the greatest importance to Soviet policy-makers. In the context of the fears expressed by Marshal Kulikov and many other Soviet spokesmen, the above means that the Palestine question in effect constitutes the primary obstacle in the face of the strategic consensus which the Reagan administration has made the corner-stone of its regional policy. This helps to explain the great interest shown by Soviet writers in the Arab response to US Secretary of State Haig's visit to the area in April 1981, and their manifest relief at its meagre results. Thus a *Pravda* article in April talked of Haig receiving an "outright rebuff" to his calls for a strategic consensus in Saudi Arabia and Jordan,[53] while a Tass report said that in both states Haig was told "unequivocally that it was not the Soviet Union which was threatening the Arab people, as Washington maintains, but Zionism ...".[54] Both items stress the emphasis laid by these moderate Arab governments in the talks with Haig on the necessity of solving the Palestine question, as did a more in-depth piece by Soviet Orientalist Dr. Igor Belyayev in *Literaturnaya Gazeta* the following month. Belyayev also described Saudi Arabia as, since the US's "loss" of Iran, "the weakest link in the United States' military-strategic plans in the Middle East." He concluded by making the point explicitly:

> The Arabs have never considered the Soviet Union their enemy. No matter how they view Communist ideology, Arab politicians *(even the conservative ones)* do not take the cock and bull stories about "Soviet interventionism" and "Soviet imperialism" seriously. We have not made war on the Arabs or occupied their lands. But in their experience they have known both American intervention and American imperialism. Arab politicians *(even the conservative ones)* have never refused Soviet assistance in their struggle against their real enemy – the Israeli expansionists. The Arabs will hardly become accomplices in an anti-Soviet crusade under the aegis of the United States.[55]

This argument, for all that it contains in the way of wishful thinking, was both aimed at and meant to describe the moderate states which were candidates for inclusion in Wash-

---

[53] *Pravda*, April 12, 1981, "Hawk's Flight" by S. Vishinsky, cited in *CDSP*, XXXIII, 15, p. 17.

[54] Leonid Ponomaryov, "Haig's Middle East Mission Ends in Failure," cited in *SN*, No. 6066, p. 122.

[55] "The Middle East – Time to Decide," May 27, 1981, cited in *CDSP*, XXXIII, 21, pp. 11-13. The emphasis is in the original.

ington's "strategic consensus." And since the most important of these were the Arab Gulf states led by Saudi Arabia, it can be seen clearly that the Palestine question, the constant thorn in these states' relations with the US, had a definite and important connection with the issue of the Gulf for Soviet policy-makers.

To quote Belyayev again, this time writing earlier on the Iran-Iraq conflict, there is no support in the region, outside Israel and Egypt, for the thesis that the Soviet Union represents the greatest threat to the area's stability and security:

> The position taken by other Arab countries is diametrically opposite. Thus, in the opinion of Kuwait and Bahrein, *the security of the Gulf depends on whether the Arab-Israeli dispute is successfully resolved.* From their viewpoint, the Knesset's official annexation of Arab East Jerusalem is much more alarming and fraught with a much greater danger of destabilizing the region.[56]

(b) Clearly, if the Arabs were fully to accept this thesis, and more important, to act on it, there would result a momentous shift in their relations with the US. And just as Belyayev was fairly faithfully summing up the *stated* positions of most Arab regimes, it was and is an unspoken truth that most have failed to back their words with actions. Nevertheless, just as the Palestine question has been important to the USSR in keeping the Arabs away from its rival, so has it helped to bring them closer to it. And this fact, that the problem of Palestine is and always has been a major incentive in Arab-Soviet relations, is the second reason for its importance in Soviet policy.

---

[56] "Concerning the Iran-Iraq Conflict," October 1, 1980, cited in *CDSP*, XXXII, 39, pp. 1-2. Emphasis added. In an interview with *al-Siyasa,* the Soviet Ambassador to Kuwait, Nikolai Sikechev, declared that the tension in the Gulf region was due to the "failure to reach a just and permanent settlement of the Arab-Israeli conflict." Cited in *al-Safir*, March 15, 1981, p. 1.

This was clearly the case with Egypt, from the time of the 1955 arms deal, Suez, the 1967 war and the war of attrition, until the October war, and it was similarly the case with Syria over the same period and with the Palestinians (in the case of the latter two, until the present time). But it has recently become true also of states such as Jordan and Kuwait, which because of their problems with the United States over the Palestine question, have chosen to expand significantly their ties with Moscow. Confronted by US policy on the Middle East, which seems to go from bad to worse from administration to administration in its blind and bland support for whatever outrages Israel cares to commit, these powers find themselves increasingly frustrated, and with their internal legitimacy and credibility seriously undermined. Thus, they find themselves making the same choice made by their "radical" fellow-Arabs two and three decades ago, by opening towards Moscow.

The objective in their case, as to some extent even with the so-called radicals, is to obtain leverage with the United States, via this "Soviet option", and at the same time to balance the overwhelming US regional presence.[57] Thus in the words of "diplomats in the Kuwaiti capital," cited by AP:

> Kuwait sees the necessity of establishing balanced relations between East and West, and it sees that there is an increasing danger of US-Soviet competition in the Gulf region, and that the growing American military presence provokes the threats which it is supposed to confront.[58]

---

[57] Thus the resolutions of the summit conference of the Steadfastness and Confrontation Front in September 1981 in Benghazi called for: "The continued reinforcement of relations with the Soviet Union, and entering into talks with it so as to bring about a qualitative development of relations between it and the Arab Nation, in a manner leading to a *reestablishment of the balance* in the region, particularly after the new American-Israeli alliance." *al-Safir*, September 20, 1981, p. 1.

[58] *al-Safir*, September 21, 1981.

There can be no question that there are limits to this policy on the part of these states, particularly in the Gulf, and there can be no better illustration of these limits than the hesitations of Saudi policy-makers since Moscow began energetically wooing them over the past few years.[59] But, as we saw at the end of the preceding section, it will be factors other than the simple weighing of the virtues of this specific case which will ultimately decide the Saudi leadership one way or another.

(c) The third and final reason for the importance of the Palestine question to Soviet policy-makers is that their consistent stand in support of the Arab states since the mid-50's, and of the Palestinians over the past decade or so, gives their policy and their presence in the region a certain legitimacy, particularly when it is compared with that of all the other major powers. This is especially the case with the moderate regimes, in a certain sense more so than with the others. For the latter – notably Iraq and Libya, and less frequently Syria and the PLO – have often been unable to see eye to eye with the USSR on the details or format of a Middle East settlement, or on certain aspects of the Palestine question.

Thus, the Jordanian-Soviet and Kuwaiti-Soviet joint communiques show a very high degree of agreement in these questions, and include formulations reflecting the Soviet position which do not appear in joint Syrian-Soviet or PLO-Soviet documents. Perhaps the best example is the phrase

---

[59] The Soviet approaches have been modestly reciprocated by the Saudis. There is a string of Saudi statements going back to 1979 at least which recognize the USSR's "important role in world politics," and its positive policy towards Arab issues (the words are those of Foreign Minister Saud al-Faisal in *al-Hawadith*, March 3, 1979). See also Prince Fahd's interview with Arnaud de Borchgrave, *IHT*, March 19, 1979, pp. 1-2, and Belyayev's article in *Literaturnaya Gazeta* January 1979, cited in *CDSP*, XXXI, 5, pp. 5-6, as well as Prince Fahd's interview with *Der Spiegel*, cited in *al-Safir*, March 1, 1981, p. 1. For a more recent Saudi response to Soviet overtures, see the Saudi paper Ukaz of January 10, 1982, for a favourable editorial on the subject of relations with the USSR.

"guaranteeing the right of all states in the region to an independent existence and to security," which occurs in the Soviet-Jordanian communique as one element of a comprehensive Middle East settlement.[60]

This legitimacy is reflected not only in the formal praise of both Kuwait and Jordan for Soviet Middle East policy in their respective joint communiques with their Soviet hosts – the former declaring: "Kuwait places a high value on the assistance and support that the Soviet Union is giving to the Arabs' just cause;"[61] and the latter repeating nearly the same formula. It even finds an echo in the occasional statements of Saudi policy-makers, eagerly picked up and repeated by Soviet authors, such as the following quotation by Belyayev of Saud al-Faisal, the Saudi Foreign Minister, that "we have found much that is positive for the Middle East in Soviet leader Leonid Brezhnev's report (to the 26th Party Congress). The new Soviet proposal contains features that will make it successful..."[62]

"GOLF PERSIQUE – PALESTINE, MEME COMBAT"

These three reasons why the Palestine question is important to Soviet policy-makers also show why, for them, the Gulf and Palestine are in some measure two aspects of the same strategic competition with the United States over the Arab world. Just

[60] *Pravda,* May 30, 1981, cited in *CDSP,* XXXIII, 21, pp. 10-11.

[61] *Pravda,* April 26, 1981, cited in *CDSP,* XXXIII, 17, p. 13.

[62] *Literaturnaya Gazeta,* May 27, 1981, cited in *CDSP,* XXXIII, 21, pp. 11-13. These three points should *not* be interpreted as meaning that the USSR has no interest in a solution of the Palestine question; quite the contrary, for such a solution would (*a*) prevent a new Middle East war, with its dangerous potential for escalation; (*b*) obviate the possibility of another Arab defeat at the hands of Israel, and therefore of another perceived Soviet defeat; (*c*) eliminate or reduce the danger of.nuclear proliferation in the region, and (*d*) increase Soviet prestige and regional standing, since any durable settlement would have to involve the USSR and be satisfactory to its regional allies, Syria and the PLO.

as the US, sensitive to its own vulnerability over the question of Palestine in its relations with the Arabs, tries to keep it separated from other problems such as that of the Gulf, so is it on the contrary in the interest of the Soviet Union to see to it that they are kept linked as closely together, particularly in Arab perceptions. For as we have seen, any mobilization by the Gulf powers, however unlikely that may currently seem, to solve the Palestine question, would lead to a confrontation with the US assuming no change in that power's present policy. And that would clearly be in the Soviet interest.

It is in this light that we can best explain the constant and repeated calls by Soviet leaders and commentators for greater Arab unity and solidarity, which they describe the US as trying to prevent. The imperialists, Brezhnev declared in his October 1980 dinner speech for Asad, "would like very much to strike a crushing blow at Arab unity"[63]; Washington desires, in the words of Colonel Ponomaryov, in an article cited earlier, "to divide the Arab peoples, whose strengthened unity is hindering imperialist reaction in carrying out its plans and is blocking the path to Israel, the US's chief henchman in the Middle East;"[64]   a *Pravda* article says the US is trying "to split the Arab front of opponents of Camp David"[65]; while Soviet Vice-President Kuznetzov, in Damascus in December 1980 for the signing of the Soviet-Syrian treaty, declared that "the main strength of the Arabs in this struggle is their unity. That is why the imperialist forces are seeking to sow discord, aggravate relations between Arab countries..."[66]   The Camp David policy of the US, Brezhnev declared to the Party

[63] *Pravda*, October 9, 1980, cited in *CDSP*, XXXII, 41, pp. 5-6.

[64] *Krasnaya Zvezda*, October 26, 1980, cited in *CDSP*, XXXII, 44, pp. 2-3.

[65] "Operation Persian Gulf," Y. Glukhov in *Pravda*, November 3, 1981, cited in *CDSP*, XXXII, 44, pp. 3-4.

[66] *SN*, No. 6049, p. 382.

Congress, was aimed at "dividing the Arab world"[67]; and the Soviet-Kuwaiti joint communique "stressed the importance of the Arabs' solidarity, on the common platform of the decisions of the Arab states' summit conferences."[68]

What we have here is in effect a new theme in Soviet policy, a call not for "Arab solidarity on an anti-imperialist basis," the previous formulation which evolved in the 1950's, 60's and 70's, but for a broad Arab front including both radical and moderate powers. The old theme can still occasionally be heard, as in the praise in the Soviet-Libyan joint communique for the Libyan-Syrian union and for the Steadfastness and Confrontation Front,[69] or in a Novosti commentary on Qadhafi's visit to Aden praising the Libyan-Ethiopian-South Yemeni treaty, which it held up as an example to the Arabs and added:

> Arab history knows of many examples which demonstrate that unity, cohesiveness, and work in a unified front with the forces hostile to imperialism has achieved success. We recall the Algerian liberation war, the Suez War and October war.[70]

However, much more frequently we now find Soviet writers talking of "the need for reinforcing Arab solidarity and for the creation of a unified Arab national front."[71] Thus, according to a Palestinian report, during Qaddumi's June Moscow visit, "the Soviet leadership praised... PLO efforts exerted to unify

---

[67] *Moscow News*, No. 9 (March 9, 1981) Supplement, pp. 4-5.

[68] *Pravda*, April, 26, 1981, cited in *CDSP*, XXXIII, 17, p. 13.

[69] *Pravda*, April 30, 1981, cited in *CDSP*, XXXIII, 17, pp. 11-13. The Soviet-Syrian and Soviet-Algerian joint communiques mention only "strengthening united action by the Arab states" and "strengthening the cohesion of the Arabs" respectively: the former is cited in *Moscow News*, No. 43 (Oct. 26, 1981), supplement, pp. 6-7; and the latter in *SN*, No. 6075, pp. 196-7.

[70] "Musku tushid bi-jawlat al-Qadhafi al-akhira wa bil-mu'ahada al-libiya-al-yamaniya-al-ithiopiya, *al-Safir*, September, 6, 1981, p. 16.

[71] Novosti commentary dated July 11, 1981, published in *al-Safir*, September 12, 1981, p. 1.

Arab ranks to confront the Zionist and imperialist threats."[72]

In conclusion, it might be said that to the extent the Gulf and Palestine questions are kept separate, the United States has a chance of achieving a "strategic consensus" and building a new alliance-system directed against the USSR stretching across the Middle East. To the extent that these two questions are kept together as far as Arab public opinion and Arab diplomacy are concerned (whether as a result of Soviet efforts or otherwise), does the USSR have a chance of foiling this plan. It is thus perhaps ironic that, for reasons related to its interests as a super-power in conflict with another, the USSR has the chance to appear as one of the leading champions of a cause which is central to the concerns of classical Arab nationalism. As a result, it may very well come to terms with this force in this decade over the very issues of the Gulf and Palestine.

[72] WAFA English Bulletin, No. 138/81, July 2, 1981, pp. 4-5, "Abu Lutf: 'Positive Results from USSR Visit; Moscow Considering Ambassador Status for PLO'." More recently, a Novosti report on Arafat's meeting on October 18, 1981 with Brezhnev said the two sides had emphasized "the importance of consolidating the unification of steps taken by the Arab states and all patriotic forces in the Arab world, as one of the decisive factors in' the struggle against imperialist and Zionist intrigues, and towards the realization of a genuine peace in the Middle East." WAFA English Bulletin, No. 233/22, October 1981, p. 6.

8

The Emergence of the Palestinians in American Strategy for the Middle East: Issues and Options

by Robert J. Pranger

For the United States, national security in the world outside the Western Hemisphere is now divided into three rather than two parts; this fact, not its dependency on imported oil, represents the most important effect of the 1973 Middle East War on American international policy. Or better put, what began as strictly a matter of dependence of the West on Middle Eastern oil has evolved into a complex web of interdependent relations between the Arab world and the West, including significant defence relationships with the United States. As a corollary to this change, the shift from a dual to a triple focus for American national defence has not been affected by decreasing consumption of petroleum products nor will this transformation of US policy be influenced by a declining reliance on oil from the Persian Gulf. Although the initial shock of the 1973 war was felt in the area of world energy supplies, the war brought the Arab world into an ascendancy in global affairs and made Southwest Asia strategically significant to the United States and Soviet Union in ways which have now transcended oil itself. In turn, as the Arab position in world politics has become enhanced in the past decade, so has the role of the Palestinians become more evident in strategic terms.

My study will focus on the emerging strategic importance of "the Palestine question" in American policy, an importance linked to the interest of both superpowers not only in the Gulf but in the broad band of Third World countries stretching from Ghana to the Philippines (and perhaps including Central America and the Caribbean as well). The following topics will be covered in my analysis: (1) the 1973 revolution in American national security policy caused by the October War; (2) the evolution of an autonomous Arab security policy, in economic and military terms, which has given the Arabs a collective status of potentially great power; (3) Israel's suspicion about the evolution of American security policy in the Gulf toward a greater Arab emphasis; (4) the emergence of the Palestinians in US strategy in the Middle East; (5) Soviet interest in American policy shifts in the Gulf; and (6) options for the United States in its policy on the Palestine question and the security of the Gulf.

1. The 1973 Middle East Revolution in American National Security Policy

Before the October 1973 Middle East war, those in the United States who espoused a strategic conception of the Middle East were largely confined to persons advocating indirect American support for indigenous forces against threats of intervention by the Soviet Union and its allies. In this respect the Nixon Doctrine, when applied to the region, was something of an extension of the containment policies of Truman, Eisenhower and their successors, whatever the Nixon policies meant for US withdrawal from Southeast Asia; there was to be no American withdrawal from the Middle East, but neither was there to be much direct involvement.[1] Détente

---

[1] The Nixon Doctrine's central thesis was: "the United States will participate in the defense and development of allies and friends, but... America cannot – and will

would have only limited applicability in the Middle East, with the period from 1970 to 1973 one of American emphasis on the Soviet threat in this region.[2] Hence, American assistance to the Shah of Iran under Nixon represented a sales-oriented version of the Eisenhower grant assistance programmes for the Shah in the 1950's, with Nixon's variant all the more generous because it had a pecuniary as well as a security dimension. In the instances of both Eisenhower and Nixon, Iran became a special instrument for American strategic policy — especially important in Nixon's case because of US withdrawal from Southeast Asia at a time when Great. Britain was moving its forces out of the Gulf — an instrument doubly attractive because (a) it spared the United States from having to assume a major direct presence in the troubled Middle East and (b) it provided the recycling of billions of petrodollars in military sales otherwise destined for other countries.

A similar policy of indirect support was adopted by the United States in Israel's special case where one key rationale for American support (though not the only justification) was that such assistance alleviated the need for the United States to station forces in the region for Israel's defence.

Jordan and Saudi Arabia were no exceptions to the pre-1973 rule in American Middle East policy of indirect assistance, although in the 1970 Jordanian civil crisis the US contemplated direct intervention, but finally turned to less direct means.[3] There was no talk in Washington of bases in the

not — conceive *all* the plans, design *all* the programs, execute *all* the decisions and undertake *all* the defense of the free nations of the world. We will help where it makes a real difference and is considered in our interest." Richard M. Nixon, *United States Foreign Policy for the 1970's: A New Strategy of Peace,* A Message from the President of the United States (Washington, D.C.: Government Printing Office, 1970), p. 6.

[2] See William B. Quandt, *Decade of Decisions: American Policy Toward the Arab-Israeli Conflict, 1967-1976* (Berkeley: University of California Press, 1977), pp. 124-127. Quandt considers the anti-Soviet emphasis a mistake.

[3] *Ibid.,* pp. 115-119; Henry Kissinger, *White House Years* (Boston: Little, Brown, 1979), pp. 617-631.

Arab world, and most certainly no interest in assistance programmes for Egypt. Turkey was the one exception to the American doctrine of indirect support, but it was the only member of NATO located in the Middle East.

Such a policy of indirect defence on the part of the United States before 1973 meant that the strategic position of the Middle East in American thinking was secondary when compared to Western Europe and East Asia. Before the war in Indochina appeared unwinnable to the United States, at least in the terms the Johnson administration chose to fight it, Europe and Asia were each considered possible theatres of military action for a full-scale conventional and even nuclear war under the so-called "two-and-one-half war" defence strategy. The "half war" concerned minor contingencies, although few thought the Middle East even a region for a lesser American military intervention. In the Arab-Israeli struggle the greatest emphasis in American policy was placed on peace-making, especially after the 1967 war with Security Council Resolution 242, negotiations with the Soviet Union, and the Rogers initiatives — a peace settlement process generously endowed with arms for Israel.

While the quest for peace by the United States in the Middle East continued after the 1973 war and achieved some of its most spectacular achievements (at least in American terms) from the 1974-75 disengagements to the 1978 Camp David accords, these initiatives were increasingly accompanied by moves on the military side, bringing American forces more directly into the Middle East, either connected to or separate from these initiatives. First there developed greater interest in how the Gulf might be included in "half" or "plus" war contingencies, then how the Gulf could become a third major theatre together with Western Europe and East Asia.[4] The

---

[4] The evolution can be found in the annual budget reports of three American Secretaries of Defence — Schlesinger, Rumsfeld and Brown — from fiscal years 1975 through 1981.

American peace undertakings after 1973 were themselves a reminder that war in the Middle East may be the most potent agent for change in the international relations of this region — change for good or evil as far as American interests are concerned. By 1981 a new and separate military command for the Gulf had been announced by Secretary of Defence Weinberger.[5]

The 1973 war in the Middle East was motivated by Arab intentions to make it clear to the West — especially to the United States — that Israel's continued occupation of territories seized in June 1967 was both unacceptable to the Arab world and dangerous for the Western industrialized world. The most immediate danger, of course, came from the oil embargo; memories of the boycott continue to haunt Western capitals and financial centres. There can be no doubt that part of the reason for America's increased defence awareness about Southwest Asia has come from its determination to safeguard sources of oil in the Middle East that cannot be replaced elsewhere. Yet the 1973 war also succeeded in what was the primary political motive for this war in the first place, Arab determination that the West take seriously the demand that Israel withdraw from the occupied territories and accept Palestinian self-determination. Certainly the West, including the United States, has become increasingly impressed by these intentions.

In other words, the 1973 Middle East war created a revolution in American thinking about the Middle East, by forcing on Washington the importance of developing a strategic policy where the Arab world would play a major role from the standpoint of its own, independent interests. Collectively speaking, the Arabs emerged from the 1973 war as a potential great power in world affairs and moved quickly, a

---

[5] Weinberger statement of April 24, 1981. See Richard Halloran, "U.S. Plans Persian Gulf Combat Command," *New York Times,* April 25, 1981.

year later at Rabat, to link the fortunes of the PLO and Palestinian self-determination to their own ascendancy. The period between October 1973 and October 1974 may be called a historical watershed of profound significance in world affairs, a year that clearly established Arab and Palestinian power in global terms.

American policy has been evolving since 1973 with the Arab states gaining ever greater prominence in the national security calculations of the United States. What only a few of us urged on our government before the 1973 debacle — a genuine Arab policy formulated within the broad global plans of the United States — has now become a more commonplace argument in American strategic thinking.[6] In this respect the Soviet Union has consistently been ahead of American foreign policy — especially on the question of Palestinian self-determination which is a key element in any contemporary Arab-oriented policy — so that the balance of power in the Middle East, while in principle on the side of the United States because of the strongly anti-communist nature of most of the Arab world, remains wavering between American and Soviet affinities. As I will note, the best that the United States can hope for under these circumstances is an autonomous Arab security policy, clearly establishing the Arabs as a great power, which might add an entirely new dimension to the world balance of power, turning this balance from a bipolar to a multipolar structure, including, as well, new centres of national power in Western Europe and East Asia.

[6] See the Haig rationale for sale of AWACS to Saudi Arabia on ABC News programme "Issues and Answers," August 23, 1981: it is important for American strategic interests in the region; Bernard Gwertzman, "Haig Says Reagan Is Ready to Meet Soviet Halfway," *New York Times,* August 24, 1981. The strategic importance of the Arab world and the Palestinians to the United States has reached deep into American military thinking; for example, see Lt. Col. Benedict F. Fitzgerald, USA, *US Strategic Interests in the Middle East in the 1980's,* Strategic Issues Research Memorandum (Carlisle Barracks, Pa.: Strategic Studies Institute US Army War College, 1981), pp. 11-13.

2. An Autonomous Arab Security Policy

Before 1973 it was meaningful and appropriate to speak of great power patrons and regional clients in the Middle East. Such relationships were forged in military and economic terms with either the Soviet Union or the United States. From time to time new relations might be made. The concept of "partnership" under the Nixon Doctrine was, in this sense, not much different from the older military assistances programmes of the 1950's and 1960's. In the Soviet case there were also patron-client linkages, though perhaps Sadat had already given Moscow a hint of what was to come in 1973, when he peremptorily asked Soviet advisers to leave Egypt in 1972. Even though clients might exhibit a certain degree of independence, however, they seldom possessed enough national power of their own in world politics to have much leverage over their patrons.

In 1973 the word "interdependence" became central to international affairs as far as the Middle East was concerned: both patrons and clients now had autonomous power as oil-rich Arab states not only developed their own policies but provided leadership for others in the Arab world. Also, Egypt and Syria, having led the Arab armies in the October war, achieved a new semblance of independence through their military capabilities; in Egypt's case this allowed Sadat to make his startling initiatives for peace with Israel, while for Syria this meant capabilities for interventions in Lebanon. The 1973 war permitted most Arab states to pursue their most fundamental interests in ways more independent than ever before. Collectively speaking, the Arab nation was encouraged by the war to demand, with greater assertiveness, nationhood for the Palestinians, just as the events of October 1973 gave greater incentives for the Palestinian movement to make its demands for self-determination on the Arab nation and the broader international community.

No better evidence of the new post-1973 Arab autonomy

can be found than in Kissinger's shuttle diplomacy of 1974 and 1975: prior to the war Kissinger avoided the Middle East as a main focus of his global strategy, an omission he subsequently regretted and made efforts to change. Kissinger's efforts after 1973 on behalf of US interests in the Middle East stand in marked contrast to his disinterest before, but in both cases his attitudes can be explained by the shift of the Arab world from client status to autonomy in world affairs during the final months of 1973. As in so many major transformations of power in world affairs, war proved midwife for this drastic change of Arab status, a fact that Kissinger, the realist, could appreciate.[7]

The lessons of 1973 were not lost in the United States.[8] Part of the American reaction to the events of October was to send its most prominent statesmen to mediate a ceasefire, disengagement and peace. Quite logically the main focus was on the Arab power providing the main inspiration for the 1973 war, Egypt. Hence, the Sinai became the major target for Kissinger's and Carter's efforts. Yet the deterrence of further warfare through expanded security efforts in the Middle East also became a more salient objective of American statecraft: emerging in US strategic thinking was the idea that in some way the Gulf, source of oil resources so dramatically and unilaterally curtailed by the Arabs in 1973 and 1974, must be better guarded against a possible repetition of the 1973 events. The Shah's fall and the Soviet invasion of Afghanistan in 1979 added enormous urgency to this idea. Saudi Arabia became the logical point of emphasis in this new security concept.[9] Egypt

---

[7] See Edward R.F. Sheehan, "Step By Step in the Middle East," *Foreign Policy*, No. 22 (Spring 1976), pp. 3-70.

[8] We await the next volume of Kissinger's memoirs for his interpretation of the October 1973 Middle East war.

[9] See Robert J. Pranger and Dale R. Tahtinen, "American Policy Options in Iran and the Persian Gulf," *AEI Foreign Policy and Defense Review*, I, 2 (Washington, D.C.: American Enterprise Institute, 1979), 24-28.

and Saudi Arabia would become the main foci of American diplomatic, economic and military energies in the Arab world after October 1973; Egypt for its potential to bring an Arab-Israeli peace by eliminating one front of Arab confrontation with Israel, and Saudi Arabia because of its vast oil resources and strategic geopolitical position. Sadat had been determined to convert his diplomatic gamble with Israel into a strong military relationship with the United States. Needless to say, the revolution in Iran has given special importance to a Saudi-American defence relationship and improved Sadat's bargaining power for military assistance from the United States.

Few relationships in world affairs have changed as quickly as that between the United States and Saudi Arabia during the last months of 1973 and the early months of 1974. Central to this historic transformation, of course, was the success of the OAPEC boycott led by the impressive economic might of Saudi Arabia.[10] With the embargo ended, the United States established closer economic and defence relations with the Saudis than ever before, but, more importantly, the terms of the relationship had changed: American policymakers would now listen with greater attention to Riyadh's own strategic conception of Middle East security. In other words, Saudi Arabia was now no longer purely a client state within a patron's strategic vision, but a patron of considerable power itself with a unique foreign policy viewpoint.

The Saudi international outlook begins with vast financial power as an Arab and Islamic state. Hence, while Saudi Arabia's leadership in the Middle East has obvious global consequences, it sees this leadership in quintessential Arab and Islamic terms. Those who wish partnership with the

---

[10] A good appreciation for this startling transformation is found in George Lenczowski, *Middle East Oil in a Revolutionary Age,* National Energy Study No. 10, (Washington, D.C.: American Enterprise Institute, 1976).

Saudis, as the United States does, must adopt a security policy that accounts for Saudi interests and perspectives.[11] Foremost among these perspectives is a view toward the Arab-Israeli confrontation adamantly pan-Arab and pro-Palestinian and, to a considerable extent at this point, anti-Egyptian. Also of importance is Riyadh's wish to create an autonomous Arab-centred security system in the Gulf, exemplified in the six-nation, conservative Gulf Cooperation Council established in May 1981. The Council stands for non-interference of both superpowers in Gulf affairs and has similar views about the rest of the Arab world; recently it accused the United States of "cowboy politics" in the American downing of two Libyan planes over the Gulf of Sidra.[12]

In retrospect it was a mistake for the United States to have divided Egypt from Saudi Arabia in its approach to peace-making in the Middle East, because in relying on both for the building of its own Arab strategy after October 1973, American policy should have integrated their separate strengths. This still remains an American objective, but the spirit of Camp David has contradicted this aim. As we shall note, this integration runs counter to Israel's current objective of separating the Egyptians and Saudis. President Sadat was partly responsible for this separation of Cairo and Riyadh — divorce might be a more appropriate term — by accepting the division at Camp David between his peace with Israel and a more comprehensive settlement for the Palestinians (or "inhabitants of the West Bank and Gaza," the language of the

---

[11] See three very interesting short presentations by HRH Prince Bandar Bin Sultan of the Royal Saudi Air Force (Harvard University, John F. Kennedy School of Politics and Government, September 19, 1979; New York Council of Foreign Relations, January 28, 1980; and a working paper for the Air University, US Air Force, September 1979-February 1980), collected in HRH Prince Bandar Bin Sultan, *Strategic Priorities* (1980).

[12] "6 Persian Gulf Nations Assail US on Dogfight," *New York Times,* August 23, 1981.

accords), a move he must have known would harm his relations with the Saudis. Yet one cannot but speculate that the United States was unduly persuaded by Prime Minister Begin's willingness to settle with Sadat; the prospect of a diplomatic victory, at a time when such victories were in short supply, seemed irresistible to President Carter, and Begin was only too anxious to tempt Carter on this account. What Begin's motivations were are not easy to fathom, but he possibly saw this summit as an opportunity, among other things, to separate Egypt and Saudi Arabia and thereby destroy the relationship they had jointly established with each other and the United States during the October 1973 war and the subsequent Kissinger disengagement efforts. There is no doubt that Sadat would like to re-establish a close linkage with the Saudis today, something also desired in Washington but probably not in Jerusalem (the Saudis seem overtly anti-Egyptian).

After Camp David, Egypt would appear as the "peace partner" of the United States (and Israel), while Saudi Arabia would be seen as the "national security partner," the greatest threats of violence now feared in the Persian Gulf and to Israel's north, and not in the Sinai. In the Saudi case, as far as American strategy is concerned, the national security role would be ambiguous, at times the Saudis appearing as the new "pillar" of security in the Gulf replacing Iran, but at other times seeming a potential source of instability, because of internal factors, as well as Iran.

Neither Egypt nor Saudi Arabia has been entirely happy with its current status in American policy, however, each placing great emphasis on a matter that divides them both from Washington — the status of the Palestinians. Both insist on the importance of recognizing Palestinian self-determination as a moral and strategic necessity for the United States in pursuit of its Arab security policy. Israel has become uneasy about the growing closeness of the United States, in military terms, to Saudi Arabia and even to Egypt precisely because of the centrality of the Palestinians in the Egyptian and Saudi strategic viewpoints — through it must be admitted that Egypt has not put the Palestinians ahead of its own national interest to make peace with Israel. We shall first examine Israel's uneasy relationship with the United States under circumstances of Washington's growing strategic intimacy with the Arab world, and then turn to the increasingly central role the Palestinians play in any American strategy for defence of the Persian Gulf.

Only after the central actors in the Arab-Israeli struggle, Israel and the Palestinians, have been identified within the context of American Middle East policy, will it be possible to look at the Soviet Union's strategy in the Persian Gulf; at this point in history the global strategies of both superpowers are in a very fluid or indeterminate phase, no more so than in the Middle East, and under these circumstances both Moscow and Washington will be as interested in the transformations of each other's policies as in the continuities.[13] In other words, just as American global policy has been significantly affected by the Soviet invasion of Afghanistan, thought to be a drastic shift of Soviet policy toward direct intervention in the Third World, so a dramatic movement of US international security policy toward closeness with the Arab world, despite traditional American commitments to Israel, may well be seen in Moscow as a fundamental change in strategic orientation.

3. Israel's Suspicion About the Evolution of American Security Policy in the Gulf

During May 1979, in a talk given at the Tel Aviv University

---

[13] See Robert J. Pranger, *Defense Implications of International Indeterminacy,* Foreign Affairs Study 4 (Washington, D.C.: American Enterprise Institute, 1972); "Six U.S. Perspectives on Soviet Foreign Policy Intentions," *AEI Foreign Policy and Defense Review,* I, 5 (Washington, D.C.: American Enterprise Institute, 1979).

Centre for Strategic Studies on the future of American defence policy in the Middle East, I argued that greater American strategic emphasis on Saudi Arabia seemed almost inevitable in the wake of the Iranian revolution.[14] Given my audience as well as my convictions, I also noted that Israel and Egypt were obviously of greater strategic significance to the United States than ever before. After my talk it was pointed out to me by a member of the audience that I had focused too much on the threat posed to US interests by the Soviet Union and had not really noted the danger growing out of a peculiar combination of Arab strength (oil) and weakness (domestic instability); most notably was this combination present in Saudi Arabia. The suggestion was made that, in certain respects, Saudi Arabia presented a greater threat to American interests than the Soviet Union itself, a perspective shared by others in the audience, I am sure. I think my interlocutor was also politely hinting that my view recommended appeasement of the Saudis at the expense of interests shared jointly by Israel and the United States. If anything, Israeli strategic thinking has always been firmly anti-Soviet, even in its preoccupation with the Arab threat to Israel's security. Yet with growing American involvement in the Arab world during the 1970's, the Israeli argument seems to have shifted somewhat: increasing power and societal problems in the Arab world, some caused by fissiparous forces more conservative than Begin himself, now pose threats to Western interests quite independently of Soviet policies though ultimately in congruence with them.

One senses in Israel's reaction to the post-1973 rapprochement between the United States and the Arab world a growing sensitivity to this new mood of strategic as well as economic cooperation. For example, despite smooth implementation of

---

[14] See Robert J. Pranger, "The Future of American Defense Policy in the Middle East," Tel Aviv University Centre for Strategic Studies, May 27, 1979 (unpublished).

the peace treaty between Israel and Egypt, concerns persist in Jerusalem over the return of key Sinai bases to the Egyptians even though this return is envisioned in the treaty itself; among Israel's supporters in the United States there continues an interest in somehow Americanizing these airbases. (Sadat had countered by offering the US base facilities at Ras Banas and had become perplexed by legalistic American standards for the use of these facilities.) On the subject of Saudi Arabia, Israel and its supporters have bitterly fought against every major US arms sale to the Saudis from the F-15 in 1978 to the Airborne Warning and Control Systems (AWACS) in 1981. In my estimation, Israel's 1981 air attack on Iraq's nuclear facility and its bombing of Beirut were further signs of increasing Israeli sensitivity about possible closer relations between the United States and key Arab powers: Iraq will no doubt figure more prominently in future American policy, while the United States has moved to the brink of a new focus on Lebanon's territorial integrity against all outside powers, Arab and Israeli, with the powerful support of Saudi Arabia and perhaps Syria itself. Begin in particular seems beset by prospects of America's desertion of Israel, his party always having been more chauvinistic in its orientation than the Labour Alignment.

Over no issue in the expanding Arab-American dialogue has Israel been so uneasy, however, as on the Palestine question and its leadership to Gulf security concerns of the United States. While there has been an obvious evolution of influential American thinking on the matter of Palestinian self-determination toward greater appreciation of the importance of this question to those Arab states Washington wishes to integrate in its global security policy,[15] Israeli viewpoints have actually

---

[15] See William J. Baroody, Sr., "What a Palestinian Solution Will Solve," *Washington Post,* November 7, 1979; also the treatment of Palestinian self-determination by Edward A. Said, *The Question of Palestine* (New York: Vintage Books, 1980), Chapter Three.

approached even more of a consensus against the PLO than before the October 1973 war. Indeed, the war produced in Israel a peculiar contradiction; on the one hand, a greater respect for Arab economic and military power, yet on the other hand a greater fear that somehow this power would be used to coerce the world community into recognition of a Palestinian nation. The main battleground for Israel in its resistance against this Arab strategy has been the United States, and it was no accident, I think, that Israel exacted the price of prior consultation on Palestinian contacts from Kissinger for its agreement to the disengagement accords. The rest of the world might support Palestinian nationhood and the PLO, but as long as the most powerful nation of all does not recognize the Palestinian question as a legitimate issue there will be no such conundrum on the serious agenda of world politics. At the centre of American Middle East policy today lies an Israeli anxiety over a possible American desertion of Israel on the question of Palestine.[16]

On the question of Palestine, the only Middle Eastern power with influence at all comparable to Israel's in the United States is Saudi Arabia. It is true that Sadat probably heads the list of favoured Middle East leaders in Washington, his 1981 visit significant because he was the first major Middle Eastern figure invited to see President Reagan, but this is primarily because of Sadat's role in making peace with Israel and not because he is feared as someone who can damage American interests (unless he were to fall from power). The Saudis hold autonomous power in the world community and in the United States because they have demonstrated their willingness and capability to use coercive influence of a kind that can harm US interests. The key to eventual American

[16] On the psychological reality of the "Holocaust syndrome" among Israel's leadership see Michael Brecher, *Decisions in Israel's Foreign Policy* (New Haven: Yale University Press, 1975), pp. 333-334, 508, 514.

support of Palestinian self-determination, in Israel's view, is Saudi Arabia, the power Jerusalem fears most in the Middle East and perhaps in the entire word, not excluding the Soviet Union itself.[17] It is significant that the more Sadat aspired to a leadership role in Arab security relations with the United States, the more he also became a champion of the PLO, as his August 1981 visit to Washington demonstrated.[18]

With its capacity for autonomous economic and political action and its potential for genuine great power status, Saudi Arabia has deliberately linked the question of Palestine to the issue of Persian Gulf security. From its strategic vantage point, Riyadh sees the Arab-Israeli struggle, not the Soviet Union, as the paramount security issue in the Middle East (not that it ignores the threat of the USSR to Saudi interests), and considers the Palestinian issue and the status of Jerusalem central to this struggle. With military capabilities and influence in America that give it a measure of independent status, the Saudi perspective cannot be ignored by Israel because Saudi Arabia has growing influence in Washington.

In Israel's mind, appeasement of the Arabs by the United States and its oil-starved Western allies (even when such starvation is purely symbolic) is always a possibility; this inevitably makes the Palestinians and their Saudi allies the main security threat to Israel, and makes any American policy aligned with Saudi Arabia menacing as well. Talk about an American sponsored strategic alliance against the Soviet Union involving Egypt, Israel and Saudi Arabia seems utopian under these circumstances, the diplomatic equivalent of squaring the circle. It is small wonder then that Israel would think

---

[17] On Israel's fears of Saudi defence capabilities see Charles Mohr, "U.S. Aides Concede Saudis Bar Limits on Use of Awacs," *New York Times,* August 23, 1981.

[18] On Sadat's security aspirations see Loren Jenkins, "Sadat Indicates US Receptive to His Bid for Area Security Role," *Washington Post,* August 20, 1981. This paper was written before Sadat's assassination on October 6, 1981.

its national interest – even the US interest – served by disruption of improved American relations with the Arab world, especially with Saudi Arabia, except in those circumstances where these relations are improving equally with Israel. For example, it may well have been an intended or unintended consequence of Israel's raid on Iraq's nuclear facility during 1981 that seeds of doubt were sown in Saudi Arabia's thinking about the sincerity of US assistance in operating the Awacs system for the Saudis. Distrustful themselves of the West's possible betrayal, Israelis think they know Arab doubts as well. One improvement in US relations with the Arab world is eliminated from the start by Israel, however, and that is the subject of independent nationhood for the Palestinians, which means, by definition, that all those supporting this improvement as a pre-condition for improving their own relations with Israel, including the Saudis, become adversaries.

For most Americans, including the Reagan administration, it might seem odd that the United States could actually reach the point where Israel would see Americans as possible adversaries; perhaps the idea is exaggerated. Yet, one should not underestimate Israeli foreboding about Saudi influence over American security policy, especially since 1973 and even more since 1979, and the possibility that at least some persons in the United States and even some participants in the Reagan administration would be seen in Jerusalem as having moved to the side of Israel's foes. Even before 1973, the so-called "Arabists" in the US State Department were considered "anti-Israel", as were those who favored a more "even-handed" American Middle East policy, and Israel has exerted strong efforts to discredit these people.

To be close to the Saudis is to be near to independent power of significant influence in Washington which has, as its first strategic priority, the freeing of the territories occupied in 1967 (including East Jerusalem) and the establishment of an independent Palestinian state separate from pre-1967 Israel.

For Israel and some of its supporters a major interest exists in discrediting Saudi Arabia as well as the Palestinians; the PLO may have no power in American councils of state, but the Saudis have increasing influence. The Saudis have such influence because the Gulf has now become a major security concern of the United States and an Arab power friendly to the United States now exercises paramount influence there. It is through this concern with Gulf security that the Palestinians themselves will no doubt achieve the status of a strategic rather than a purely moral issue for American policy. Once such status has been achieved, under the auspices of the conservative Gulf Arabs led by Saudi Arabia, Israel will have an almost impossible task arguing in the United States against Palestinian self-determination. During 1981 or 1982 this realization of the strategic importance of the Palestine question and its linkage to the Gulf may finally come to the United States, under a Reagan administration ironically more opposed to Palestinian self-determination than its predecessor was. Lebanon may be the vehicle for this realization, since the issue of Lebanese independence, of some interest to the present administration, is closely linked to settlement of the Palestinian question; both the Lebanese and Palestinians are important future leaders in the Arab world and the regional balance of power.[19] Israel may well fear that this development is near and take drastic steps to prevent it, as in its vigorous military assault on the Palestinians in Lebanon, the sudden raid on Beirut, and the abrupt rejection of Prince Fahd's peace proposal — all during 1981.[20] We now turn to the strategic importance of the emergence of the Palestinians in American strategy in the Middle East and Gulf.

[19] Discussed in Elie A. Salem, *Prospects for a New Lebanon* (Washington, D.C.: American Enterprise Institute, 1981).

[20] *Time,* in its August 24, 1981 edition, termed Crown Prince Fahd's peace proposal "bold" and "new." See William E. Smith, "A Bold New Plan by the Saudis," *Time,* August 24, 1981.

4. The Emergence of the Palestinians in American Strategy for the Middle East and Gulf

Although the Palestine question and the issue of Palestinian self-determination were clearly important topics on the agenda of world politics before 1973, this was not the case for American policy. From June 1967 until October 1973 the Palestinians emerged, under PLO leadership, as those most affected by the real tragedy for the Arab world of the 1967 Middle East War: having been deprived of part of their homeland when Israel became an independent nation in 1947, those Arabs in Palestine lost the remainder of their land in the six days of Israeli preemptive military action in 1967. In other words, an Arab people had become completely stateless by mid-1967, depriving it of an effective voice in world councils. The PLO has obviously supplied this voice. Yet, the United States concentrated its attention during its peace initiatives prior to 1973 on various withdrawal schemes for Israel which would at once protect Israel's future security and return a portion of the 1967 occupied territories to Syria, Jordan and Egypt. At no time in the six-year period between 1967 and 1973 did official American Middle East policy see the Palestinians as a primary issue in its peace settlement proposals; quite the contrary, the prevailing position in Washington was that the Palestinian issue was not a serious bar to peace in the Middle East and that with the proper redivision of Palestine between Israel and the three Arab confrontation states, the question of Palestine would solve itself. This solution was most often seen as taking place when portions of the West Bank were returned to Jordan.

Even the Jordan Civil War of 1970 did not disabuse American thinking of the idea that the Palestinians were a secondary item on the Middle East peace agenda. Still, it was obvious by late 1970 that the centre of the Palestinian movement had shifted from Jordan to Lebanon and that the direction of West Bank and Gaza action was now more oriented toward the PLO in Beirut than Hussein in Amman. Hussein's abortive federation plan, rejected by all Arab states, the Palestinians and Israel and greeted with silence by the United States, demonstrated his growing impotence in the politics of the occupied territories. Nonetheless, American thinking stubbornly refused to see the Palestinians as a legitimate national movement and, in any case, rejected the idea of dealing with an organization it considered devoted to terror instead of positive government.

The October 1973 war itself did not change American ideas on the Palestinians. Avoiding anything that would put an American seal of approval on Palestinian aims, Kissinger even agreed to the famous prior consultation provision with Israel in the disengagement accords, as we have noted. By insisting on this provision, however, Israel demonstrated characteristic shrewdness about its own interests, because it perhaps saw better than the United States that the longer term consequences of closer American ties with the Arab world, especially with Egypt and Saudi Arabia, would be changes in American policy toward the Palestinians. This Israeli perspective was no doubt reinforced by events at Rabat during October 1974.

It is doubtful that American strategy toward the Middle East would have taken the Palestinians seriously even after October 1973, if it were not for the Rabat Arab summit in October 1974. Seizing on opportunities for leverage against the West provided for them in the aftermath of the October War, the PLO and its Arab allies managed to produce the unprecedented Rabat declarations on behalf of Palestinian self-determination and the PLO as the sole legitimate leader of the Palestinian movement. Still holding to the secondary status of the Palestinians in a future peace settlement, the United States seemed completely unprepared for the results of Rabat. While in some Washington circles there was characteristic disbelief that all the Arab powers really meant what they solemnly declared at Rabat, a new realization seemed evident in American policy after 1974 that, indeed, there could be no long-term Middle East peace without settlement of the Palestinian issue. Like most major transformations in world affairs, this new realism in American policy resulted from a shift in the global balance of power toward greater Arab autonomy after the October 1973 war, rather than from any change of spirit. From Rabat to the present the mood of American policy toward the Palestinians has generally been truculent. Nonetheless, adaptation to new realities, a cardinal principle for maintaining great power status, has led the United States to a greater appreciation of the importance of the Palestine question in defence of its vital national interests in the Middle East and the Gulf.

Changes in official American attitudes toward the Palestinians can be seen in a number of instances since the October 1973 Middle East war, but always in the context of continual ambivalence caused by profound US commitments to Israel's defence. What is important, I would argue, is that the context for American policy toward the Palestinians is now one of *ambivalence* – a conflict in US thinking between the realities of Arab power in the regional and world balance of power on the one side, and the realities of Israel's close ties to the United States on the other – a transformation of American strategy for the Middle East of no small consequence. The latter view of the PLO, held by those closest to Israeli thinking in the United States, sees the Palestinian national movement as a terrorist organization. In policy terms the ambivalence in US policy is between the idea of the Palestinians as a potential strategic asset versus the view of the PLO as a Soviet-supported terrorist organization that threatens American strategic interests.

Ambivalence is the best the Palestinians can hope for from the United States, with perhaps some movement of American realism still further toward the Arab position at crucial points in the peace process under the right circumstances and at the appropriate time. Elsewhere I have discussed American peace policy in the Middle East from 1969 to 1971 as a combination of "principle, manoeuvre and time," and I think this description is as pertinent for the period since 1973.[21] In this realism there has also been greater American interest — largely unofficial — in the PLO itself as leader of the Palestinian national movement.[22]

If the United States has missed numerous opportunities for rapprochement with the PLO because of America's steadfast loyalty to Israel, a steadfastness necessary if American global policy is to retain the independence and credibility of a superpower, then the PLO has also squandered chances to make a more positive impression on the United States. Fortunately, events in Lebanon during 1981 seem to demonstrate that the United States and PLO may, at long last, understand the necessity of cooperation without official ties, but such has not always been the case. The years of the Carter presidency were a time of false signals and embarrassing reversals. Yasir Arafat's first appearance before the United Nations was not calculated to appeal to an American audience, even though the New York headquarters of the UN insures that no other public in the world so closely follows events there as Americans do. Anti-terrorist causes in high places of the Reagan administration have included the PLO, though this policy line should be seen as but one Reagan approach to the PLO, balanced to some extent by the usual noncommittal position and by talk

---

[21] Robert J. Pranger, *American Policy for Peace in the Middle East 1969-1971: Problems of Principles, Maneuver and Time,* Foreign Affairs Study 1 (Washington, D.C.: American Enterprise Institute, 1971), p. 3.

[22] See Doyle McManus"US, PLO: 7 Years of Secret Contacts," *Los Angeles Times,* July 5, 1981. McManus insists that the Reagan administration has continued these alleged contacts despite official policy.

from Secretary of State Haig about the importance of the Saudi alliance and about "preconditions" for improved relations with the PLO; more about these policy options in the final section of this analysis.

A word should be said at this point, however, about the latest statement on preconditions by Secretary Haig in response to Sadat's strong appeal for the PLO in Washington during August 1981 — that the United States wishes the PLO to recognize Israel's right to exist and embrace Security Council Resolutions 242 and 338 before it will consider official ties. The major point to keep in mind is that Haig's position is not Israel's, since Israel will not deal with the PLO or recognize Palestinian self-determination under any circumstances. In other words, for Israel there is no "Palestine question" in the first place, while for the United States there may or may not be such a question. Cynics would argue that Haig raised these preconditions because he knew they would get nowhere. However, my argument has been that in the period from October 1973 to October 1974 — from Ramadan to Rabat — the United States awoke to the realities of emerging Arab autonomy in world affairs and, with this independence, the emergence of the Palestinians to a high place, if not the highest spot, in the Middle East peace agenda. Considerations about the balance of world power, in which the Arabs are destined to play an ever greater part, have forced certain realities on American Middle East policy and virtually guaranteed a raised level of consciousness in Washington about the place the Palestine question has in the security of the Gulf. Whether the United States turns to Fahd or Sadat, the recommendation is the same: security for the US and its allies in the Middle East must include the full participation of the Palestinians as an independent nation and the PLO as the only credible leader of this movement toward national independence. Under circumstances of strategic necessity, therefore, one can forecast a growing division between the United States and Israel on the future of the Palestinians and the PLO's role.[23]

Future directions of American policy toward the Palestinians have been increasingly influenced by events since October 1973 and by the major actors in the Arab word influential in the United States – Egypt, Saudi Arabia, Jordan and Lebanon. Israel's position must now compete with very influential Arabs; for example, before restoration of full diplomatic relations in October 1973, Egypt's access to Washington (and vice versa) was sporadic and ineffective, whereas in 1981 Sadat appears very important in Reagan's calculus, at the possible expense of Begin.[24] One may forecast continued American ambivalence on the Palestinians with further adjustments in Washington for the realities of world power and for the necessities of a closer alliance with the Arab world in pursuit of US security requirements in the Gulf. The Palestine question and its linkage to the Gulf has emerged as a central strategic issue for the United States, a conflict between those who see in the Palestinians and the PLO a potential ally of considerable importance (I am among these persons and will develop the argument further in the final section of this study), and those who hold that the PLO is a terrorist organization operating as client for radical, Soviet-inspired objectives.

5. Soviet Interest in American Policy Shifts in the Gulf

The Soviet response to an emerging American Arab policy

[23] The latest well-placed strategist to argue for direct contacts between the US government and the PLO is Zbigniew Brzezinski on August 12, 1981; see Bernard Gwertzman, "Brzezinski Urges Talks with P.L.O.," *New York Times,* August 13, 1981. Israel's most dedicated American supporters tend to see Sadat's backing of the PLO as mere rhetoric, a view no doubt held by some of the PLO's most fervent partisans as well.

[24] See Rowland Evans and Robert Novak, "Sadat's Rising Influence," *Washington Post,* August 19, 1981. They note Sadat's cordial reception from American Jewish leaders during his August 1981 visit to the United States, not one of whom offered a defence of Begin.

in the Middle East and the Gulf since 1973 has until very recently varied between cautious cooperation and ineffective opposition. While it is true that Moscow's troubles in the Middle East may have begun as early as Sadat's ouster of Soviet advisers in 1972, the success of Kissinger's disengagement efforts, bringing Egypt and Syria into accords with the US and forgoing closer ties with Saudi Arabia, did not enhance the USSR's position; in fact, in the American rhetoric on disengagement there was a distinctly anti-Soviet bias. All of Kissinger's success was preceded by renewed diplomatic relations between the United States and most Arab countries who had severed relations in 1967, an outcome of the 1973 war especially ironic since early Arab success on the battlefield was achieved with Soviet arms. A casual observer might have thought that the Soviet Union would emerge from October 1973 with at least equal status to the United States in the subsequent peace process, a belief Moscow itself held as it cooperated with Washington in arranging the ceasefire and providing for Geneva peace talks in Security Council resolutions. In order to protect its own interests in the Gulf, however, the United States somewhat frantically seized the initiative with the Arabs as well as Israel.

Until the collapse of the joint Soviet-American statement on the Middle East and Sadat's overture to Jerusalem for direct talks in late 1977, however, Soviet interest in American policy shifts in the Gulf continued to waver between cooperation and opposition. The Carter administration reversal after agreeing with the Soviet Union on basic principles for a Middle East peace in 1977 must have been an unsettling experience for a Soviet foreign policy until then looking somewhat cautiously for expanded forms of cooperation with the new Carter administration (one might add that the March 1977 Carter SALT II proposals were an even earlier example to Moscow of intrinsic contradictions inside Carter's national security policy between the so-called Vance and Brzezinski schools). Generally speaking, the Soviet reaction to Sadat's offer to negotiate directly with Israel was one of great suspicion that the Americans and Israelis had coaxed the Egyptians into a separate peace, thereby dividing and con- quering the Arab world and isolating the Soviet Union from a vital strategic path into the Middle East (Sadat's initiative had been preceded, of course, by the victory of Likud and Menahem Begin in mid-1977, an event greeted with great foreboding in the USSR). With the enthusiastic entry of the United States, as third party, into the emerging entente between Egypt and Israel in 1978, it is likely that the Soviet Union came to the conclusion that all hopes of cooperation with American policy in the Middle East had vanished and that it was time to pursue its own interests relentlessly in South- west Asia. Camp David may have proved the final chapter in Soviet disenchantment with the idea of cooperation in the Middle East begun in October 1973 by Kissinger himself as a means of ending the war with minimal damage and eventual advantage for the interests of the United States. If the Americans could work for unilateral advantages, so would the Soviets.

This analysis of Soviet interests in American policy shifts in the Gulf would suggest that the idea of superpower cooper- ation, if not condominium, in the Middle East has always been an option for Moscow and Washington in the region. Some- times one or the other will play the option for reasons of manoeuvre, though at times both may work together out of mutual interest as in the case of Security Council efforts in October 1973 where each hoped to gain some special objective from this cooperative effort. As is usually the case with great powers, however, the particular objectives sought in cooper- ation rather than competition may be as different as those desired in competitive behaviour; it is only the pattern of action in pursuit of objectives that changes. This does not mean that, at certain junctures in history, the superpowers may not share similar objectives and cooperate for these ends, but the range of cooperative policy can be as broad as the range of competitive policy between the Soviet Union and the United States. By the end of 1978, however, the prevailing policies of both superpowers in the Middle East were intensely competitive and no more so than in the Gulf area.

Instability in Iran and Afghanistan during 1978 and 1979, perhaps in part caused by the aftershocks of October 1973 which moved Soviet-American relations in the Middle East from hopeful signs of cooperation to vigorous rivalry, provided the ground of opportunity for a Soviet counteroffensive against American policy initiatives in the Gulf. As 1978 began, the United States had become apparently hegemonic in the Gulf with the strength of both Iran and Saudi Arabia firmly on its side, a hegemony which could not be viewed in Moscow as anything other than threatening. This American policy of virtual monopoly in the Gulf had been motivated by questions of sheer survival in 1973 and 1974, though by 1978 it had become part of an emergent US strategy of world leadership in various sectors of the Third World under Carter administration priorities often framed in an explicitly anti-Soviet way. Perhaps if the earlier policies of cooperation would have worked to the mutually beneficial advantage of the two superpowers, the United States would have continued this path, but for very complicated reasons concerning Soviet competitive action in the 1973-78 period (e.g., in Angola) as well as American policy during this time-frame, competition became the centrepiece of Soviet-American relations during 1978. The Shah's troubles brought Soviet rhetoric into full stride against his regime and in obvious encouragement of dissident factions. Of supreme importance for American policy in the Gulf, however, was the actual fall of the Shah himself, a disaster for US hegemony only in part related to Soviet moves. What clearly was a direct Soviet move during this crisis in the Gulf was the decision by the USSR to intervene politically and then militarily in Afghanistan.

It may well be that the entry of the USSR into Afghanistan was, at least in part, an expression of Soviet frustration with American unilateral initiatives in the Middle East and the Gulf, all of them apparently designed by the United States to exclude Soviet influence in the region. In this respect Camp David, following as it did on the heels of the abortive Soviet-American joint statement on the Middle East in 1977, may have been the last straw for the Soviet Union as far as its own conduct in the Middle East was concerned: no longer would Moscow concern itself with. American reactions to Soviet moves, but instead the Soviets would take their own unilateral steps to define their interests in stark opposition to the United States, not only in the Middle East but elsewhere as well. In other words, the successful American policy toward the Arabs after 1973 was seen as a series of classical manoeuvres to regain advantages for US and Western interests at the expense of the Soviet Union, the objective being a shift of the Middle Eastern and world balance of power against the Soviets through skilled diplomatic, economic and military actions. How else could one explain the shuttle and summit forms of diplomacy being used so publicly by the United States in the Middle East? In what other way could Sadat's dramatic initiative be explained but as something devised in Washington (and Jerusalem)? If the game was to be unilateral advantages through manipulation of the balance of power, Moscow might argue, then two could play at the game and, indeed, both superpowers must play if one does. Certainly the military power of the Soviet Union, as well as its worldwide ideological influence, allowed it plenty of opportunities.

Soviet political and military intervention in Afghanistan may have served Moscow's interests in tipping the Asian balance of power in its favour, but the action was hardly applauded in the Arab world: the invasion gave the United States more immediate − though probably not long-term −

leverage with the Arabs and the wider Islamic community; other steps would be necessary to develop credible Soviet competition with the United States in the Middle East after 1973. It was not until its friendship treaty with Syria in 1980, following on the heels of Soviet support for the Arab rejection of Camp David, that the Soviet Union seemed to recover its composure after the reversals it apparently suffered in the contradictory outcome of the 1973 Middle East war: while Egypt and Syria achieved their spectacular early successes against Israel with Soviet arms and support, they immediately moved to re-establish full diplomatic relations with the United States, a move followed by certain other countries who had broken ties with Washington in 1967. The 1980 treaty and backing for the general Arab position against Camp David and for the PLO, however, restored a measure of ambiguity and manoeuvre to Soviet policy in the Midddle East; indeed, the very enigma of the Syrian-Soviet treaty, with its rumoured secret clauses, added a note of mystery to Soviet (and Syrian) intentions, especially for Lebanon. Similarly, in the 1981 Lebanon crisis and even before, the Soviet approach to the tragedy has been adroit and perhaps rewarding, over the longer term, for Soviet interests. Such subtleties might also be seen in various overtures to Saudi Arabia, in Brezhnev's appeal for no arms or outside interference in the Gulf,[25] and in Moscow's comportment during the Iranian revolution and its aftermath. All of these careful policies stand in sharp contrast to the

---

[25] Karen Elliott House notes the increasing desire of Arab leaders to keep their options open with the Soviet Union on the grounds they should manoeuvre somewhat independently of both superpowers. While this reflects growing Arab autonomy in world politics, it is also an indication of some subtlety in Soviet policy; see "Soviets and the Middle East," *Wall Street Journal,* June 3, 1981. See also Yevgeny M. Primakov, "Is Peace Feasible in the Middle East? " in Judith Kipper, ed., "The Middle East Conflict: Views from Abroad," *AEI,* Foreign Policy and Defense Review, III, 1 (Washington, D.C.: American Enterprise Institute, 1981), 20-25.

power politics of Soviet intervention in Afghanistan, effective as this was in impressing on Asia the growth of Soviet might, and the shrillness of Moscow's complaints against most US diplomatic initiatives since October 1973.

One Arab asset in the Middle East the Soviet Union can ill afford to lose is the Palestinians and PLO, because on this issue Moscow has been applauded throughout the Arab world for the steadfastness and justice of its support. Even the intervention in Afghanistan was to some extent counterbalanced in the Arab view by Israel's continuing occupation of territories seized in 1967. One must add that in this view the United States is usually seen as giving de facto support for continued Israeli occupation, despite official, formal American opposition: this tacit support is often credited as the real force behind Israel's obduracy about withdrawing, just as most Arabs think real American disapproval of the occupation, backed by deeds as well as words, would free the West Bank and Gaza from Israeli control. In the Reagan administration it is not clear just how firm even American pro forma opposition to Israel's occupation of the territories is, because certain parts of the administration hold that Israel is actually not an occupying power, thereby sharing the Israeli self-perception that they are an "administering" not "occupying" power; some say that Jordan's claim is no more legitimate than Israel's to actual sovereignty over the West Bank (Gaza is seen as Egypt's at some future stage, because Sadat is now at peace with Israel).

As it has already been noted, however, as American policy in the Middle East becomes more influenced by the growing power of the Arab world in regional and world politics, the Palestine question climbs higher and higher on the ladder of US strategic priorities in defence of the Gulf: if the Soviet Union cannot afford to lose the Palestinians, the United States cannot avoid the Palestinians, because of (a) its need for friendship with the Arabs, (b) its own security within the

Middle East balance of power, and (c) its global rivalry with the USSR. The result of this American policy shift — within the general ambivalence toward the Palestinians noted earlier — could well become a battle between the US and the USSR for the hearts and minds of the Palestinians, and, by extension, of the entire Arab world. What the Soviet Union continues to hold as high cards on the side of justice for the Palestinian movement may eventually be matched and even surpassed by what the United States seeks to gain in its expanded security policy for the Gulf. What are the options for the United States in its policy on the question of Palestine and the security of the Gulf?

6. Options for the United States on the Palestine Question and the Security of the Gulf

The world balance of power today may be in the midst of a fundamental transformation from bipolar or multipolar organization in economic, military and political terms, although this structure still appears basically bipolar. In each of the regions of major security interest to the United States and the Soviet Union — Western Europe, Southwest Asia (which includes the Middle East and the Gulf), East Asia and perhaps even Latin America and the Caribbean — new powers are emerging with the potential to become great ones. I have a special interest in the power adjustments underway in the Middle East and East Asia[26] but one need only look at the once familiar terrain of Western and Eastern Europe to see important changes underway as well. The Soviet Union and the United States still stand

[26] The East Asian dimension of the world balance of power I have addressed in a paper presented to the Fifth Annual Shimoda Conference at Oisa, Japan, September 2-4, 1981, sponsored jointly by the Japan Society and Japan Centre for International Education. The paper was entitled "How to Deal with the Soviet Threat to Japan and the United States," to be published in a conference volume during 1982.

as the only two superpowers in world affairs, meaning that they have interests in the balance of power in every major area of global politics and yet, they tacitly recognize even if their explicit strategies do not, that they confront not only each other in competitive relations but other important nations as well. The whole of world politics today is not as subordinated to the Soviet-American rivalry as it once was, but now includes other players with significant autonomous power or claims to great power status of their own; the Arab community is included among these newly ascendant actors. I believe it is in the interest of the United States to encourage, as the central policy of its global strategy, a transformation of world politics from a bipolar to a multipolar balance of power.[27]

United States options on the Palestine question and the security of the Gulf are quite limited — either accommodate the Arabs or get out of the Middle East. Obviously, within the realm of accommodation between the United States and the Arab world there are various courses of action for American policy on the Palestinians and security of the Gulf within the general ambivalence noted earlier; these will be the options considered here. From the standpoint of its own position as a superpower, one option is prima facie closed to the United States, that of simply withdrawing from the power game in the Middle East. One of the five options within the range of ambivalence, faithful American adherence to Israel's position on the Palestinians and PLO, is nearly the same thing as withdrawal, but I will nonetheless deal with it because Israel is a Middle Eastern state. The options for US policy on the Palestine question and the Gulf are: (1) strict conformity with Israel's position, tantamount to accepting Israel as the most important strategic power in the Middle East; (2) adherence

---

[27] *Ibid.* My argument is that Japan is a better candidate for great power status in the short run, in terms of economic and military potential, than China is; but its domestic politics may prevent Japan from reaching this status.

to a noncommital US role in the Palestine question, equivalent
to playing an unbiased umpire between Israel and the Arabs;
(3) revival of Soviet-American cooperation in sponsorship of
a comprehensive peace settlement; (4) establishment of preconditions by the United States for its own direct linkages
with the Palestine question and PLO, but with the future open
as to the nature of a Palestinian nation; and (5) acceptance of
the main body of Arab opinion on the Palestinians with full
Israeli withdrawal from the West Bank and Gaza and establishment of a Palestinian state. After reviewing all the options, I
will express my preference.

Option 1: American conformity with Israel's position.
Israel rejects the idea of a Palestinian nation and the PLO's
leadership of this nation. Hence, there is little or no support
among Israel's political leadership for an independent Palestine
on the West Bank and in Gaza, no matter what position the
PLO takes on Israel (although Palestinian acceptance of Israel
would very likely change some minds). While the Labour
Alignment has favoured some kind of partition plan for the
occupied territories, it does not accept the PLO as anything
but a terrorist organization and rejects the notion of Palestinian self-determination. Likud and the religious parties favour
a peace settlement with one or another form of limited
"autonomy" for the inhabitants of the West Bank and Gaza,
but this autonomy would incude Jewish settlers as well as
Arabs, would not be "full" autonomy specified in the Camp
David accords, and would under no circumstances have its own
national sovereignty.[28] Labour tends to phrase its main

---

[28] The latest Israeli affirmation of its stand on autonomy was announced on
August 23, 1981. See William E. Farrell, "Israeli Cabinet Affirms Stand on
Autonomy Talks," *New York Times,* August 24, 1981. Begin and Sadat agreed at
Alexandria in late August to resume the talks on September 23, something Begin
urged during the Alexandria meetings.

objections to the PLO in security terms, but the Likud coalition adds to security considerations the ancient claim of Israel to Judea and Samaria.

American support for the Israeli position, whether it be Labour or Likud, on the Palestinians would be a refusal (*a*) to hold open the possibility of Palestinian self-determination and PLO legitimacy, and (*b*) to connect the Palestine question to the security of the Gulf. No American administration has taken such an extreme position, although this point of view is strong among Israel's supporters in Congress and in the Reagan administration. I doubt that this viewpoint will gain ascendancy in the Reagan administration however, even if it is clear that this option has powerful support. Were the United States to adopt this option as official policy, American security interests in the Middle East and Gulf would be fatally undermined.

Option 2: Noncommittal American role in Palestinian question. The option of a noncommittal American role in the Palestinian question was favoured until October 1973 because official thinking held that the Palestinians were not a key element in a peace settlement. It has continued to be an American option even after 1973. Jordan was the logical choice as that power likely to regain large parts of the West Bank and rule the Palestinians under some kind of federal arrangement. As noted earlier, even as early as September 1970 and the Jordanian civil crisis this ideal became more illusion than reality; subsequent events between 1970 and 1973 confirmed the illusory quality of a Jordanian-Palestinian federation – the exodus of the PLO from Amman to Beirut, the failure of Hussein's federative proposal, and his decision not to enter the October 1973 war. Nevertheless, American policy has continued to be attracted to this option, even after the October 1973 war, since it provides an opportunity to avoid the Israeli option without having to suffer the consequences in American domestic politics of being more explicit about Palestinian self-determination. A certain language is typical of this policy, the rhetoric of "process" and "transition" generally used in American peace plans including the Camp David accords.

The problem with this option is that it really satisfies none of the parties in the Middle East conflict and is, therefore, an option without foreign policy effectiveness, whatever safety it provides in domestic politics (any policy without consequences is obviously ineffective). All sides see a lack of American commitment as pure vacuousness: the Arabs suspect that it is a cover for American support of the Israeli position and the Israelis think it masks a subtle evolution of American thinking toward a pro-Palestinian position. For the Palestinians the non-committal American option is contrasted to strong Soviet support for the PLO, with the consequence that the American position is seen as pure negativity because it says and does nothing. The noncommittal option has the virtue of buying time for the US, but the parties to the conflict will not wait forever.

Option 3: Soviet-American cooperation. Any honest history of the superpowers in the Middle East since the end of the Second World war would include chapters on Soviet-American cooperation as well as conflict. This cooperation was evident in the 1947 partition of Palestine, the peace talks of 1969, the principles enunciated at the Nixon-Brezhnev summit in 1973, the Security Council votes of 1973, and the joint statement of 1977. It is not clear that this cooperative activity favoured one side more than the other in the Arab-Israeli struggle. Until 1977 the Palestinians and the PLO were not the main focus of Soviet-American dialogue. Both Moscow and Washington have tended to believe that no final, comprehensive peace settlement can take place or be effective without the cooperation of both superpowers, though the

United States has worked to exclude the Soviets from the peace process as much as possible since 1973 on the grounds that only in the later stages would it be appropriate to have a broader international conference. Naturally, the Soviet Union disagrees vehemently with this view, suspecting that the American position is a transparent means of diminishing Soviet influence in the Middle East.

I believe strongly in the importance of the option of Soviet-American cooperation, if a way can be found to keep the option from exacerbating relations between the superpowers (the same thing can be said about SALT as Middle East cooperation).[29] Unfortunately, the record has not been good on this count: the Sisco-Dobrynin talks of 1969 ended in recrimination, the votes of 1973 to Soviet charges they had been cooperative for naught, and the joint statement of 1977 to collapse before the ink was dry. In fact, the disappointment of the Soviets over the sharp Carter reversal after the joint statement may have sparked actions and reactions by the superpowers in the Middle East that have brought both to their present stage of strategic confrontation in the region. Given the intense suspicion that now exists between Moscow and Washington, the cooperation option will have to wait until the global agenda between the superpowers can be framed in a more détente-oriented direction. With such sharp differences between regional powers in the Midde East over the Palestine question, supported in various degrees by the Soviet Union and the United States, any effort at this point to revive cooperation between the two in this region, before the overall strategic relationship shifts, could lead to further conflict and even a war involving the superpowers. In Soviet-American relations cooperation is no magic elixir for reducing conflict,

---

[29] See Robert J. Pranger, "U.S. Foreign Policy in the 1980's: A Speculation," Address at Fort Bragg, N.C., June 7, 1977, *AEI Reprint No. 74* (Washington, D.C.: American Enterprise Institute, n.d.)

but may itself be a form of latent conflict finally breaking down into overt confrontation: in addition to cooperation per se the time and general mood must be oriented toward détente — the "atmospherics" so to speak — before cooperative actions will lead to a genuine reduction in tensions.

Option 4: Direct American relations with PLO with preconditions. The chief problem with the noncommittal American option on the Palestinians, as far as security in the Gulf is concerned, is that neither of America's major defence partners in the Arab world, Egypt or Saudi Arabia, will accept this option as sufficient for the mutual security interests of the United States and Arab world. As I have argued, America's thinking on the Palestinians after 1973 has been increasingly influenced by its closer relations with major Arab powers in the Middle East and this inevitably means that the United States will not only be interested in an Arab policy appropriate for itself, but will also be more drawn to making some kind of decision on a positive policy for the Palestine question.

Even in 1981 direct, official American relations with the PLO have been foreclosed by US commitments to Israel, though it may well be that an ambivalent attitude toward the PLO has intensified. On the one side are those who see no choice for improving security relations with Egypt and Saudi Arabia except through American approval of Palestinian self-determination and PLO leadership, among them persons with considerable influence in Washington, such as Prince Fahd and, formerly, Sadat. On the other side are those who see the PLO as a strategic liability threatening the interests of the United States and its allies in the Middle East through terrorism supported by the Soviet Union. Both positions start from the premise that American interests require greater strength against the Soviet Union in the Middle East, but come to diametrically opposed conclusions. A global policy that places the highest priority on containing the Soviet Union, as the

Reagan administration proposes, need not be an anti-Arab policy at all; Eisenhower demonstrated this.

In what may be a move to find a way out of this ambivalent impasse on the Palestinians in American policy, certain pre-conditions have been put forth, most lately by Secretary Haig, for American acceptance of the PLO as something more legitimate to US interests than a terrorist organization; the preconditions are Palestinian recognition of Israel's right to exist and acceptance of Security Council Resolutions 242 and 338. This is no place to analyze the various nuances of this approach − the possible subtleties are themselves extremely complicated (for example, will Israel accept Palestinian nation-alism on any terms?) − but as noted earlier, it is very important to see that the option of American relations with the PLO, with preconditions, is different from the Israeli position and also avoids the negativity of the noncommittal option. I am not competent to judge Haig's motives and cynics may well argue that since Israel rejects the idea it is easy enough for Haig to recommend it for purely symbolic reasons. Yet, the preconditions option is the best of the five options, as I will make clear.

Option 5: American conformity with the Arab position. The majority Arab position on the Palestine question and the Gulf is obvious: the chief security problem for the Arab states is Israel, not the Soviet Union, and this danger will continue until there is a peace settlement acceptable to the Arab world (indeed, Soviet influence has been enhanced by the conflict). After settlement the Arabs will turn full attention to Soviet threats to their interests. Yet, no peace settlement is possible without self-determination for the Palestinians and recognition of the PLO as their sole legitimate representative. If no such peace transpires, security interests of the United States in the Gulf will suffer because (*a*) it will be rejected by the Arabs, at least in terms of close defence relations (Sadat may not have gone so far); *(b)* the Soviet Union will benefit because it supports the PLO: and (c) instability in the Arab world will intensify with increased radicalization stemming from the unsettled Palestinian issue. With these considerations in mind it is argued that the United States and its Western allies should explicitly disavow Israel's opposition to the PLO and Palestinian self-determination and firmly support Palestinian aspirations and leadership; this is not a call for abandoning Israel. The "balanced" model for this reversal is the European Economic Community position on peace in the Middle East which has sparked a new era in "Euro-Arab" cooperation and provides an example for the United States and other industrialized nations (such as Japan) should they wish lasting, mutually beneficial relations with the Arab world.[30]

The option of American conformity with the Arab position on the question of Palestine is probably unacceptable because of US defence commitments to Israel. Arab insistence that this option be seen by the United States as no more extreme than the pro-Israeli position, however, gives one some idea of how much the dynamics of Middle East politics have changed since 1973. Washington must listen attentively, even if it disagrees.

I believe that the option of direct American relations with the PLO with preconditions, even if this does not include official recognition in the beginning, is the best for protection of American security interests in the Gulf. It allows for an inevitable ambivalence in American policy toward the Palestinians caused by strong and necessary commitments to Israel, yet it also accords with the realities of shifting balances of world and Middle Eastern power toward the Arab community

[30] Note the role of the new "Center for U.S.-European Middle East Cooperation" in Washington, D.C., under the new leadership of its president, John P. Richardson. The Center's brochure notes: "The most vital consideration is for the United States and Western Europe to develop a *complementary* approach to Middle East peace that will incorporate the best elements of each of the respective policies."

and thus guarantees that American defence needs in the Gulf will be safeguarded. It also permits a certain ambiguity or openness for American policy that could allow this policy to swing more toward the Arab position at crucial times, as on the matter of defining "autonomy" for the West Bank and Gaza.[31] In longer term competition with the Soviet Union, the option of US acceptance of the idea of Palestinian self-determination will work to prevent the Middle East regional balance of power from tilting more sharply in Moscow's direction: such acceptance and recognition may also offer American policy special advantages. If the United States is now seriously approaching the Middle East and other regions from the perspective of a global strategy seeking to curb "Soviet intervention in regional conflicts," as Secretary Haig proposes,[32] then America will recognize the strategic significance of the Palestine question in the Gulf as a positive rather than a negative factor.

---

[31] Some would look on the problems of defining "autonomy" as a hopeless and useless project, fiddling while Rome burns, so to speak. For American policy, however, the matter is important because only the United States, of all the major actors in the Middle East, stands *between* the Arabs and Israelis; both sides must be taken seriously and for Begin the idea of "autonomy" is serious indeed. Flexibility on other matters, such as conversations between the US and the PLO on ideas for negotiation, would also be possible under option 4. For a good survey of conflicting points of view on common topics between Israelis and West Bank/Gaza Arabs see four volumes published by the American Enterprise Institute: Emile A. Nakhleh, *The West Bank and Gaza: Toward the Making of a Palestinian State*, AEI Studies 232 (1979); Daniel J. Elazar, *The Camp David Framework for Peace: A Shift Toward Shared Rule*, AEI Studies 236 (1979); Emile A. Nakhleh, ed., *A Palestinian Agenda for the West Bank and Gaza*, AEI Studies 277 (1980); and Daniel J. Elazar, ed., *Israeli Views on Judea, Samaria and Gaza* (1981).

[32] See the speech of Alexander Haig to the American Bar Association in New Orleans, August 11, 1981; excerpts in the *New York Times*, August 12, 1981. "The most persistent troubles in US-Soviet relations," argues Haig, "arise from Soviet intervention in regional conflicts, aggravating tensions and hampering the search for peaceful solutions. Unless we can come to grips with this dimension of Soviet behavior, everything else in our bilateral relationship will be undermined — as we have seen repeatedly in the past."

Bibliography

Bandar Bin Sultan, HRH Prince. *Strategic Priorities.* 1980.

Baroody, William J., Sr. "What a Palestinian Solution Will Solve," *Washington Post.* November 7, 1979.

Brecher, Michael. *Decisions in Israel's Foreign Policy.* New Haven: Yale University Press, 1975.

Elazar, Daniel J., *The Camp David Framework for Peace: A Shift Toward Shared Rule.* AEI Studies 236. Washington, D.C.: American Enterprise Institute, 1979.

Elazar, Daniel J., ed. *Israeli Views on Judea, Samaria and Gaza.* Washington, D.C.: American Enterprise Institute, 1981.

Evans, Rowland and Robert Novak. "Sadat's Rising Influence," *Washington Post.* August 29, 1981.

Farrell, William E. "Israeli Cabinet Affirms Stand on Autonomy Talks," *New York Times.* August 24, 1981.

Fitzgerald, Benedict F. Lt. Col. *US Strategic Interests in the Middle East in the 1980's.* Strategic Issues Research Memorandum. Carlisle Barracks, Pa.: Strategic Studies Institute, US Army War College, 1981.

Gwertzman, Bernard. "Brzezinski Urges Talks with PLO", *New York Times.* August 13, 1981.

Gwertzman, Bernard. "Haig Says Reagan Is Ready to Meet Soviets Halfway," *New York Times.* August 24, 1981.

Haig, Alexander M., Jr. Speech to the American Bar Association in New Orleans, August, 11, 1981. *New York Times,* August 12, 1981.

Halloran, Richard. "US Plans Persian Gulf Combat Command," *New York Times.* April 25, 1981.

House, Karen Elliott. "Soviets and the Middle East," *Wall Street Journal.* June 3, 1981.

Jenkins, Loren. "Sadat Indicates U.S. Receptive to His Bid for Area Security Role," *Washington Post.* August 20, 1981.

Kissinger, Henry. *White House Years.* Boston: Little, Brown, 1979.

Lenczowski, George. *Middle East Oil in a Revolutionary Age.* National Energy Study No. 10. American Enterprise Institute, 1976.

McManus, Doyle, "U.S., PLO: 7 years of Secret Contacts," *Los Angeles Times.* July 5, 1981.

Mohr, Charles. "U.S. Aides Concede Saudis Bar Limits on Use of Awacs." *New York Times.* August 23, 1981.

Nakhleh, Emile A. *The West Bank and Gaza: Toward the Making of a Palestinian State.* AEI Studies 232. Washington, D.C.: American Enterprise Institute, 1979.

Nakhleh, Emile A., ed. *A Palestinian Agenda for the West Bank and Gaza.* AEI Studies 277. Washington, D.C.: American Enterprise Institute, 1980.

Nixon, Richard M. *United States Foreign Policy for the 1970's: A New Strategy of Peace.* A Message from the President of the United States. Washington, D.C.: Government Printing Office, 1970.

Pranger, Robert J. *American Policy for Peace in the Middle East 1969-1971: Problems of Principle, Maneuver and Time.* Foreign Affairs Study 1. Washington, D.C.: American Enterprise Institute, 1971.

Pranger, Robert J. *Defense Implications of International Indeterminacy.* Foreign Affairs Study 4. Washington, D.C.: American Enterprise Institute, 1972.

Pranger, Robert J. "Six U.S. Perspectives on Soviet Foreign Policy Intentions," *AEI, Foreign Policy and Defense Review,* I, 5. Washington, D.C.: American Enterprise Institute, 1979.

Pranger, Robert J. "U.S. Policy in the 1980's: A Speculation." Address at Fort Bragg, N.C. June 7, 1977. *AEI Reprint No. 74.* Washington, D.C.: American Enterprise Institute, n.d.

Pranger, Robert J. "How to Deal with the Soviet Threat to

Japan and the United States." Paper presented at the Fifth Annual Shimoda Conference. Oiso, Japan. September 2-4, 1981.

Pranger, Robert J. "The Future of American Defense Policy in the Middle East." Tel Aviv University Centre for Strategic Studies. May 27, 1979 (unpublished).

Pranger, Robert J. and Dale R. Tahtinen. "American Policy Options in Iran and the Persian Gulf." *AEI Foreign Policy and Defense Review*, I, 2. Washington, D.C.: American Enterprise Institute, 1979.

Primakov, Yevgeny M. "Is Peace Feasible in the Middle East? " in Judith Kipper, ed. "The Middle East Conflict: Views from Abroad," *AEI Foreign Policy and Defense Review*, III, 1. Washington, D.C.: American Enterprise Institute, 1981.

Quandt, William B. *Decade of Decisions: American Policy Toward the Arab-Israeli Conflict, 1967-1976*. Berkeley: University of California Press, 1977.

Said, Edward W. *The Question of Palestine*. New York: Vintage Books, 1980.

Salem, Elie A. *Prospects for a New Lebanon*. Washington, D.C.: American Enterprise Institute, 1981.

Sheehan, Edward R.F. "Step by Step in the Middle East," *Foreign Policy*, No. 22 (Spring 1976), 3-70.

"6 Persian Gulf Nations Assail U.S. on Dogfight," *New York Times*. August 23, 1981.

Smith, William E. "A Bold New Plan by the Saudis," *Time*. August 24, 1981.

9

The Present Situation in the Middle East and the Policy of the Soviet Union

Oleg V. Kovtounovitch

The significance of the Middle East in present-day international relations can hardly be overestimated. There is every reason to believe that political, economic and military stability in the world largely depends on the situation in that region. Almost all Western countries, as well as Japan and the Third World countries, are vitally interested in an uninterrupted flow of oil from the Middle East. The states of the region have sovereign rights to their natural resources and only peace and stability there, it would seem, can guarantee mutually advantageous and equal trade exchanges. However, for decades now tension has prevailed in the Middle East. What is more, it has been increasing over the last few years.

As noted by Academician Y. Primakov:

... the development of the Arab-Israeli confrontation unquestionably influences the energy problem. The situation is aggravated by the fact that oil will evidently remain, until the end of this century, the principal component in the world balance of energy consumption, and the Middle East will continue to be the world's largest oil reservoir. Recently, the oil problem has taken on a new dimension: the US attitude toward it has become a major cause of the growing militarist trends in Washington's policy in the region.[1]

---

[1] Yvegeny M. Primakov, "Is Peace Feasible in the Middle East? " in Judith Kipper, ed., "The Middle East Conflict: Views from Abroad," *AEI Foreign Policy and Defense Review,* III, 1 (Washington, D.C.: *American Enterprise Institute,* 1981), p. 20.

The reason for this lies in the US policy aimed at turning this region, like any other region of the world within the framework of its general geopolitical strategy, into an object of active imperialist interference. This phenomenon is not new. It is quite obvious that for several decades the United States has been fanning local conflicts, including the Arab-Israeli one, to strengthen its positions. At present we are witnessing a new, sharp exacerbation of tension and the emergence of dangerous features in the Middle East situation. The point is that the course of finally abandoning détente has firmly established itself in Washington. This course had already been started by the Carter Administration. Back in 1979, President Carter emphasized that the people of the region should take into account the fact that the United States has "real national interests" in the peace and stability of that region, especially as regards ensuring the deliveries of oil and protecting the routes by which this oil is delivered to the USA and its friends and allies.[2] Naturally, in this context peace and stability are understood in the "American way," that is, they should be protected and controlled by American arms. US foreign policy should contribute to the realization of claims to American world supremacy. The military doctrine advanced by Washington includes not only Europe, but also the Middle East; it proceeds from the possibility of waging a "limited nuclear war." The American brass hats are openly preparing for waging "two and a half wars," that is, two major and one limited, local wars. The US actions in the Middle East, in the Gulf area, in the Indian Ocean and in the so-called Horn of Africa show that the United States is ready to turn this region into the theatre of a "local war" threatening to grow into a major one with the use of nuclear weapons.

The Iranian revolution provided an additional stimulus to these plans, for it excluded the possibility of Iran ever being

---

[2] *Time,* March 12, 1979.

used as a pro-American "centre of force" in that region. Evidently, it is precisely that event that made the United States re-appraise its concept of reliance on satellite-states. True, it stepped up the formation of an Egyptian-Israeli alliance after the developments in Iran, but that alliance as such has not turned out to be a sufficient guarantee of American interests in that region. It was necessary to ensure a direct US military presence.

It is with these aims in view that the United States naval forces have entrenched themselves in the Persian Gulf and the Arabian Sea. Washington is persistently trying to obtain agreement from the states of the region to build military bases, as well as the right to use airports and ports in crisis situations. Americans are supervising the construction of military bases in Egypt, Israel, Oman, Somalia and Kenya. Roads, ports, airports, storehouses and barracks are being built in these countries which could be used by US troops in case of a "local war." Military equipment is being brought there, including tanks, artillery and ammunition, so that the "Rapid Deployment Force" dispatched there could immediately start military operations. US-Egyptian manoeuvres conducted in Egypt have the aim of contributing to the military preparedness of US men and officers and checking military equipment, etc. in the natural conditions of the region.

An agreement signed in Washington on the so-called multinational forces which are to replace the Israeli occupation forces in Sinai, envisages that they be placed under US military command and that the number of American troops there should reach 1,000. This is a dangerous precedent. When the US deputy Assistant Secretary of State, Michael Sterner, who headed the negotiations, was asked whether this agreement would mean the deployment of American troops in the Middle East, he replied: "That is essentially correct, yes."[3]

3 *Newsweek,* July 6, 1981.

Simultaneously, the United States is trying to create, under its aegis, a regional defence bloc for which purpose it has to bring Israel and the conservative Arab regimes closer together. Certain prerequisites for this, in the opinion of American politicians, have been created by the Camp David agreements. Concentrated US military and financial aid to Egypt should serve as a bait for other Arab states. But a question arises: for whose sake and against whom should this bloc be created?

An answer to this question can be found in the ideas expressed by the US Secretary of State, Alexander Haig, during his trip to a number of countries in the Middle East last April. He attempted to persuade the governments of Israel, Egypt, Saudi Arabia and Jordan that the "Soviet threat" to countries in that region was so great and real that it should command main attention, whereas the unsettled Arab-Israeli conflict and the unresolved Palestinian problem are matters of secondary importance, whose solution could be postponed indefinitely in the face of the "Soviet threat."

The response to such an approach by the United States to the Middle East problem is characteristic enough. The most favourable attitude to it was, naturally, on the part of Israel, which received additional assurances that the United States would continue to devote particular attention to its security and render it massive assistance; Israel was satisfied with the fact that the present Administration placed the Palestinian question even farther down on the list of priority problems of US foreign policy than had been the case with the Carter Administration. The Zionist rulers of Israel well realized that the United States considered Israel, as before, to be its main pillar and ally in the Middle East. The subsequent aggressive actions of Israel in Lebanon and the bandit raid on Baghdad prompt one to think that agreement on making the situation more tense in the Middle East was already reached during Haig's visit.

This goes to show that the United States sometimes follows

in the wake of Tel Aviv's aggressive "initiatives," which it later includes in its political plans in the Middle East.

Haig's anti-Soviet statements have been met with complete understanding in Cairo. However, even President Sadat could not agree to the United States according only secondary importance to the Palestinian problem. This could be explained by the fact that Sadat had hoped that he would be able, with the help of the United States, to make Israel move, at least ostensibly, towards a solution of the Palestinian problem. This could have led President Sadat out of his isolation in the Arab world.

American references to the "Soviet threat" have, apparently, not received the desired response on the part of the Gulf states. Indicative in this respect is a statement made by Zaid ibn Sultan al-Nahayyan, President of the United Arab Emirates, who said:

> I am not convinced that at present the USSR poses any threat to us or to any other Gulf state, for that matter. If one has in mind the Soviet presence in Afghanistan, the Soviet troops are there in accordance with an official request of the country's legitimate government... We do not regard the USSR our enemy. We consider Israel the genuine enemy of the Arab peoples and an aggressor.[4]

The sentiments prevailing in the countries of the Gulf region were reflected, to some extent, in a communiqúe on the results of the talks in Moscow between the USSR Foreign Minister, Andrei Gromyko and the Deputy Premier and Foreign Minister of Kuwait, Shaykh Sabah al-Ahmad al-Jabir al-Sabah. It said, among other things, that during the negotiations:

> it was emphasized that the US actions to bolster up its military presence in the region, its desire to hammer together a military-political alliance there under its aegis were the chief reason for the aggravation of the situation and created new and serious difficulties in the way of establishing a just and stable peace in the Middle East.[5]

---

[4] *al-Mustaqbal* (Paris), June 6, 1981.
[5] *Pravda*, April 25, 1981.

Until now Oman has been an exception; its being turned into a US military springboard constitutes a menace to the independence and national sovereignty of the Gulf States.

The principal elements of the present strategy of US imperialism took shape in the first half of the 1970's, when Washington made energetic attempts to split the united front of Arab states against the Israeli aggressor and undermine progressive regimes in Arab countries. That was the aim of the so-called shuttle diplomacy of the White House, which was carried on in violation of the Geneva peace conference, and which ultimately resulted in the Camp David deal and the capitulation of the Sadat regime to Israel.

The American Administration is less inclined to regard the Middle East conflict as a local situation. This conflict is a component part of Washington's global geopolitical strategy based on US claims to world supremacy. According to the Palestine researcher Rashid Khalidi, the United States, in its approach to the Arab-Israeli conflict for a number of years

> has focused virtually all of its attention and energy on the establishment of a regional political and military alignment directed against the USSR and organized around Egypt and Israel, to include other states of the area if possible. This policy has been enacted at the expense of any effort to solve the real problems at issue, primarily that of Palestinian self-determination, which has been sacrificed to the US desire to maintain strong links with Israel.[6]

Washington's desire to force on the states of that region aims alien to them, while ignoring the core of the Middle East conflict — the Palestine problem — in order to prevent the notorious "Soviet penetration" and to bolster up US positions and, consequently, the positions of Israel as its traditional ally, undoubtedly aggravates the situation and postpones the prospects of a stable solution.

[6] Rashid Khalidi, *The Soviet Union and the Middle East in the 1980's* (Beirut: Institute for Palestine Studies, 1980), p. 8.

Israel is assigned a special role in US plans. Naturally, the Israeli leaders are rendering Washington maximum assistance in the implementation of its hegemonistic plans in the Middle East, while pursuing their own expansionist aims. Israel continues to remain the main element in the realization of American strategy in the region, as the most powerful military force which could be used in an emergency situation to protect US interests. Washington also regards Israel as a base for the "rapid deployment force." If need be, the Israeli authorities are ready to place at the disposal of the US army the Ramon and Ovda military bases being built in the Negev, to replace the Israeli bases in Sinai that are to be evacuated in April 1982 under the Egyptian-Israeli treaty. These bases are being constructed under the supervision of American army engineers. Moreover, the Israelis have undertaken to ask the Egyptian authorities for permission for the American military to use, through the mechanism of the "multinational forces," the Etzion military base that is being evacuated by Israeli troops in Sinai.[7] Apart from that, Israel with its Zionist leadership, is a bulwark of anti-communism in the Middle East.

The Sadat regime tried to rival Israel in assuming the role of the chief instrument of US policy in the region. However, that attempt was doomed to failure. Not to speak of the influential pro-Israeli lobby in the United States, Egypt is unable to vie with Israel, first of all, because it is unable to ensure mass support for its pro-American policy on the part of its own population. In an attempt to stifle mass opposition to its policy of capitulation, the Sadat regime threw thousands of Egyptian citizens into prison. Simultaneously, the Egyptian authorities fabricated absurd allegations that some members of the USSR Embassy staff and officials of other Soviet organi-

---

[7] *US Security Interests in the Persian Gulf: report of a staff study mission to the Persian Gulf, Africa, Oct. 21-Nov. 13, 1981 to the Committee on Foreign Affairs* (Washington: U.S. Government Printing Office, 1981), pp. 77-78.

zations in Egypt were involved in the exacerbation of the political situation inside Egypt. This crude anti-Soviet action was needed in order to divert public attention from the growing discontent of broad sections of the Egyptian population over the country's domestic and foreign policies. It is not accidental that these events coincide with new attempts to step up negotiations on so-called "autonomy" and to consolidate the US military presence in the Middle East. It can also be assumed that these reprisals against the opposition were taking place on the eve of new moves, already planned, in the field of Egypt's capitulation to Israel on the question of autonomy. Egypt's educational and technical level is lower than that of Israel, and this will not allow Egypt to play, even if only theoretically, the role of the "big stick" to protect American interests in the region, a task which Israel has taken upon itself.

US Middle East policy backed by Israel has remained unchanged for decades. Some modifications have been made, though, since the October 1973 war. It was previously believed in the White House that to protect American interests it was enough to maintain Israeli military superiority. However, the 1973 war and the oil boycott declared by the Arabs showed that this was not the case. It was then decided to bolster up that superiority by political efforts which could demonstrate that the United States allegedly took into account certain demands of the Arab side of the conflict. In essence, these efforts were aimed at consolidating the positions of Israel and, ultimately, the United States itself.

Washington's desire to direct the process of solving the Middle East crisis into the channel of the strategic and economic interests of the United States has become especially pronounced since the 1973 war, although the outcome of that war, it would seem, created the necessary prerequisites for a positive solution of the Arab-Israeli conflict. The collapse of Tel Aviv's military doctrine based on the idea of the Arab states' inability to resist the Israeli military machine was one of the consequences of that war. Besides, the oil boycott has demonstrated that the unresolved Middle East conflict will continue to generate tension and instability, thereby jeopardizing the unhampered extraction and delivery of oil from the Persian Gulf states, so essential for the Western countries' economies.

However, instead of exerting efforts to reach a just and stable settlement, the United States preferred to thwart the Geneva peace conference and, together with Egypt, did everything possible to debar the Soviet Union from participating in the process of settlement. The United States has virtually ignored not only the Soviet Union, but also the UN and all other Arab states. Washington has chosen a course aimed at reaching a separate Egyptian-Israeli agreement, thereby trying to remove the key problems of settlement from the agenda.

All US actions along the road to reaching a separate deal have been keynoted by a flagrantly slighting attitude to the vital interests and aspirations of the Arab peoples. This is why, as early as the stage of the preparations for the second Sinai agreement, that policy met with growing resistance in the Middle East whose public regarded a "stage-by-stage" solution of the Middle East problem as a pro-Israeli course which fanned still more the expansionist appetites of Tel Aviv. In this situation both the United States and Israel resorted to the well-tested practice of creating local crisis situations. In an attempt to disunite and set the Arab countries against one another, as well as to weaken the Palestine resistance movement as much as possible, Washington, by all means at its diposal, contributed to social and religious contradictions in Lebanon growing into a bloody civil war. With American blessing, Israel went so far as to resort to open armed interference in the events in Lebanon, helping the local reactionaries, and taking part in military hostilities.

In November 1977, Sadat made his "historic" trip to

Jerusalem. In September 1978, the Camp David agreements were signed by Egypt and Israel, under US patronage. On March 26, 1979, a "peace treaty" between Egypt and Israel was signed in Washington.

Imperialist and Zionist propaganda is trying to represent these stages of Sadat's capitulation as an important achievement on the road to a comprehensive settlement. It would seem that the two countries that have been at war for more than three decades have at last decided to establish normal relations between them. In this connection Academician Y. Primakov wrote:

> it is precisely the 'normalization' of Egyptian-Israeli relations on a separate basis — contrary to the interests of Egypt, of the other Arab countries, and of the Palestinian people — that obstructs the establishment of a genuine peace in the region. It is not a step forward, but rather a step backward, away from a comprehensive peace settlement.[8]

The Camp David agreements envisaged the exclusion of Egypt from the number of the countries confronting Israel, which would weaken the position of the Arabs and at the same time create conditions for Israel to receive more freedom in its expansionist actions in the Arab world and acquire certain "rights" to colonize further the Arab lands on the West Bank and in Gaza. As a result, a virtual Washington-Tel-Aviv Cairo axis has been created. However, all efforts by the White House to find followers of the Camp David course even among the conservative Arab states that traditionally preserve "special relations" with the United States, proved futile. The main reason for this lies, evidently, in the fact that a settlement in the "American way" does not solve the key problem — the Palestinian question — or rather presupposes its "solution" in the form of the virtual annexation of the occupied Arab lands, with their population being granted a fictitious "auto-

---

[8] *AEI Foreign Policy and Defense Review*, Primakov, *op. cit.*, p. 23.

nomy". The conservative Arab regimes cannot disregard Arab public opinion which resolutely denounces the course of capitulation to Israel. Besides, such capitulation would inevitably mean following in the wake of US policy in the region which, it is now quite clear, under any conditions assigns the priority role to Israel. Despite the close ties of these regimes with the United States, they would not wish to transfer their responsibility for their own security – one of the principal functions of a sovereign state – to the overseas patron. Naturally, the loss of that essential part of sovereignty would signify the beginning of a complete subordination of these states' political and economic interests to the global interests of Washington. This would lead, in the first place, to the loss of the relative independence of the Gulf states in establishing the level of oil extraction and setting oil prices. It is common knowledge that the United States considers the "arbitrary actions" taken by OPEC to be one of the main reasons for the present crisis situation in the world capitalist economy.

Under the guise of the "normalization" of Israeli-Egyptian relations, the Zionist rulers of Israel have stepped up the construction of military settlements in the occupied territories, thereby disclosing their intention to completely annex them. Israel has also escalated military actions in Lebanon directed against the Palestine resistance movement and the national-democratic forces of Lebanon and Syria. Israel does not stop at mass murders of peaceful civilians – women, children and old people. The aim justifies the means, as Israeli rulers cynically declare. And the aim is to intimidate the Lebanese people, to set them against their Palestinian brothers who are fighting for their legitimate right to independent existence in their own land.

Up to now Washington has been trying unsuccessfully to solve a dilemma in its Middle East policy, namely, how to encourage the Israeli aggression against the Arabs and at the same time to ensure an uninterrupted and abundant flow of

Arab oil. Obviously the aim of the brazen raid of the Israeli air force on the atomic research centre near Baghdad was to show the Gulf states that Israel has a long arm with which to punish them if necessary.

From time to time, Washington makes statements denouncing Israeli aggressive actions, or even applies "sanctions" against Israel. Thus, following the raid on Baghdad, the delivery of American F-16 planes to Israel was suspended, albeit only for six weeks. However, there can be no doubt that all these "protests" and "sanctions" are no more than an attempt to conceal from a world public opinion enraged by the barbarous actions of the Israeli military, the fact that it was the United States that inspired and organized these actions. Israeli troops are using the latest American arms. But the main thing is that Israel's aggressive course is part and parcel of the hegemonistic policy of Washington. To pursue a course aimed at militarizing one's own country and to persuade one's allies of the need to do it, it is necessary to increase tension in various regions of the world. The provocative military exercises of US troops jointly with other NATO member-states in the Caribbean, the invasion of independent Angola by large units of the racist RSA (Republic of South Africa), the piratical attacks by US aircraft on Libyan planes, the aggressive actions of Israel against Arab States – all these are links in one chain, are parts of the general course of American imperialism striving for the global aggravation of international tension. The prevailing situation completely unmasks Israel as the executor of Washington's policy in the Middle East. Of course, one can assume that individual actions of Israel are sometimes undertaken without agreement with the White House. However, even if this is the case (though, this is hardly likely), the American patron only pretends to find itself in an awkward position. On a broad and long-term basis, Israel's aggressive actions are indeed a component part of US policy. Israel's services in fanning anti-Sovietism and anti-communism, intimidating Arab countries and disrupting peaceful efforts for a just settlement are invaluable to the United States. Take, for instance, the fact that Israel agrees to stage dirty provocations, bloody terrorist acts, including those against peaceful citizens, relieving American men and officers from having to do "dirty" work and giving Washington an opportunity to pose as a "peacemaker" and "defender of "human rights." To this should be added that these services rendered by Israel cost the US comparatively little. According to J. Churba, American military aid to Israel amounts to less than one per cent of the US defence budget.[9]

To justify its bellicose foreign policy and to persuade the Arab states to follow in its wake, the US Administration is making extensive use of the myth of a "Soviet threat" looming over the region. Various "proofs" are being adduced to bolster up these assertions. Among them is the traditional policy of Russia aimed at securing access to the "warm seas," which was initiated back in the 18th century by Catherine the Great and has allegedly been continued by the Soviet Union. Indeed, the Empress's grandson Alexander, the future Emperor Alexander I, made a thorough study of Greek, in preparation for ascending the throne of a Greek kingdom with its capital in Constantinople. After the Great October Socialist Revolution of 1917, the Soviet Government made public the secret documents of the Entente known as the Sykes-Picot agreements, according to which Russia, in case of victory in World War I, was to receive large territories in the south at the expense of Turkey. The young Soviet state resolutely dissociated itself from the expansionist, colonialist policy of the czarist regime. All assertions about the USSR's participation in such a policy are completely groundless.

Another argument is based on the claim that the Soviet

[9] Camille Mansour, *Israel in American Strategy in the 1980's* (in Arabic), (Beirut: Institute for Palestine Studies, 1980), p. 11.

Union will, by the mid-1980s, face a serious need to import oil. Consequently, it should be assumed that it will try to seize the rich oil deposits in the Gulf region. But even if the Soviet Union did in fact need to import oil, it could obtain it by regular, peaceful means — through trade and economic cooperation, and not by seizing or establishing its control. Besides, those experts who maintain that the possibilities of increasing oil output in the Soviet Union have almost been exhausted, are either in error or are wilfully distorting the real state of affairs. The development plans for oil producing in the 1980's, including the 11th Five-year Plan for 1981-1985, envisage a considerable expansion of the output of oil. The Soviet Union firmly holds first place in the world in oil extraction, and does not intend to cede it. Naturally, we are faced with serious difficulties in this field, but we do not conceal them and have every chance of overcoming them. These difficulties are connected, above all, with the fact that the main reservoirs of oil are situated in far-off, hard-of-access and sparsely populated Siberian regions with a severe climate. Consequently, the development of these regions requires large investments, and the transportation of oil to the European part of the country, which is envisaged by the 11th Five-year Plan. The Soviet Union also has colossal coal and gas deposits. The task facing Soviet industry is to improve the structure of the fuel-and-energy balance of the country by lowering the proportion of oil through replacing it by gas, coal, atomic energy and other sources of power.

As for the assertions about Soviet "ideological expansion" they do not hold water, any more than the previous ones. The USSR is indeed supporting the countries that have taken the road of progressive development. But its policy has nothing in common with the "export of revolution," inasmuch as the Soviet Union maintains that the conditions for revolutionary transformations mature within a given society, and the degree of their maturity depends on concrete historical, economic, social and other circumstances.

It is common knowledge that the Communist Party and the Government of the Soviet Union invariably emphasize the Leninist character of Soviet foreign policy. This means that it is based on the principles elaborated by the great theorist and leader of revolutionary struggle and the founder of the world's first socialist state. Here is what Lenin wrote in 1918:

> Of course, there are people who believe that revolution can break out in a foreign country to order, by agreement. These people are either mad or they are provocateurs. We have experienced two revolutions during the past 12 years. We know that revolutions cannot be made to order, or by agreement. They break out when tens of millions of people come to the conclusion that it is impossible to live in the old way any longer."[10]

And he said also: "revolution is not made to order; it results from an outburst of mass indignation."[11]

Thus, the Soviet Union has no economic or other motives for seizing the sources of oil in the Gulf region. The USSR has set as the main goal of its foreign policy the strengthening of peace and international détente.

The US imperialists have been especially zealous in their exploitation of events in Afghanistan to prove the "Soviet threat" to the Gulf countries. But this argument is utterly false. The revolutionary development in Afghanistan that began in 1978 proceeded without any interference on the part of the Soviet Union and even the most rabid anti-Sovieteers cannot deny this. The USSR has never had anything to do with the struggle among the Afghan revolutionary forces themselves. A limited contingent of Soviet troops has been dispatched to Afghanistan at the request of the Afghan government in connection with foreign intervention in the internal affairs of that sovereign country. There is no doubt

10 V.I. Lenin. *Collected Works,* Vol. XXVII, p. 480.
11 *Ibid.,* Vol. XXVI, p. 345.

that the situation in Afghanistan would have been normalized a long time ago, had it not been for active military and financial aid from the United States, China, Egypt and some other countries to the Afghan tribal feudal reactionaries. The Soviet Union has stated time and again that a limited contingent of its armed forces is stationed in Afghanistan temporarily, that is, as long as there is a threat of armed intervention in that country from outside. The Afghan government has repeatedly advanced proposals to reach an agreement with its neighbours on reliable guarantees that there shall be no new intervention from their territories. However, these proposals have not met with any positive response.

It is a known fact that the Soviet Union is ready to conduct concrete negotiations on measures of trust in the Persian Gulf area as an independent problem. Taking into account the fact that some people insist that this problem cannot be isolated from the question of the Soviet military contingent's stay in Afghanistan, the Soviet Union is ready to discuss this matter in coordination with the questions of security in the Gulf area. Of course, it is only the international aspects of the Afghan problem that can be discussed, and not the domestic issues that come under the jurisdiction of Afghanistan as a sovereign state. Such is the consistent and flexible position of the USSR on this question. The reason why this stand providing for sound compromises does not find a response, should be sought in the policy of the United States, whose aim is to fan conflicts.

The Soviet Union is interested in peace and security in the Middle East. It proceeds from that fact that peace between the Arabs and Israel can be stable, provided it has a just and realistic foundation. Peace should inevitably answer the following three conditions: Israeli troops should be withdrawn from all Arab territories occupied in 1967, including the eastern sector of Jerusalem; the right of the Arab people of Palestine to self-determination, including the creation of their own independent state, should be implemented; the sovereignty and security of all states in the region should be guaranteed. If even one of these principles is violated, the entire process of peaceful settlement will be thwarted. Naturally, this process should provide for non-interference in the internal affairs of the countries and peoples of this region.

As is known, the Arab-Israeli conflict has two aspects: internal and external. The first is the conflict between the Arabs and Zionist Israel, and the second its international implications. The latter are connected with the direct or indirect involvement of many states in the conflict. Their aims vary from the desire to establish a stable peace between the two parties to the conflict, which could exert a favourable influence on the general situation in the Middle East, to a desire to maintain, and even aggravate, the conflict situation, with a view to using this state of affairs in their neo-colonialist interests in the region. Undoubtedly, the US Administration's global strategy of concentrating on the achievement of military-political superiority over the USSR and trying to subordinate the policies of other states to these aims where it is possible, regards the Arab-Israeli conflict as a means of maintaining tension in the region, which is in line with the interests of that strategy. US policy operating in conjunction with that of Israel, is the main obstacle in the way of reaching a genuine settlement.

The Arab-Israeli conflict, so it seems, acquires an ever-growing regional significance. This is connected, on the one hand, with the fact that the American imperialists are trying to tie in one knot all existing and potential conflicts so as to establish their control over the region. On the other hand, the confrontation of the Arabs and Israel goes beyond the boundary dividing Israel and the neighbouring Arab states and has become a national cause of all Arabs.

The extensive support for the struggle of the Arab people of Palestine on the part of all Arab states cannot be ignored even by the rulers of those countries that are connected with the United States by firm economic and political ties. In other words, the stability of the situation in the region directly depends on how the Arab-Israeli conflict develops. This also concerns the Persian Gulf countries and consequently, the preservation of these countries' sovereignty and their right to independently dispose of their main natural wealth – oil.

The Soviet Union has invariably displayed an interest in ensuring security in the Persian Gulf region, as well as in the entire Indian Ocean basin. Back in 1968, the USSR resolutely opposed the plans of the US and Britain to set up in the Persian Gulf region the so-called joint defence system. A Tass statement emphasized at the time that the Soviet Union condemned Western plans to interfere in the affairs of the Persian Gulf states; the USSR maintained that it was only the peoples of these countries that had the right to shape their destinies.[12] The USSR has invariably come out for détente, for its proliferation in all regions of the world, including the Indian Ocean and the Gulf basin. At the 1971 UN General Assembly session, the USSR actively supported its Declaration proclaiming the Indian Ocean a zone of peace. The Soviet Union has repeatedly reaffirmed its stand ever since. It is important to emphasize in this context that ensuring the security of sea routes across the Indian Ocean is of especial significance for the USSR, inasmuch as ours is the only state in the world whose all the year round sea communications between its European and Far Eastern parts pass through that ocean.

In 1977-1978 the Soviet Union conducted direct negotiations with the United States on limiting and subsequently curtailing military activities in the Indian Ocean. An agreement on these issues could be a tangible contribution to the implementation of the UN General Assembly Declaration on

[12] *Pravda*, March 4, 1968.

turning this region into a zone of peace. However, the US again suspended the talks, thus demonstrating its unwillingness to implement the Declaration.

At the 35th session of the UN General Assembly, the coastal states put forward an initiative for the convening in Colombo in 1981 of an international conference to prepare an agreement on turning the Indian Ocean into a zone of peace. The Soviet Union supported a similar resolution to this effect. Washington's refusal to take part in that conference has caused serious alarm. For the United States not only refuses to resort to political means to alleviate tension in the region, but exacerbates it, by stepping up its direct military presence there. Denouncing US attempts to put the blame for the militarization of the region on the Soviet Union, the newspaper *Times of India* noted that it was not the Soviet Union but the United States that refused to participate in the conference, and that it was the US that had rejected Soviet proposals for negotiations on the Indian Ocean.[13]

Speaking in the Indian Parliament in December 1980, L.I. Brezhnev proposed that the United States, other Western states, China, Japan and all other countries interested in the situation in the Gulf region, should reach an agreement on the following mutual commitments:

• not to create foreign military bases in the Persian Gulf region and the adjacent islands; not to deploy nuclear or other weapons of mass destruction there;

• not to use, or threaten to use, force against the Gulf countries, and not to interfere in their internal affairs;

• to respect the status of non-alignment chosen by the Gulf states; not to draw them into military groupings to which the nuclear powers are parties.

• to respect the sovereign right of the countries of the region to their natural resources;

13 *Times of India,* May 4, 1981.

• not to create any obstacles or threats to normal trade and the use of sea communications connecting the states in the region with other countries.[14]

Such an agreement, to which the states of the region would be full-fledged parties, would accord with their vital interests and be a reliable guarantee of their sovereign rights and security. It would considerably hamper imperialist interference in these countries' internal affairs and attempts to plunder their natural wealth. The Soviet proposals are fully in line with the principles of international law.

Washington's rejection of these Soviet proposals shows that the general improvement of the situation in the region is not to its liking, although the lifting of tension would have a definitely positive impact on the search for a just solution of the Arab-Israeli conflict.

The Soviet Union puts forward constructive proposals for breaking the deadlock. At the 26th Congress of the CPSU, the General Secretary of the Party Central Committee, L.I. Brezhnev, proposed the convening of a special international conference for the purpose. The Soviet Union is ready to take part in this conference, in a constructive spirit and animated by good will, together with other interested parties — the Arabs (naturally, including the Palestine Liberation Organization), Israel and the USA, with which we had a definite experience in this respect. The USSR is also prepared to cooperate with European countries and all those who sincerely desire to ensure a just and stable peace in the Middle East.

The Palestine problem should be solved with the most active and efficient participation of the only legitimate representative of the Palestinian people — the PLO. Time can only consolidate the PLO's position. For many years already, the Israeli rulers, who were later joined by Anwar Sadat, have not

[14] *Pravda*, December 12, 1980.

been able to find any puppet organization which they could oppose, even nominally, to the PLO.

The Soviet Union realizes full well that to search for a just and stable settlement is a difficult task. This is especially true in the present international situation, when the most aggressive circles of imperialism have become more active and are striving to aggravate tension, put up a stubborn struggle against the socialist community and the national-liberation movement, and gain the dominant role in world affairs.

It seems premature now to consider the consequences of the Egyptian President's departure from the political scene, particularly because there actually have been no changes in the regime. Nevertheless it is now clear that this event brings new momentum to the Middle East situation. The assassination of President Sadat, which bears witness to the deeprooted disagreement of wide circles of the Egyptian people with the pro-imperialistic policies of the regime, caused a new outburst of American military activity in the Eastern Mediterranean. This activity has been followed this time by threats against Libya by the Sudanese President Numayri. Urgent military assistance was promised to Sudan. At the same time, military supplies to Egypt will be increased. The US-Egyptian manoeuvres "Bright Star" were planned as a demonstration of the cooperation between two countries with an anti-Arab and especially anti-Libyan character. Washington is anxious to create an impression that after the assassination of Egypt's President there exist threats to that country on the part of some forces, as though this justifies US military actions undertaken for its alleged "defence."

On October 20 a meeting was held between President L. Brezhnev and the Chairman of the Executive Committee of the PLO, Yasir Arafat. During these talks the two sides condemned the actions of the US aimed at creating a dangerous zone of tension in the Mediterranean by bringing the American fleet and the so-called "rapid deployment forces" to a state of high readiness. The two leaders consider this action as an attempt by the USA to interfere in the internal affairs of Egypt and other Arab states, and to exert pressure on them.

But it should be borne in mind that this new feat of adventurism is caused by the profound economic and social crisis of the capitalist world. It can safely be asserted that the Leninist policy of peaceful coexistence with countries of different socio-economic systems, in conjunction with a firm course aimed at rebuffing the aggressive schemes of the imperialists and with the cooperation of all nations and progressive-minded forces interested in peace and security, is able to thwart the plans of the most reactionary imperialist circles in the world, and the Middle East in particular.

III
THE REGIONAL ACTORS

10

Palestine and the Gulf:
A Palestinian Perspective

by Shafiq al-Hout

When one refers to the "Middle East" or the "Near East," what specific countries is one talking about? And where do these imaginary lines that de-limit the "East" start or end? Judging by what we read and write, we cannot ignore the fact that these ambiguous terms are susceptible of political exploitation in the service of certain specific goals.

If it were a question of purely geographical terms it would be unimportant. It does not disturb the Frenchman or the Italian to have his country described as "West European," or the Czech or Bulgarian when his country is described as "East European," because such references do not involve any implied menace to the national identity of these peoples.

But in our case, the matter differs radically. This is because the obscurity of such terms, by denying our national identity as an Arab nation and an Arab homeland, imply the possibility of new entities being created. Thus, the fragmentation and division of the Arab homeland initiated by the Sykes-Picot agreement could be followed by further fragmentation and division, to the point where the Arab identity is completely dissipated and replaced by so-called "Middle Eastern" or other non-national affiliations.

In the case of "the Gulf,' here too is an apparently innocent, simply geographical expression. Yet here too is the same dangerous ambiguity — an ambiguity that is in fact directed against the national identity of the land and people of "the Gulf," especially since the discovery of oil, a vital resource with a great impact on the world economy as a whole.

Is it not strange that all the gulfs in the world should have names except this "Gulf" we are talking about? We are all aware of the dispute between the Arabs and the Iranians over the naming of the Gulf. The Arabs call it "the Arab Gulf" and the Iranians "the Persian Gulf," and both parties may have support for their claims, especially as they both have long coastlines on either of its sides. We know this and we grieve for it, and both parties should be urged to reach agreement so as to close this gap which is open to the unceasing interested ambitions of international forces attempting to breach the ties of Arab unity and bolster tribal and sectarian ties as a step towards transforming the region into a chain of weak and artificial entities.

Just as on the Arab coast of the Gulf there are numerous entities instead of a single entity within a national framework, so on the opposite coast, attempts are being made to fragment Iran. Thus "the Gulf" has no fixed identity, and this will continue to be the case until the conflict is resolved. If international ambitions are successful, then it will no doubt continue to be referred to by the same ambiguous terms, and may even come to be known as "the Middle Eastern Gulf."

There is another point to be made clear in discussing the "Gulf," and its relation to the Palestinian cause. Since it is obvious that the Kingdom of Saudi Arabia, by virtue of its coastline on the Gulf and of its political and economic weight inside and outside the region, is included in this expression, we find ourselves compelled to consider a larger regional framework than "the Gulf" that is "the Arabian Peninsula." In fact the picture can only be complete within this framework, which also includes some non-oil, but influential and important states, i.e. Northern and Southern Yemen. I would like to point out here that the term "Arabian Peninsula" is the most valid historically, geographically and politically, and one more in line with the national aspirations to unity which govern our political thought, and constitute our starting point in conception and analysis.

We in the PLO consider ourselves part of the Arab liberation movement, opposed to colonialism, Zionism and all forms of racial discrimination and struggling for the achievement of freedom, unity, progress and social justice. Moreover, our Palestinian Arab people are the most committed of all the Arab peoples to the cause of Arab unity. The reasons for this have to do with our people's political experience ever since the great Arab revolt against Turkish colonialism, through the era of European colonialism, and up to this very day when it is confronting the Zionist entity that was created by force at the expense of Palestine and its people, and at the expense of the whole Arab nation. If the cause of Arab unity is seen by some Arabs as a luxury, a long-term ambition, for the Arabs of Palestine it is a question of destiny, because it affects their very existence.

In this paper I have tried to present the conceptions of our revolution, and its approach to the topic we are considering, as reflected in its literature. Therefore, although the views I will present have no official character, I believe they are close to our movement's political line.

In order to discuss the subject of the relation between Palestine and what has been referred to by this symposium as "the Gulf" — what I would prefer to call "the Arabian Peninsula" — it is necessary to conduct a rapid review of the historical background of this relation.

The relation of Palestine and its people to the Arabian Peninsula goes back thousands of years. It is a relation determined by the nature of the vast desert areas of the Peninsula and of the surrounding areas, including Palestine, which are rich in vegetation and water. The waves of migration and settlement by Arab tribes in these areas heavily influenced the region's demography, as the Arabs grew numerically predominant. The settlement of these Arab tribes in Palestine and other regions, such as Syria and Iraq, did not sever their relations with their original regions. This relation was preserved for many centuries until Islam appeared from the very heart of this desert, qualitatively transforming the tribes into a single nation under a single banner.

The conquest of Jerusalem by the Caliph Omar ibn al-Khattab in the year 636 AD constituted a historical turning-point in the determination of the Arab identity of Palestine. Even though Palestine later witnessed many wars and conquests, resulting in the establishment of foreign entities, some of which lasted for dozens of years, yet Palestine preserved its Arab identity and only those who were Arabs, or who were Arabized, remained permanently on its land. It is hard to envisage the fate of the present racist entity of "Israel" in Palestine outside this historical framework which shows that force alone cannot guarantee the perpetual existence of any artificial entity that contradicts the nature, heritage and identity of the land on which it was set up. History shows that any balance of forces is liable to be upset, and if the factor of "force" is eliminated, then what was imposed by force will also come to an end. The Arabs of Palestine, like all other Arabs, include Moslems, Christians and Jews, and any disputes that exist between them were created by colonialist ambitions and racist ideologies with the aim of fragmenting this nation and preventing the establishment of a unified national state.

Perhaps the tragedy of the Zionist movement, and the entity that embodies it, goes beyonds its fears of a shift in the balance of forces, even though it short-sightedly does not perceive other grounds for concern, because peace too is a source of fear and concern for it. If the Arab-Israeli wars have allowed the Zionist leadership to avoid dealing with contradictions in the society it created, then the absence of wars will cause these contradictions to explode into fierce conflicts, particularly between the Ashkenazim and Sephardim, in other words between the European Jews and the Oriental Jews. The signs of such a potential conflict exist, discussion of it has increased lately, and more than one Israeli intellectual has warned of it. The attempts of the Zionists to solve their historical problem by exterminating or expelling the Moslem and Christian Arabs and by limiting the increase in the number of the oriental Jews, are futile and anachronistic.

To return to the relation between Palestine and the Arabian Peninsula, all these countries we are talking of constituted a single country and a single nation within a single political framework up to the fall of the Ottoman state, the last of the Islamic Caliphates.

When the Arabs declared their first Arab national revolt against Turkish despotism and oppression and allied themselves with Britain and her allies — a clear case of national allegiance outweighing religious allegiance — they were unaware of the fact that they would soon have to confront this ally under the same banner and for the very same goal, that national independence in their homeland.

If we examine that period of our history, the reasons that led to such a confrontation become obvious, as do the reasons for the faltering of the Arab revolt. Without too much elaboration, we can say that in spite of the success of European colonialism in replacing Turkish colonialism, it found itself facing a resolute Arab awakening and heroic resistance. The people of Palestine played an important role in this field, even though the regional terms we use today were not employed in those days, except for geographical description.

European colonialism, from the superior scientific, technological and cultural position it occupied in those days, was no doubt aware, and perhaps more so than some of the Arabs, of what a dangerous menace the establishment of a United Arab State would be to its position and its future. It was also aware of the great strategic potential of a state extending from the Atlantic Ocean to the Gulf, all along the southern coast of the Mediterranean, linking two ancient continents and controlling the most important routes between Europe and this part of the world.

In the light of this, colonialist strategic planning was based on two complementary lines:

The first aim was to fragment the Arab nation into statelets, kingdoms and sheikhdoms governed by mistrust and manufactured disunity.

The second aim, and this is where the role of the Zionist movement fits into the scheme, was to set up a human barrier, alien to the people of the region that would create a breach in the Arab nation, exhaust its resources and potentials and deprive it of the chance of developing and modernizing or even benefiting from its resources.

Of course, Palestine was the most suitable location for the achievement of this goal, because of its vital geographic position, and because of the sentiments it aroused, as the cradle of the revealed religions, in the European world in general and in particular among the Zionists, who used religious myths as a cover for their activities.

European colonialism was able to accomplish the first part of its scheme during World War I, as was disclosed later when the Sykes-Picot Treaty was exposed and artificial thrones, emirates and statelets were established. Then came the second stage, that of the establishment of a racist, colonialist, Zionist entity which started with the issue of the Balfour Declaration, and continued until the full tragedy was enacted in 1948 and Israel was established.

Before going into the reasons for the faltering of the

national movement and its failure to thwart this Zionist colonialist scheme, mention must be made of the magnificent resistance put up by the Palestinian Arab people, between 1917 and 1937, especially to the British mandate authorities. The Palestinian people revolted in 1920, 1921, 1929 and 1936, when the revolution reached its peak and spread to every village, town and city in Palestine. These uprisings and revolts aroused sympathy throughout the Arab world, and popular participation in and sympathy with them often embarrassed some Arab states whose rulers had surrendered to the mentality of fragmentation and disunity.

Thus, as an arena of conflict, Palestine was the pole that induced the Arab movement to continue the struggle throughout that period, just as from 1945 until today the cause of Palestine has been the centre of polarization. There can be no doubt that the Arabs at the mass level have been, are and will remain the strategic ally of the people of Palestine in their unceasing struggle, but we have to admit the discrepancy between the position of the masses and the position of the Arab regimes. No Arab regime has been able to adopt an overtly negative position towards this struggle, with the exception of Egyptian President Anwar Sadat, whose deviation from the Arab consensus caused him stifling isolation, internal crises, and ultimately his death.

I will briefly mention what I consider to be the reasons for the faltering of the Arab leadership in confronting the Zionist colonialist aggression in the period between the years 1917-1943.

1. The members of this leadership were conservative and traditional, their main concern being to make compromises with colonialism in order to safeguard the regional, class or tribal advantages they had inherited.

2. The failure of the ruling leadership to comprehend the profundity of the colonialist scheme, each leadership keeping itself to its regional borders and narrow interests.

3. This leadership participated in the political, military and economic confrontations from positions of fragmentation and disunity, led by regional and not pan-Arab interests. Such forms of confrontation were not up to the level needed to confront such complex colonialist schemes.

The establishment of Israel in 1948 meant the usurpation of a large portion of Palestine and the expulsion of over a million Palestinians from their homeland into compulsory exile. The Zionist movement's switch from alliance with Europe to alliance with the US, whose leadership of the West had been consolidated at a time when the domination of world politics by the two super-powers had been established, resulted in escalation of the conflict, and was the reason for the series of wars which ensued in the region.

Before the Palestinian diaspora, the Arabs heard and read about the cause of Palestine and the people of Palestine, but without any direct contact with that people. And the same applied to the Palestinians with regard to the Arabs. Mass contact was not easy in those days, and was limited to educational or health missions or to the commercial sector.

After the diaspora, the picture changed radically because of the degree and intensity of contact established and the relations that were developed thereby between the Palestinians and their Arab brothers.

Because of their geographical proximity, Jordan, Syria and Lebanon were the first and principal stop for the Palestinian emigrants, but the economic factor made the oil-producing states in the Arabian Peninsula their second stop. The Palestinian tragedy was enacted contemporaneously with the expansion of the oil industry in the Gulf states. Thus on the one hand there were the Palestinians seeking a source of livelihood, and on the other, workshops in need of labourers.

I recall vividly the scene when, over thirty years ago, two queues of Palestinians could be seen, one leading to the refugee aid centres, and the other to obtain "work permits" in oil companies. Having stood in both of them myself, I recall the emotions of pain, concern and sorrow in these queues that were to lead us to eternal exile.

Today there is no Arab country without a noticeable and influential Palestinian presence, though the states of the Arab Peninsula have the greatest density after Syria, Lebanon and Jordan. According to the best estimates, there are over half a million Palestinians in the Arabian Peninsula from the level of construction labourers to that of senior advisers on oil or finance.[1] It is almost impossible to envisage the states of the region without this Palestinian presence, the more so because the urgent need for it persists even though the doors are open to non-Palestinian Arabs and foreigners from India, Pakistan and other Asian countries.

The issue of immigration has come to be a source of concern to the states in the region and has been the subject of numerous studies, analyses and predictions. The source of this anxiety is the future "identity" of these countries in which three trends are in conflict: the Islamic, the Arab and the cosmopolitan. The political connotation of the Palestinian is not only an Arab but also an Arabist. It seems to me that fate has always placed the Palestinian people on the front lines in safeguarding the national identity of this nation, whether in their homeland Palestine or in the "host" states, the official term adopted by the Arab League.

The Palestinian has carried his cause with him wherever he

---

[1] *The Palestinian Statistical Abstract 1981,* published by the Economic Department of the PLO Central Bureau of Statistics (Damascus, 1981), gives 474,390 as the number of Palestinians in the Arabian Peninsula in 1980 – Kuwait 276,390, Saudi Arabia 137,000, the United Arab Emirates 37,000 and Qatar 24,000 in 1980. The Kuwaiti figure is taken from the Kuwaiti census, and the others are estimates. The *Abstract* notes that accurate data on the number of Palestinians in Bahrain, Oman, the People's Democratic Republic of Yemen and the Yemeni Arab Republic are not available. The 1982 total for all eight countries, however, is certainly well over half a million.

goes. In the stage of uncertainty and absence of political leadership, the Palestinian took his experience and his tragedy to his Arab brother, who realized the immensity of the calamity and the dangers of its extension.

Though many states dealt negatively with the Palestinians — both as people and as the bearers of their cause — this was limited to the official authorities and never extended to the popular level. National identification with the Palestinians, along with the need for their expertise, qualifications and services, was sufficient to secure co-existence, interaction and the consolidation of national ties.

As a result of the immense growth of the Arab bourgeoisie and the narrow chauvinistic regional trends this engendered, and of the consecutive blows dealt to the Arab national movement, culminating in June 1967, this relation was shaken. But by then the Palestinian had passed the stage of loss and uncertainty, and the stage of nationalist fluctuations which the area had witnessed, and had moved on to the stage of the national revolution with the birth of the PLO in May 1964. This was a turning point in both Palestinian and Arab political life, and a qualitative change in the life of the Palestinians in the diaspora.

The general impression prevailing at the time was that such an outcome of official Arab decision-making would be like all similar cases and end in oblivion. But this view neglected the fact that in this case the decision was of vital importance to the Palestinian people. The Palestinian mass base was alive with militant political groupings and organizations dedicated to the goal of resuscitating the Palestinian national identity and its national and political institutions. In fact, a considerable and influential sector of active and politicized Palestinian youth was concerned at the extent of official Arab influence on the PLO, and their cooperation with it was limited and cautious. All the developments during the three years that followed the birth of the PLO, and the June war in particular, led in 1968 to a radical turning point in the structure and destiny of the PLO when Palestinian "legitimacy" and revolutionary spirit were fused together, whereby all the organizations and political forces of the resistance participated in the new National Council and a new leadership was elected, led by Yasser Arafat, the Commander-in-Chief of the Forces of the Palestinian revolution.

Thus the PLO acquired a much weightier stature which enabled it to continue the struggle at all levels, and to become the sole legitimate representative of the Palestinian people, and then to gain international recognition, including decisive Arab recognition. At this stage the relation between any Arab or any other state and the Palestine cause was determined by its attitude to a specific party, the PLO.

Thus the attitude to Palestinians developed everywhere (and of course this included the Arabian Peninsula), from one of sympathy for "refugees" or guilt feelings towards "the victim," to respect for the "revolutionary," mingled with concern over what this revolutionary might initiate in the war of new transformations. The masses of Palestinians in exile also transformed into communities with a role and an impact in supporting the revolution and the PLO, and in consolidating the relations between the host country and the PLO.

These years that witnessed the rise and growth of the PLO also witnessed the beginnings of transformations in the centres of Arab leadership, and the emergence of oil, economy and finance as important weapons in the struggle to insure and accomplish the national aspirations of the Palestinian people according to principles which have been the subject of international approval, with Israel and the US as the only deviants.

Thus this time-span witnessed two important events, the rise of the PLO and the growth of the role of the Arabian Peninsula in the planning of general Arab policy. This is a remarkable coincidence, but what is much more surprising is the fact that they coexist, mutually incompatible though they appear.

The PLO represents a revolution that regards armed popular struggle as the main tool in achieving the required change.

The states of the Arabian peninsula, with the exception of Democratic Yemen are characterised by attributes that are the complete opposite of everything revolutionary. Their structures are traditional and conservative, their links with the West are very old, and the discovery of oil has enhanced these ties and deepened them.

How can there be co-existence between the Palestinian revolution, which regards imperialism, colonialism and Zionism as its enemies, and these regimes, some of which are more staunchly hostile than the US itself to any anti-Western force? Saudi Arabia, for example, has no diplomatic relations with Moscow and combats communism outside her own borders, yet finds no embarrassment in supporting the PLO and its struggle whenever she can, regardless of all she knows about the alliances within the PLO and the alliances of the PLO on the Arab and international levels.

I think the answer lies in the 1960's, from the first year of the decade to the last. In September 1961 the United Arab Republic, the first Arab Union in modern history, broke up into two regions; in September 1970 Gamal Abdel Nasser, the first Arab leader to adopt the Arab liberation movement while in power, departed. These two dates summarize a long story, full of events and interactions, that has led us to where we stand today.

The break-up of the UAR weakened confidence in the effectiveness of Arab struggle. The Arab nationalists were split, some turning sceptical over the Arab national cause itself, others retrogressing to regional left — or right-wing positions, while others again were sceptical only as regards the ability and responsibility of the leadership, and kept their faith in Arab nationalism.

This event was a shock that demanded a re-assessment of attitudes by all the forces in all the Arab arenas. It was only natural that the nationalist Palestinians should be the most grieved because the failure of the Egyptian-Syrian unity meant the temporary eclipse of the slogan "Unity is the way to liberation." It also meant the break-up of the unified Syrian-Egyptian state along the southern and north-eastern frontiers of their homeland.

This may have been the main reason why the Palestinians started to consider new organizational frameworks to replace the old ones though no doubt the Algerian revolution, which was on the brink of victory at that stage, caught the imagination of the revolutionary Palestinians, and the Algerian example was seen as one to be followed and learnt from.

The most important new strategic lessons taught by the Algerian experience were the need to bear arms, to ensure the independence of the national will and to avoid involvement in inter-Arab conflicts over side issues.

It may well be that *Fateh,* because of the background of its founders, was the first to be thus inspired by the Algerian revolution, because all the other organizations were still drawn, ideologically and organizationally, to Arab nationalism, and the political forces which embodied it.

Since its foundation, *Fateh* has been anxious to seem new, and to hanker after either the glories or the burdens of the past stage. Its most important new feature has been that it initiated armed revolution before putting out any political programme, as if to say that armed revolution would put out its own programme, and its own ideology. The other new element was its rejection of the existing classifications and titles for the regimes and parties, depending on a single touchstone for differentiation between what was national and progressive and what was the opposite. *Fateh* decided to reject any interference in the internal affairs of any Arab country, and all this was inspired by the Algerian experience.

These slogans did not gain popularity at once, and were the subject of extensive and profound theoretical argument. However, developments, especially after the 1967 defeat and the acceptance of the cease-fire — which *Fateh* and other organizations of the resistance rejected — confirmed the importance of these slogans and their popularity, particularly in the Arabian Peninsula. Why was this?

1. Because it was the first to benefit from dropping of the classification of Arab states into the categories of "progressive" and "reactionary," which the Gulf states and Saudi Arabia in particular had suffered from more than any others.

2. Because once the sole criterion for acceptability became their attitude to the Palestine question, these states were no longer condemned for their negative attitudes on other issues.

3. Because the countries of the Arabian Peninsula were preparing themselves for a leadership role in the region, a role they had to assume following the immense development in their resources, which they wanted to safeguard. As they were aware that the issue of Palestine was the core of the issues of the region and that it had to be faced up to in one form or another, for there can be no power without responsibilities, they chose to deal with this revolutionary line, particularly that represented by *Fateh*. For no matter what risks were involved, they were calculated risks especially, that could not be evaded. We should also recall the importance of Jerusalem especially to Muslim regimes, the largest and most important of which, Saudi Arabia, was responsible for safeguarding Mecca and the Medina, the Muslim holy places. So it was impossible for the Arabian Peninsula states to wash their hands of the Palestine cause without destabilizing their own home ground. The Iranian revolution at the end of the 1980's increased their sensitivities, as comparison started between this version of Islam and that.

Another reason was the Palestinian presence in the Peninsula, and its role and influence in those societies, to which we have already drawn attention.

This was the situation in the 1960's, and these were the

factors governing the relations between the states of the Arabian peninsula and the Palestine cause. But in discussing the state of this relationship in the 1980's, I would like to point out that, if I have concentrated somewhat on *Fateh,* this is due to three objective reasons: (1) Most of the *Fateh* leadership embarked on its mission from the Arabian peninsula. (2) *Fateh* alone offered something new, whether as regards means of action or the criteria of action, and though the rest of the organizations later adopted the same methods, most of them remained ideologically committed to their previous basic principles. (3) *Fateh* became the backbone and the axis of the revolution.

Nevertheless, commitment is to the PLO and to its decisions, adopted by the conferences of the National Council, the highest political authority of the PLO. For over a decade the decisive word has been that of the PLO and not that of any single organization. This is why the relation between the Palestine cause and the countries of the Arabian Peninsula means the relation between the PLO specifically and these states.

During the past decade many important developments have taken place in the resistance organizations, whether in their positions or in their practice. No doubt the continuation of the struggle with the enemy on all fronts has been the most influential factor in bringing about such developments. I will try to be brief:

1. The PLO adopted political and mass struggle for the achievement of its goals, in addition to armed struggle, and regarded all these forms of struggle as complementing each other.

This decision was followed by the return of the Palestine cause to the United Nations and the PLO's achievement of observer status in the organization in 1974. This in turn was the beginning of PLO participation in regional and international blocs, such as the Non-aligned nations bloc, the

Organization of African Unity and the Islamic conference, in
addition of course to the Arab League. Thus the PLO attained
international legitimacy, with all that this involved in the way
of commitments to the charters and rules of these organizations.

2. There was a revival of the emphasis on Arab national
efforts and their role in the conflict in the region. This meant a
realization that the task of liberation cannot be achieved by
Palestinian struggle alone, though the Palestinians have to be in
the vanguard. This left its impact on Palestinian-Arab alliances
during this stage, regardless of their ups and downs.

3. The Palestinian revolution came to be considered part of
the international liberation movement against imperialism,
colonialism and all forms of racial discrimination. This development reflected itself on our alliances with international
liberation movements, and with the socialist countries, led by
the Soviet Union.

4. The PLO adopted the policy of non-alignment, and
defended this political line and the bloc that embodies it.

Not one of the organizations that make up the PLO
deviates from these points. Any observer of the history of
these organizations is aware of how much their positions have
developed due to the spirit of alliance on a front basis and the
striving for national unity, and to the experiences of the last
ten years. Yasser Arafat was once asked what was the secret of
the PLO's steadfastness and the inability of its enemies to
strike at it from within. He said: "Our democracy is such that
it makes decisions enabling me to be, probably, the first
person to fly direct from Riyadh to Moscow."

What, then, are the current relations between the Peninsula
countries and the PLO, and our expectations for their future,
and what is the impact of these developments on the Peninsula
countries and how do they deal with it?

Let us take a closer look at the map and be more precise as
to why we call them the states of the Peninsula, so as to ensure

that it is permissible to answer this question with generalizations that include all of them.

The countries of that region have been subject to change, some for internal reasons and social development, and others for reasons going beyond that to the overall Arab atmosphere and to international conflicts.

We can divide these countries into three groups:

1. The first includes the Kingdom of Saudi Arabia, Kuwait, the United Arab Emirates, Bahrein and Qatar. In spite of the apparent discrepancies in the regimes and policies of this group, we can say that in the final analysis they all belong to the same school. Saudi Arabia, as the largest and richest among them, has an especially influential role, but that does not invalidate the role of the others. This group has close ties with the West in general and with the US in particular due to the oil relations between the two parties, and to their fear of the possibility of internal change that is growing as a result of the contradictions arising from huge and unplanned growth and the Arab and Islamic revolutionary trends that are developing all around them.

Thus concern to safeguard the status quo is the strongest motivation behind the planning of the general political lines of this group. What increases this concern is that it also applies to the American "ally," whose credibility has been greatly weakened since the fall of the Shah, one of the most important former friends of America in the region. It may well be that the least important specific source of concern for this group is just what the US is trying to present as the greatest danger, i.e. the Soviet danger.

2. The second group is the two Yemens. It may seem strange to place them in the same group in spite of the sharp difference in the type of regime ruling each of them. Democratic Yemen is a socialist republic, which is guided by Marxism-Leninism in its policies and the administration and organization of its life, whereas North Yemen is still under the bondage

of tribal traditions in spite of the power and persistence of the trends working for change, and especially those calling for the unity of the two Yemens, which almost every single Yemeni, in both Yemens, desires and believes to be inevitable.

Democratic Yemen has decided who are her enemies and who her friends, both in the Arab and international spheres, in accordance with her ideology and on this basis has formulated her political theory and practice. North Yemen, on the other hand has neither closed nor opened wide her doors to all, so that she cannot easily be classified with this or that party, whether on the Arab or the international level. And any regime in North Yemen that does not carefully calculate its local, Arab and international policy cannot hope to save itself from unrest and perhaps collapse.

3. At the end of our list comes the Sultanate of Oman which, in brief, is a base open to the Western states. The only preoccupations of its regime are Democratic Yemen and the danger of the revival of the revolution in Dhofar, especially since the fall of the Shah, who frequently came to the rescue of the regime, striking at the revolution with his advanced military machine.

Having examined this political map, with its many complexities and linkages, we can realize how difficult it is for the PLO in dealing with its relations with all the countries of this region, and preventing itself from falling victim to these complexities while at the same time mobilizing these relations to the advantage of the central contradiction it faces, the Arab-Zionist conflict.

Let us specify some of the main convictions that govern the "relation" between the PLO and all the Arab states, before going into details regarding the states of the Arabian Peninsula.

The first conviction which derives from a realization of the importance of the Arab national role in the struggle to recover the national rights and the land of the Palestinian people, is that the mobilization of the resources and potentials of the

Arabs demands unceasing struggle for the establishment of at least a minimum of Arab solidarity.

The political practice of the Palestinian leadership during recent years gives clear evidence of this position. Yasser Arafat once described the PLO as "the bridge of confidence" between the Arab states.

The second conviction is that with the accumulation of events over more than thirty years, the Palestine cause has become a very complex issue and cannot be solved by simple means. This demands a careful distinction between strategy and tactics. The strategy should be stable and firm, but tactics should be flexible, and this demands special attention to each stage of the struggle.

The third conviction is that, although relations with the Arab regimes are important and necessary, they should not be at the expense of relations with the forces of revolutionary change in the Arab world, and especialy those which call for support for the struggle and revolution of the Palestinians. These days the Palestinian arena hosts most of the Arab militants and political leaders who have not been tolerated in their own countries.

The fourth conviction is insistence on the independence of Palestinian "decision-making." This does not at all mean insistence on Palestinian "isolation"; that would be a grave political and national mistake: the "independence" of decision-making remains within the general framework of Arab nationalism. As for marginal inter-Arab disputes, the PLO tries its best to avoid taking sides, and to help the parties settle these disputes.

The fifth conviction is insistence that the PLO should always be the embodiment of the Arab conscience, and must allow the voice of truth and justice to be raised in its arena without any fear; this is the aspiration of every free Arab.

In the light of these convictions the PLO tries to consolidate its relations with the Arab countries. This is no easy task, but it has no other choice. The shocks the PLO has suffered at the hands of more than one Arab party and in more than one arena throughout the last decade, came as no surprise. Nor can we rule out the possibility of this happening again in the future and in any arena, including the Arabian Peninsula. Good will alone is not enough to resolve the contradictions that may arise at moments crucial to the fate of our people.

The Arabian Peninsula is at present the scene of important political moves related to the Palestine cause, under the leadership of Saudi Arabia and with the official endorsement of the Gulf Cooperation Council. This activity has been dictated by the circumstances of and developments in the Arab-Israeli conflict, especially since the October 1973 War, in which for the first time oil played an effective role, especially in the international arena, so that any discussion of this strategic commodity now involves, to a great extent, discussion of the Palestine cause.

Oil in itself is a complex issue because of its effect on international industry and economy and world politics. The linking of this issue to the Palestine cause was bound to increase the dangers and the risks. We are now seeing how far this inter-linking has gone, and we have to be on our guard to ensure that oil, which we wanted as a weapon in our hands, is not used as a weapon against us, a danger of which the PLO is well aware.

In fact all the resistance organizations have reached a stage of maturity that goes beyond hasty, rigid and over-simplified reactions. This is primarily a sign of self-confidence and an indication of awareness gained through bitter experience, of how to deal successfully with initiatives and manoeuvres and how to distinguish between the two. Our cause has often witnessed initiatives and manoeuvres that ended in nothing.

The moves of Saudi Arabia, along with all the forces they represent and the states that support them, gain their importance from several factors which I will briefly state:

1. The immense economic weight of Saudi Arabia, along with other influential Gulf states such as Kuwait, the UAE and Qatar.

2. The political complexion of the Saudi regime in particular and the Gulf regimes in general, which are ideologically of the type deemed desirable by the West. The links of the Saudis with the US in particular and the West in general are of a very profound and special nature.

3. The strategic position of the Arabian Peninsula, especially within the framework of the present strategy of the US administration.

For these basic reasons, and for others of secondary importance, any political move by the states of the Arabian Peninsula, as well as being particularly important, is particularly dangerous, regardless of its success or failure.

Success would mean that the US had given the green light to the move and approved of it, so that both those accepting and those rejecting the move would have to reappraise, at more than one level, the existing alliances in the region.

Failure would mean that the US had rejected the move, and this would necessarily be reflected in US-Gulf relations. The effect would not necessarily be dramatic or radical, but the embarrassment the Gulf states suffered because of the contradiction between their close friendship with the US and the policy of the US government would increase considerably.

After Begin's visit to Washington in September 1981 and the declarations about agreements in principle on Israeli participation in the general American strategy in the Middle East, it came as no surprise when a Saudi official, Prince Bandar Bin Sultan, declared that his country might resort to the devil himself to defend its dignity in the face of American insults. This is the first time this has happened, and its implications are very clear. These include rejection of the view held by some that any collaboration between the Gulf states and the USSR is impossible. The attitude of Kuwait in particular and, to a great extent that of the Emirates to the USSR, as embodied in the official and unofficial contacts made and the comments issued by these two states, provide further evidence of this development.

In order to assess whether the Saudi move will succeed or fail we have to first comprehend the American position.

In spite of the many evaluations and analyses, both positive and negative, that have been made of the personality of the American President Ronald Reagan, Palestinian experience during the administration of eight American presidents together with a political understanding of the general policy of the US have given us grounds for nothing but pessimism and despair as regards any change taking place in the attitude of the US government.

This pessimism reached its climax when President Reagan entered the White House with an electoral programme which so far, it seems, he has adhered to, and will try to put into effect. This programme provides for a return to the policy of arrogance, power and confrontation, or at least the threat of confrontation, which reminds us of the policy of cold war, and seem likely to bring us to the brink of a hot war.

In spite of what is being said to the effect that no American president these days has the power to take decisions on his own, and that this president in particular gives priority to American national interests over any other consideration, including the alliances of his government with other states, from what we have observed so far it is clear that he has decided that the higher national interests of his country do not conflict with those of Israel, but that both complement each other and must be energetically promoted, but within the framework of a new strategy "to stop the spread of Soviet influence." He is trying, through the exertion of strong pressures, to include Arab countries in this American-Israeli strategic alliance, although his Secretary of State has not specified which countries these are. After Begin's September visit, General Haig tried, by means of his meeting with Prince Fahd ibn Abd al-Aziz, the first Arab leader he met after that announcement, to play down the importance of the agreement with Israel in the eyes of the Arabs. He claimed that the Saudi Prince was not troubled by the agreement "because it was directed against the Soviets and not against the Arabs." But that was not a very satisfactory explanation, because Saudi Arabia and the other Gulf states, in spite of all talk to the contrary, have no interest in turning the Soviet Union into an enemy, since it is a great power and a state with alliances and friendship with the Arabs.

It is true that Gulf diplomacy, and Saudi diplomacy in particular, has for many years been very deliberate and patient and has avoided overt and angry reactions. But it is also true that the developments that have taken place throughout these years have not left much more scope for the practice of this type of diplomacy without risking internal and inter-Arab crises. The Gulf states, and notably Saudi Arabia, have to take into account these developments, the most important of which are:

1. The Palestinian revolution and its role in the region, with all it represents in terms of its subjective forces, its alliances and the locations of the Palestinian communities in the diaspora.

2. The Iranian revolution has proved beyond any doubt that no regime in the world, and in particular no regime in our region, is secure from violence, revolution and change. The US with all its capabilities and resources, cannot provide any regime with guarantees.

3. The overwhelming Arab trend of opposition to American imperialism. especially in the context of the Arab-Zionist conflict, and the fact that this trend has powerful strongholds, especially within the framework of the Steadfastness and Confrontation Front states. One of these states is actually in the Arabian Peninsula — Democratic Yemen, while Syria is

located on one of the most important borders of the Peninsula. In addition, though at a greater distance, there are Libya
and Algeria.

4. The unchanging fact of the importance of the USSR as a
great power which cannot be excluded from any settlement of
the Palestine question, if such a settlement is not to be
sabotaged or deadlocked.

5. Since the Israeli raid on the nuclear reactor in Baghdad
and the raid on civilian quarters in Beirut a month later,
Israel's menace to the Gulf states, and to all the Arab states,
has increased and developed from a possibility to a certainty.
As a result of this qualitative development, the Zionist menace
has now spread beyond the frontiers of the Arab states
bordering Israel, to the Gulf states themselves.[2] It is a
striking confirmation of all that has been said in the past about
Zionism's true expansionist ambitions, which some have described as propaganda exaggerations. This was followed by the
US-Israeli strategic cooperation agreement, which is further
proof that the Zionist-imperialist alliance is going to continue,
perhaps for ever, and which will ultimately have radical
repercussions on overall Arab policy.

We can thus see clearly how dangerous a situation the Gulf
states are in when they hope to achieve the impossible goal
they have so long put their money on, that of neutralizing the

---

[2] A speech by Israeli War Minister Ariel Sharon, reported in *Ma'ariv* on 18
December 1981, specifies the extent and range of this menace. Sharon declared:
"Israel's security interests are affected by developments and events beyond the area
of direct confrontation on which Israel has focused in the past. Beyond this
traditional first circle of confrontation states surrounding Israel, Israel's strategic
concerns should expand to include two other geographic regions which have great
security importance: The second circle includes the other more distant Arab
states...; while the third geographic region of importance to Israel's strategic
interests includes those foreign countries which ... could pose a threat to Israel's
security in the Middle East and on the shores of the Mediterranean... and the Red
Sea. Thus we must expand the area of Israel's strategic and security concerns in the
1980's to include states like Turkey, Iran and Pakistan, and areas like the Persian
Gulf and Africa, particularly the states of North and Central Africa."

US as far as Israeli policy is concerned, or at least reducing its pro-Israeli bias.

On September 16, in the aftermath of the uproar resulting from the Reagan-Begin meeting and the talk about the strategic cooperation agreement between the US and Israel, the Saudi Foreign Minister Prince Saud al-Faisal, a man well-known for his careful choice of words, commented: "The vote of Congress against the US selling AWACS planes to Saudi Arabia will raise questions about the future of relations between the two countries." He added: "The time has come for a fundamental assessment of the relations of the US with Israel and the continuous flow of arms to her which have allowed her to increase her aggressive actions." He urged the American administration to treat the Palestine question seriously, it being the core of the problem in the Middle East. He also said: "Without such a step there will be no peaceful solution in the region." He praised the Soviet attitude, affirming the Saudi point of view to the effect that "Israel, and not the Soviet Union, is the main enemy in the region."[3]

This is only a sample of what we will hear plenty of in the future. Even if Saudi Arabia is careful and retains her moderate phraseology, some of her allies among the Gulf states will be much more explicit and clear in their rejection of the current American position.

Here it should be noted that Kuwait has for some time realized the danger of alignment with the West, has sought to develop its political, military and economic relations with the USSR and the socialist countries and has concluded some significant deals with them. The UAE, too, is seriously considering the establishment of similar relations with the Eastern bloc; it is only a matter of time, which US policy may help to shorten. No doubt such developments will leave their impact on the Arab Republic of Yemen and remove some of the

---

[3] *Al-Safir*, 16 September 1981, p. 12. citing a UPI report from Taif.

obstacles that have been delaying the development of its relations with the USSR and the socialist countries. They will also lead to increasing efforts to unify the two Yemens.

It is hard at present to predict the developments that will take place during the coming period.

In this context it is to be noted how similar the West European attitude is to that of the oil states of the Arabian Peninsula as regards this subject. It is an attitude that fluctuates between intentions and the ability to implement such intentions. The main impediment to this ability is the American position. Both groups want to maintain their relations with the US, but they cannot endorse its policy on the Palestine issue, because they are aware of the dangers of this policy. There is only one difference between the two attitudes — the Arab character of the states of the peninsula, which increase the internal dangers and the possibility of popular uprisings. Although the question of Jerusalem is part of a whole, if the city's Judaization continues, this is in itself sufficient to remain a source of grave concern to any Muslim Arab leader, and more so to the Saudi leadership.

So how does the PLO act with regard to all this? There is no PLO leader, indeed there is not one Palestinian, who does not perceive all the dimensions and possibilities inherent in this complex picture. Throughout the sixty years of the history of our struggle, we Palestinians have learned, have been politicized, and have raised the level of our consciousness and awareness. Our bitter experience may have brought us to the brink of paranoia, but we have not lost the ability to classify attitudes and make the necessary distinctions between them to distinguish an "initiative" from a "plot," and a serious proposal aimed at reaching a political solution from one that merely seeks to abort the military solution. In other words, we have become mature in our political assessments.

From this long and bitter historical experience, and from our current revolutionary experience, the PLO has derived a methodology somewhat similar, although there are differences, to the Zionist methodology as regards action.

This methodology demands firm adherence to the final goal, which Yasser Arafat describes as "the dream of our revolutionaries," the establishment of a secular democratic Palestinian state. We believe that the process of history will make the achievement of this goal inevitable for, regardless of the obstacles, our goal is in line with the movement of history. This methodology also demands simultaneously, and along the path towards the same strategic goal, acceptance of the establishment of a Palestinian national state on any Palestinian soil that is liberated from Zionist occupation by the strength of the revolution or by international political pressures.

It is a methodology that could be desribed as speaking the same language in two dialects: the ideological dialect and the political dialect, the first to address the future and history; the second to address the present and the current scene. There is no contradiction between the two dialects; they are, in fact, complementary. If they seem contradictory at times, that is only the fault of these who cannot pronounce them correctly, and sometimes the fault of those who do not want to comprehend them.

11

Israel and the Gulf

by Elias Shoufani

What does Israel have to do with the Gulf?

On the surface, Israel should not have anything to do with the Gulf area. Ostensibly, Israel was established to solve the "Jewish Question" in a Jewish nation-state. That question was conceived of by the Zionist political leadership as a national problem necessitating a national solution. A Jewish state in Palestine, to be founded through a settler project, was seen to be the solution to that problem; hence, the *raison d'être* of the Jewish aspect of Israel from the Zionist Movement's point of view. The Gulf, however, is oil — a vital commodity for the industrialized West, with the United States dominating its production and distribution. Israel gets its oil needs from Egypt, in accordance with the "Egyptian-Israeli Treaty."

Following the fall of the Shah's regime in Iran, and the Soviet intervention in Afghanistan, the US has been actively engaged in building a military-political formation in the Middle East, on the basis of the "Carter Doctrine," a task continued by the Reagan administration. The declared aim of that formation is the creation of a "strategic consensus" among certain pro-Western states in the Middle East, under the auspices of the US. The parties to this multilateral alliance claim that their only purpose is to defend their national interests against Soviet "expansionist and subversive activities." The "Carter Doctrine" emphasized the "security" of the Gulf, and gave it high priority, which made Saudi Arabia the focal point of interest in this formation, and hence, of US strategy in the area. At the same time, Israel has shown a keen interest in integrating itself in that formation, and has expressed concern about every step Washington takes in that direction. It claims that this interest and concern are dictated by the needs of what it considers to be its "national security."[1]

Obviously, the formation of this "strategic consensus" guided the Carter administration's policy in the negotiations for a "peaceful settlement" in the area, leading to the "Israeli-Egyptian Treaty," and hence, Washington's obscure behaviour in the extensive process of those negotiations. As the Reagan administration embarked upon implementing the second stage of the "Carter Doctrine," two highly indicative steps in that direction were announced: (a) the declaration on "strategic cooperation" between Israel and the US; (b) the proposition of the Saudi initiative for peace in the Middle East, in the form of the Fahd plan. It is interesting to notice that while the Saudis remained silent about the upgrading of the relationship between Israel and the US to the level of a de jure alliance, Israel attacked the "AWACS" deal, did everything possible to block it, and rejected the Fahd plan out of hand. This paper will attempt to expose Israel's attitude towards the American-initiated "strategic consensus," whose main concern is the Gulf.

Israel's unique concept of "national security"

As a colonial-settler project, founded on the basis of an imbalanced partnership between the Zionist Movement and one imperialist centre or another, and still under construction,

---

[1] See, for instance, Shimon Peres, (ex-Prime Minister of Israel), "A strategy for peace in the Middle East," *Foreign Affairs* (Washington) Spring 1980, pp. 887-901.

Israel is a unique political entity. Hence, the unique concept of what its leadership considers its "national security" on both levels — current and strategic. On the strategic level, which is the main concern of this paper, the security of Israel, as conceived by its leadership, depends on the accomplishment of the "Zionist Project." That project has two sides: (a) Jewish, reflected in the Zionist idea of presenting a "national" solution to a "national" problem, i.e. the "Jewish Question," (b) imperialist, reflected in Israel's role in the area as a policeman. And, just as the two sides of the project are interdependent, so is their security dialectically connected.

Strategically, the security of the Jewish aspect of Israel depends on the ability of the Zionist settlers in Palestine (the *Yeshuv*) to Judaize that country — land, people, and market. The *Yeshuv* in Palestine, which started from zero in its relationship with the newly-acquired territory, cannot become secure, according to this view, until it develops new ties with the land, replacing those of the natives. In the case of Israel, such security remains conditional on two major factors: (a) a Jewish consensus around Zionism, warranting a steady flow of immigrants who move from their homelands and settle in Palestine; (b) nullification of the native Palestinian society, leading to the liquidation of its national movement. As of now, it is quite evident that Zionism has failed on both scores.

On the imperialist side, however, the security of Israel depends on achievement, delivery, and efficiency in performing its role. In this respect, and at least from the point of view of the senior partner in the Zionist Project, the role of Israel is to help subjugate the Arab mass movement to the dictates of that partner's interests in the area. At this stage, the US is practically the "mother country" of the as yet-incomplete Zionist Project, and its support for Israel is determined by the principle of "cost and benefit." The determining factor in Washington's relationship with Israel is whether the latter constitutes an asset to, or a burden on,

American strategy in the Middle East. In this respect, although it has been a contributive factor to the enhancement of American interests in the area, Israel still feels insecure about its position in that American strategy, and hence, highly sensitive to any possible competition in this regard. Furthermore, it has to take into consideration the aspirations and anxieties of the Jewish community in the US, and the effectiveness of the so-called Jewish lobby on the American political scene.

Today, as the *Yeshuv* is about to end a century of Zionist action, it is evident that its settler institutions have failed to achieve their declared goals of Judaizing Palestine and turning it into an accomplished and secure Jewish nation-state. Only about 20% of world Jewry is to be found in Israel. And while the original Zionist idea was to assemble the majority of the Jews in Israel, which would then spread its protective umbrella over the remaining minority in the diaspora, what happened was the exact opposite. Furthermore, the establishment of Israel resulted in the creation of two intertwined questions — the Palestinian and the Israeli. The abnormal conditions under which the Palestinians live today hinder the possibility of solving the "Israeli question" in the Arab East. As a result of this major issue, and others, immigration to Israel has dwindled to a tiny trickle, that can hardly make up for the emigration from it.

In view of this failure of the colonial institutions, the Zionist leadership turned to the Israeli military machine to fill the gap. The shortcomings of the settler institutions were to be made up for by the Israeli army, which appropriated their role, and developed disproportionately with them, giving Israel its salient feature of being more of a fortress than a normal nation-state. The reliance of Israel on its military machine to solve problems emanating from the weakness of its colonial institutions led by necessity to its militarization, and hence, to the dominance of the imperialist side over the Jewish in the whole Zionist project. It is worth noticing here, that it was the Israeli military machine which determined the result of the Arab-Jewish conflict in Palestine. The establishment of Israel was made possible not by the cumulative success of the Jewish Agency, the Jewish National Fund, the Histadrut, and other Zionist colonial institutions, but rather by the brutal terror and force of arms of the Zionist military machine. This fact made the Israeli army the backbone of the state, leading to a situation in Israel whereby the military machine outstripped any other institution in the rate of growth and development.

The rapid growth of Israel's military machine triggered two complementary processes, leading to further militarization of Israel: (a) It enticed imperialist centres to utilize that available machine in their military adventures in the Middle East, in policing the area and controlling political developments adverse to their interests; (b) it lured the Israeli leadership to capitalize on that machine, and seek to market it as an asset to interested parties. The combined result of these two processes had, by necessity, to reflect itself in the Israeli concept of national security. With a developed military machine, "supply and demand" became the rule that controlled the policy of Israel's leadership in employing that machine. On the other side, and as far as Western Powers and the implementation of their plans in the area were concerned, the principle of "cost and benefit" determined the extent of their utilization of that machine. Indeed, Western Powers' need for effective local military force in the Middle East, and the Israeli army's availability, coincided to produce a sort of de facto partnership, particularly with the US. The latter, which has been increasingly involved in imperialist activities in the area since the end of World War II, was rapidly becoming the "mother country" of Israel. Under these circumstances, it was only natural for Washington to make use of the Israeli war machine.

At the same time, Israel's ever-increasing need for economic aid from the US led to the risk of its turning into a burden on the American tax-payer, leading to a possible backsliding in Washington's commitment towards Israel under public pressure, with the devastating effect that would have on Israel's future and development. In this respect, the Zionist leadership had another major consideration to take into account — the role and position of the Jewish community in the US, and hence, the effectiveness of the Jewish lobby in Washington. Therefore, American Jewry exerted pressures, which were responded to by the Israeli leadership, for efforts to improve the image of Israel in the American public eye, through picturing it as an asset to American global strategy.[2] The only thing Israel has to offer is military and intelligence services. Therefore, it began actively seeking to integrate its army into the American global strategy, particularly in the Middle East. And once the Israeli leadership embarked upon this line of action, a "special relationship" with the US and an exclusive position in its strategy became the cornerstone in its concept of "national security."

Israel seeks an exclusive position in the military-political formation in the Middle East

Since the October War of 1973, and under the cover of a "peaceful settlement" of the Arab-Israeli conflict, the US has been actively engaged in creating a multilateral "strategic consensus," aiming to safeguard the "security of the Gulf." The fall of the Shah's regime in Iran, and the Soviet intervention in Afghanistan, accelerated American pursuit of this goal. For Israel, it was only natural to seize this opportunity and seek to integrate itself into the American strategy vis à vis the Middle East. Following the overthrow of the Shah, the American Secretary of Defense, Harold Brown, visited the

---

[2] Yoel Marcus, *Ha'aretz* (Tel Aviv), September 20, 1981.

Middle East, with a proposition to "establish a new strategic formation, including Saudi Arabia, Egypt, Jordan, and Israel, to secure stability in the area."[3] In Israel, Brown was faced with anxiety concerning the future relationship between Israel and Iran. His hosts expressed their worry about Israel's position in the new American strategy towards the Middle East, and emphasized the point that Israel was the "only stable ally" of the West in the area. Brown, however, stressed the significance of strengthening American ties with "moderate" Arab regimes.[4] The military correspondent of Ha'aretz, Zeev Schiff, described the Brown visit as successful, because it gave him, "a more solid basis for a better understanding of the military, political, and economic problems of Israel."[5]

The Israeli delegation at the talks with Brown presented a thesis that could be summarized as follows: (1) Israel is the most stable, pro-Western, state in the Middle East; (2) it stands in the front line against "Soviet expansionism" in the area; (3) at present, Israel is dependent on the US and the West, and will remain so in the foreseeable future; (4) it is possible to view the Israeli military infrastructure as part of the Western military posture; (5) to maintain this situation, Israel must remain strong; (6) the power of Israel depends, *inter alia,* on the continuation of the peace process.[6] With this thesis in mind, the Israeli leadership proceeded to conclude a settlement with the Sadat regime in Cairo leading to the "Israeli-Egyptian Treaty."

That treaty, which was made possible by Sadat's initiative to visit Jerusalem, put the Egyptian regime in the same trench with Israel — in an American-dominated military-political formation, and hence, in de facto alliance with it. Sadat's

---

3 *'Al Hamishmar* (Tel Aviv), February 14, 1979.
4 *Ma'ariv* (Tel Aviv), February 15, 1979.
5 Zeev Schiff, *Ha'aretz,* December 18, 1979.
6 *Ibid.*

initiative signalled his exit from "Arab solidarity" under the oil umbrella and Saudi leadership, and indicated his determination to hook up with the American military-industrial complex, the staunch ally of Israel in the metropolis. With Washington pushing to create a "strategic consensus" in the area, Sadat vying to hook up with it, and Israel seeking to integrate itself in it, the trilateral treaty between these parties became a must.

But the fact that Israel agreed to conclude a treaty with the Sadat regime did not mean at all that it agreed to consider that regime as an equal party, on a par with it, in the prospective military-political formation in the area. Hence, in the process of negotiations leading to the conclusion of the treaty, Israel made sure to cut Sadat down to size and to prevent the slightest possiblity of his becoming a competitor to it in Washington.[7] At the end of those tedious negotiations the Begin government, enjoying Washington's support, succeeded in isolating Egypt in the Middle East, while stripping the Sadat regime of any representative status in the Arab World, and depriving the Egyptian leader of any claim to pan-Arab national leadership through a contribution to the "solution of the Palestinian problem." Furthermore, Israel prevented the assignment of a major role to Egypt in the Gulf, and objected to the idea of the Egyptian army being strengthened and supplied with advanced military equipment. The Begin government strove to limit any future activity of the Egyptian army within the framework of American strategy of Africa, thus blocking the Sadat regime from engaging in any possible competition with the Israeli role in the Arab East.

With Egypt out of the way as a competitor to Israel in its "special relationship" with the US, and the Reagan administration moving with accelerated tempo to implement the second

---

[7] See also, Elias Shoufani, *Begin's Road to Cairo* (Institute for Palestine Studies, Beirut, 1979), pp. 126-143 (in Arabic).

stage of the "Carter Doctrine," Israel is watching carefully every step Washington takes in the direction of Saudi Arabia. The Begin government fought fiercely against the AWACS deal between Saudi Arabia and the US, and lost its battle in the Senate against the Reagan administration by a narrow margin. The Israeli objection to that deal emanated from political and not military grounds. Israel was not apprehensive of the AWACS in Saudi hands; rather, it was disturbed by Saudi Arabia with the AWACS in hand. The Israeli leadership saw in the American supply of advanced weapons to Saudi Arabia an indication of a possible shift in Washington's priorities in the area, upgrading Saudi Arabia's position and importance in the American strategy. This view led to the belief in Israel that Saudi Arabia is a strong potential competitor to it for the "special relationship" with Washington, and hence, for the position of primacy Israel occupies in American strategy in the Middle East. This, in itself, was considered by the leadership of Israel as a dangerous threat to its "national security." It is against this background that Israel objected to the American supply of advanced military equipment to Saudi Arabia, and rejected the "Fahd plan" for peace in the Middle East.

It is evident, however, that both the "Fahd plan" and the announcement of "strategic cooperation" between Israel and the US came within the framework of the Reagan adminis- tration's move to implement the second stage of the "Carter Doctrine." And while the "Fahd plan" offers total Arab political recognition of Israel as a pre-condition for its possible successful implementation, Israel refused to concede to Saudi Arabia the position it aspires to occupy in American strategy. Yet, the Reagan administration, despite Israeli objection to the AWACS deal, announced the agreement on "strategic coop- eration" with Israel, which constitutes a declaration by Wash- ington that Israel holds a key position in the American strategy vis à vis the Gulf, whose focal point of interest is Saudi Arabia itself. According to this agreement with Washington, Israel is supposed to become a sort of a staging area for active American military involvement in any conflict in the Middle East, while the Israeli army becomes a complementary local force to the "Rapid Deployment Forces." This means Israel's full integration, alongside other Arab states, in the American dominated "strategic consensus," whose prerequisite is recognition by those states of Israel – the only innovation in the "Fahd plan."

In addition to its concern about a potential Saudi threat to the position of primacy it aspires to occupy in the new American strategy, Israel considers the implementation of the "Fahd plan" as a danger to its very existence. The Palestinian dimension of the Saudi initiative is viewed by the Begin government as a stratagem leading to the destruction of Israel, and hence, unacceptable. Indeed, the "Fahd plan" calls for Israeli withdrawal from the territories occupied in 1967, including East Jerusalem, and the establishment of a Palestinian state in the West Bank and Gaza. From the Begin government's ideological stand-point, such a Palestinian state hinders the possibility of accomplishing the Zionist project, at least in its Jewish side. In fact, the present ruling establishment in Israel is not only unwilling to accept a settlement of the Palestinian problem on the basis of conditions similar to those included in the Saudi initiative, but is also incapable of doing so. As a colonial-settler project, which is still under construction, Israel is not yet ready for settlement of the so-called Arab-Israeli conflict, in accordance with any programme meeting the minimal conditions of the Arab side, particularly the Palestinians. The Israeli leadership is not prepared at this point to determine the geographical, human, and political boundaries of the Zionist project. No Israeli political party is about to backslide from its Zionist principles allowing for a settlement of the Palestinian dimension of the Arab-Israeli conflict.

As things stand today, and as became quite clear from

the results of the last general elections to the tenth Knesset in Israel, the *Yeshuv* is split into two almost equal parts. While the ruling coalition, the Likud and the Mafdal, upholds the Zionist principle of the integrity of *Eretz Yisrael* (the land of Israel), the opposition, led by the Labour Party, gives priority to the principle of the "unity of the people." The dilemma at present is that the Zionist project, at this stage of its development, cannot combine the two; it occupies more territory than it can settle and Judaize. And should the Israeli leadership opt for a peaceful settlement, it would have to decide one way or the other, but it cannot have them both. The balance of forces for or against either of the two options is equal, preventing a possibility of decision in this direction or that. As a result Israel today cannot take either decision – to withdraw from the territories occupied in 1967, or to annex them. At Camp David, the parties agreed on the Begin formula of the "autonomy plan," which proved to be unworkable. That formula is an easy way out of a political problem facing the parties to the Camp David agreements. It is noteworthy here that all Zionist parties in Israel claim a "historical" right to the territories occupied in 1967, and emphasize the vitality of those territories to the "security" of Israel, and the ability of the latter to defend them under any adverse circumstances. With such indoctrination in the *Yeshuv*, no leadership in Israel can easily take the decision to withdraw from the West Bank and Gaza.

However, Israel's failure to respond positively to the dictates of the "Carter Doctrine" hinders the possibility of its implementation, and thereby deprives Israel itself of all the benefits which would accrue to it from integrating its army into the "strategic consensus." At this juncture, because of the immediate needs of American strategy in the Middle East on the one hand, and Israel's anxiousness to secure a privileged position in that strategy on the other, the security of the two sides of the Zionist project seems incongruent. Facing the new

American strategy in the Middle East, the Israeli leadership, with its colonial-settler project still under construction, found itself in a perplexing dilemma. It could neither stand as a stumbling block in the way of the American plan, nor could it run the risk of facilitating the realization of that plan through concessions, which would have severe repercussions inside Israel: hence Israel's wavering in the negotiations which led to the treaty with Egypt. Now, as Washington moves to implement the second stage of the plan, Israel, under the leadership of Begin, faces Saudi Arabia the way it did the Sadat regime before. It wants to secure a position of primacy vis à vis Saudi Arabia in the American strategy, enjoying all the ensuing advantages, without making any "concessions" in the Palestinian dimension of the problem in the Middle East.

In this light, the Begin government considers the declaration by the Reagan administration on "strategic cooperation" with Israel a great step forward in the direction of achieving this interim goal of the Zionist project, primary in US strategy, since it believes no concessions were required of it.

A dream come true

In the middle of September 1981, following a successful visit to Washington, which was his tenth since he assumed power in Israel (1977), and during which he reached the agreement on "strategic cooperation" with the Reagan administration, Begin boasted that he had realized what his predecessor, Ben Gurion, dreamed of during his long stay at the head of the government in Israel.[8] By invoking the name of Ben-Gurion, Begin wanted to recruit the prestige of that leader in support of a political step that the Labour opposition did not fully approve of. Some individuals in the Israeli political and military élite expressed their reservations about the neces-

---

[8] Dan Margalit, *Ha'aretz*, September 18, 1981.

sity to fix in a written document the nature of relationship between Israel and the US.[9] Others, however, questioned the wisdom of the announcement of a "strategic cooperation" between the "tiny Jewish state" and a Great Power against the background of the prevailing ties which bind the two. In response to a question, the opposition leader, Shimon Peres, gave the following answer: "In practice, a strategic cooperation, which has hitherto been conducted discreetly, exists between Israel and the US. We welcome the possibility of solidifying this cooperation. But who needs the noisy talk of the Prime Minister, or that of the Minister of Defence in particular, concerning a global strategic alliance, starting from Afghanistan and ending in the USSR."[10] Peres admonished the Begin government, and preached caution in playing with fire, adding that Israel should pay more attention to what happens on the banks of the Jordan River than to what takes place in the Atlantic Ocean.

Shortly before his death, Moshe Dayan wrote in his weekly column "From September to April" a very revealing article about the "strategic cooperation." In that article, Dayan was scathingly critical of Begin's government, in which he served as Minister of Foreign Affairs until a few months earlier. There follow some sections of the article:[11]

> On the whole, the negotiations on strategic cooperation seen extremely vague to me, mainly because we initiated them. The declared aim of this strategy is to curb Soviet expansionism in the Middle East. Israel – government and opposition – has seized every opportunity to announce that it sees in the US a faithful ally, and that it will be ready, at any time, to put its facilities at the disposal of the US, if and when the latter requests that...
>
> There is another aspect on which there are no differences in opinion – Israel wants very much to gain a slice of American

---

9   See, for instance, Moshe Dayan, *Yedi'ot Aharonot* September 18, 1981.
10   Interview with Shimon Peres, *Ma'ariv,* September 25, 1981.
11   Moshe Dayan, *Yedi'ot Aharonot,* September 18, 1981.

military products, as well as perform the required management, maintenance, and repair work for the American equipment. This matter is more economic than political; May God bless him who obtains American consent to such a matter... However, the emphasis, the headlines, and some plans of the strategic cooperation glide far beyond this. Joint ground, air, and sea exercises are definitely intended to secure joint military action. Where would such military action take place? In defence of Israel or of Saudi Arabia? Are we a party to an alliance with the Americans to defend the Persian Gulf? Indeed, Mr Begin announces that we and the US are allies, but where is the alliance? Is it the one within whose framework the Americans sell "AWACS" to the Saudis and plan wide-ranging military cooperation with them?

This barrage of polemics by Dayan speaks for itself. After all, the man was an outstanding figure in the Israeli ruling establishment, and a major member of the Israeli team at the trilateral negotiations at Camp David, which led to the Israeli-Egyptian Treaty. Dayan, as a disciple of Ben-Gurion, in spite of all his enthusiasm to solidify Israel's relationship with the US, felt that the Begin government had gone too far in tipping the balance in favour of the imperialist side of the Zionist project, at the expense of the Jewish side. Even Dayan, who personified the Zionist settler, an architect of Israeli statehood and its backbone, the military machine, exclaimed: "The weighty, serious, and central question in the whole matter is — what is Israel? "[12]

However, Dayan's objection notwithstanding, the Begin Government saw in the agreement with the Reagan administration a dream come true. In the Knesset session, where the agreement was discussed and voted upon, winning a majority of 57 against 53, Ariel Sharon described it as follows: "It is a turning point in Israel's position on the globe, in its political and military relations for the future, and in its ability to defend its existence and security."[13] Sharon went on to say:

[12] *Ibid.*
[13] "Voice of Israel," December 2, 1981, at 19:30 hrs.

> Instead of a network of relationships, which was based on charity, embarrassing at times, we will have a network of strategic cooperation, between two equal parties, who mutually contribute to their national security.[14]

And he added:

> I wish to say to the people and their representatives that we have indeed realized a great substantive change in our situation on the map of the world, in our position among the free nations, and in our future political and military relations. This will enable us to conclude agreements for peace and security in the area, to defend our existence, the integrity of the Land of Israel, and its safety.[15]

A review of its arguments in support of the agreement shows that the Begin government believes that "strategic cooperation" with the US brings the whole Zionist project to a new era. In general, the proponents of the agreement think that it will solidify Israel's security and guarantee firm American political backing, as well as bring abundant economic benefits, which will enable Israel to accomplish the next stage of the Zionist project. From the bulk of material on the subject in the Israeli press, it is possible to summarize the argument in favour of the agreement as follows:

1. On the international level, it will place the US squarely behind Israel. Such American backing will strengthen Israel's position in world politics, decrease its isolation among nations, and pave the way for renewal of diplomatic relations with those states which severed them after the war of June 1967.

2. In the United States, it will improve Israel's image in the eyes of the American public, which will realize that Israel is a strategic asset to the US, and not a troublesome burden. Such a shift in the American public's view will benefit the Jewish community there, and hence, increase the effectiveness of the Zionist lobby in Washington.

3. In the Middle East, the agreement will emphasize the

---

14 *Ibid.*
15 *Ibid.*

exclusivity of Israel's relationship with the US, and the primacy of the position it occupies in American strategy in the area, hindering any local Middle Eastern competition for this privileged position. Furthermore, it is believed that the unwavering American stand in this regard will convince more Arab states to follow in the footsteps of the Sadat regime and recognize Israel. This, by necessity, will improve Israel's bargaining power vis à vis the Palestinian dimension of the Middle East conflict, with the ultimate aim of denying the Palestinian people the right of self-determination.

4. Internally, "strategic cooperation" with the US is believed by the Begin government to build up an Israeli consensus around the Likud line of Zionist action. This revisionist current of Zionism had been outside the circle of decision-making since the establishment of Israel. In 1977 the Likud came to power, and since that so-called "upheaval" it has been striving to establish its legitimacy in Israeli politics and policy making. The conclusion of the agreement with the US is seen as contributing to the achievement of this end.

5. Economically, the agreement is expected to bring abundant financial returns to the slackening Israeli economy. This aspect of the agreement is given more publicity by Washington than by Israel, which prefers to emphasize the strategic dimension of it. According to Sharon, "every activity necessitates acquisitions in Israel."[16] He mentioned medicinal products, food-stuffs, and ammunition for emergency depots. Furthermore, all works of maintenance, repair, and storage will be paid for by the US.

6. Militarily, the agreement is expected to:

(a) augment the military power of Israel.

(b) put abundant military equipment and supplies at the disposal of the Israeli army.

---

[16] *Ha'aretz*, September 15, 1981.

(c) spare Israel the need for an air-lift in time of war.

(d) save Israel much military expense.

(e) make military aid to Israel, at least partially, an integral part of the US federal budget.

(f) give Israel access to advanced American technology.

(g) help Israel develop its military industry.

(h) raise the level of preparedness in the Israeli army, through joint air, ground, and sea exercises with the American Rapid Deployment Force.

In opposition to the Begin government, and to the agreement, the argument in limited Israeli circles could be briefly summarized as follows:

1. On the international level, some believe that "strategic cooperation" with the US will make Israel appear as an American satellite, and hence, become a target of the Soviet Union's animosity.

2. On the Middle East level, contrary to the prevalent notion in the ruling establishment, some liberal individuals think that an alliance with the US will increase animosity to Israel among the Arab peoples, thus obstructing the way to a true settlement of the conflict in the area.

3. As far as Israel itself is concerned, some believe that the agreement was totally superfluous, in view of the existing relationship between the Jewish state and the US. Others, however, think that it would limit the margin of Israel's freedom of independent action. Yet others doubt the validity of the Begin government's optimistic evaluation of the benefits accruing from "strategic cooperation."

All in all there is, and seemingly will continue to be, much talk about the agreement in Israel, but there is no straightforward rejection of it. Despite relatively widespread criticism of Begin's policy, the Knesset approved the agreement with a comfortable majority (57: 53).

It remains to be seen how the two sides will go about putting their strategic cooperation into effect. To a large degree, the execution of this agreement depends on the American side which, to a certain extent, is influenced by what the Arab states might, or might not, do.

A policeman and a spy

"We are in no hurry to become a policeman and a spy of the US in the Middle East."[17] In those words, Yitzhak Rabin, ex-prime minister of Israel, summed up his evaluation of Israel's role in the "strategic cooperation" with the US, as it was initiated and concluded by the Begin government. Rabin, who served as Chief of Staff during the June War of 1967, and later as Israel's ambassador to Washington, views the Reagan administration's foreign policy, particularly in the ME, as centering around two points:

(a) "the will to project a tough stand against the Soviet Union,"

(b) the tendency towards a "general reliance on Saudi Arabia, militarily, politically, and economically."[18] In this policy, Rabin detects "serious dangers" to Israel. According to him "the main danger to Israel emanates from that American policy, which focuses on Saudi Arabia as the key country in the Middle East. Should Saudi Arabia continue to be the cornerstone of this policy, the value of the Camp David Agreements in the network of relations will fizzle out."[19]

Israel's apprehension of Saudi competition, based on the above-mentioned evaluation of the Reagan administration's policy, led the Begin government to press for the conclusion of the agreement on "strategic cooperation" with the US. In the negotiations which preceded it, the Israeli side stressed the significance of Israel's contribution to American strategy in the area, while waging a battle against the AWACS deal with

---

[17] Interview with Shimon Peres, *Ma'ariv*, September 25, 1981.
[18] Yitzhak Rabin, *Yedi'ot Aharonot*, September 28, 1981.
[19] *Ibid.*

Saudi Arabia. When the Fahd plan was introduced, the Israeli leadership rejected it out of hand. In its manoeuvrings, Israel was trying to barter with Washington *quid pro quo* — the integration of the Israeli army into an anti-Soviet alliance, against a shift in American attitude towards Saudi Arabia. The higher Begin's rhetoric went in exalting Israel as a democracy, a part and parcel of the "free world," and the only reliable ally of the West in the Middle East, the more harshly he attacked Saudi Arabia as a medieval, feudal, and backward state, that does not, and could not, contribute much to the peace process in the area.

Following the conclusion of the agreement the opposition in Israel accused the Begin government of softening its position vis à vis the AWACS deal, in order to obtain American approval of "strategic cooperation," which was rashly suggested by the Israeli side in the negotiations. Ariel Sharon, the newly appointed Minister of Defence, and hence a leading member of the Israeli team of negotiators, retorted to those accusations by saying:

> In the talks with the President and his Cabinet, as well as in meetings in the Congress, the issue was forcefully raised. To say that there was no fight is an unprecedented distortion and perversion.[20] He added: In the discussion, not only the question of the reconnaissance planes was raised, but also the issue of supplying Saudi Arabia with modern and sophisticated weapons... There was not, even for a minute, any possibility that Israel would agree to accept something in return for its approval of Saudi Arabia being supplied with weapons.[21]

However, Sharon was more on the offensive in his defence of the other motive for concluding the agreement. According to him "the policy of the American President is to integrate Israel, as an ally, in a formation which is intended to deter the

20 *Ha'aretz*, September 15, 1981.
21 *Ibid.*

Soviet Union from threatening the Middle East and Africa."[22] He went on to say: "The purpose is to be able to contribute more to steadfastness against Soviet expansionist policy and aggressive strategy, which constitute the most serious danger that Israel faces."[23] Sharon explained his conception of the "strategic cooperation" as follows: "What is needed is a strategic formation, able to deter the Russians from war, and not one that pretends to fight in order to defend a country that has already fallen."[24]

After the agreement was signed, during a Knesset debate on the issue, where the Begin government faced a vote of no-confidence, Sharon said:

> The agreement constitutes the firm beginning of a process of broad strategic cooperation between two partners. This cooperation is vital to the national security needs of the two partners... During the last 25 years, Israel has been fighting against Soviet weapons, Soviet political support, and Soviet intervention, which sustained Arab confrontation with Israel. Don't we take into account Soviet military intervention, or that of forces under their control, on the side of these [Arab] states, as they did in past wars? Didn't we hold back our advance in the October War, and thus save the Egyptian army from total destruction, because the Soviets massed forces in countries which are subject to their hegemony, outside this area? Whom are you [the opposition] trying to mislead? [25]

With such an attitude towards the Soviet Union, it was only natural for the Begin government to believe the tension between the two super-powers to be in Israel's interest. Hence, when the Reagan administration assumed office in Washington, with its declared activist foreign policy against the Soviet Union, the Begin government expected an upgrading in Israel's position within the framework of American global strategy.[26]

---

22 *Ibid.*
23 *Ibid.*
24 *Ibid.*
25 *Ma'ariv*, December 3, 1981.
26 Zeev Schiff, *Ha'aretz*, September 28, 1981.

However, as the Reagan administration began to implement the second stage of the "Carter Doctrine," the Israeli leadership sensed a shift in Washington's priorities, leaning towards Saudi Arabia.[27] In the wake of the Saudi initiative, the Begin government was apprehensive of an imposed settlement in the Middle East, entailing Israeli withdrawal from the West Bank and Gaza. Furthermore, an American military presence in the area, as well as supplying Arab armies with advanced military equipment, was seen in Israel as diminishing its role in the "strategic consensus," which Washington was trying to create in the Middle East. The Begin government was intent on resisting such an eventuality.

In the talks with the Reagan administration, the Israeli team aimed at achieving two central goals: (a) downgrading the Arab-Israeli conflict, while upgrading the Soviet threat to the stability of the area; (b) securing a position of primacy in American strategy, while warding off any Arab competition with Israel over its special relationship with the USA.[28] According to the military correspondent of Ha'aretz, Zeev Schiff, the Israeli team proferred three propositions: (a) to establish emergency depots and other military facilities in Israel; (b) to strengthen technological ability of the Israeli intelligence services, which the US could benefit from; (c) to examine the possibility of the Israeli air force giving air cover to the American Rapid Deployment Forces as they move to their destination.[29] These suggestions invoked Rabin's cynical comment about Israel being "a policeman and a spy of the US in the Middle East."

The conclusion of the agreement on "strategic cooperation" with the US was seen by the Begin government as achieving the two goals it aimed at in the talks with the

---

27 *Ibid.*
28 *Ibid.*
29 *Ha'aretz*, October 2, 1981.

Reagan administration; hence it was considered a turning point in the history of the Zionist project. According to an ex-Minister of Justice in Israel, Gideon Hausner:

> Begin might have achieved what Ben-Gurion strove for: to found the security of Israel on an alliance with a Western country... Until now, the US has abstained from doing so, for fear of reactions in the Arab World. Now it has reached the conclusion that those Arab states that do not want peace should not be reckoned with, and that the others will reconcile themselves to the fact.[30]

By integrating its military machine in the American-dominated "strategic consensus" in the Middle East, the Begin government believes that it could safeguard Israel's "national security." Though "strategic cooperation," the special relationship with the US, which is the cornerstone of Israel's "national security," will be maintained. This in turn will guarantee abundant economic returns which will help Israel accomplish its settler project. Furthermore, the Israeli leadership expects its partners in the alliance, should it come into being, to refrain from demanding a solution to the Palestine problem, based on the idea of a Palestinian state west of Jordan River.

However, the Begin government's exuberance about its achievement notwithstanding, the execution of the agreement with the US remains conditional on the ability of the Arab parties concerned to go along with a "strategic consensus" of the kind that the Israeli leadership strives for. As things stand now (the end of 1981), the positions of the different parties to the multilateral "strategic consensus" seem to be irreconcilable. The focal point of interest in the American strategy is Saudi Arabia, which, to go along with that strategy, came out with an "initiative" for peace in the Middle East. The core of the Fahd plan is the formula: Arab recognition of Israel in return for its evacuation of the territories occupied in 1967, allowing for the establishment of a Palestinian state. Mean-

---

[30] *Yedi'ot Aharonot,* September 13, 1981.

while, the Fahd plan was neither approved by the Arabs, nor accepted by Israel. Under the present conditions in the Middle East, it remains to be seen how viable is the American plan for a "strategic consensus" in the area, and hence, how valid is Begin's optimism. In any case, the American strategy for the security of the Gulf, as it stands now, discloses the inherent contradiction in the Israeli concept of "national security" as it relates to the two facets of the yet incomplete Zionist project. At one and the same time, the "security of the Gulf" is the key to the solution of this contradiction. This depends on what the Arab states, particularly in the Gulf area, may, or may not, do.

12

Palestine and the Gulf:
An Eastern Arab Perspective

by Camille Mansour

The link between Palestine and the Gulf is not a Palestinian or Arab invention. As early as 1952, less than four years after the state of Israel was established, in hearings before the House of Representatives Committee on Foreign Affairs, several US administration spokesmen demonstrated a far-sighted lucidity, which cannot but astonish us today. These testimonies, which fell within the framework of legislative discussions concerning the extension of the Mutual Security Act (i.e. the US military aid programme), are an eloquent illustration of the objective link between Palestine and the security of the Middle East, including oil, and they make an apposite introduction to our subject here.[1]

The US officials developed the theme of the potential danger posed by Palestinian refugees, while discussing the need to absorb these refugees in the host countries. In this regard, Secretary of State Dean Acheson declared: "If that is done [resettlement of the refugees], it will have a very great

---

[1] US House of Representatives, Eighty-Second Congress, Committee on Foreign Affairs, *Hearings on Mutual Security Act Extension* (Washington: United States Government Printing Office, 1952).

stabilizing effect, because these people, there are about 850,000, are homeless and are in circumstances that are not good for morale, and present a great danger to that area."[2]

The same idea was taken a little futher by C. Tyler Wood, Associate Deputy Director for Mutual Security, who stated that these people are "a real and very serious threat to the stability of the area."[3] Jonathan B. Bingham, Acting Administrator, Technical Cooperation Administration, went as far as to say that the Arab refugees "constitute a potentially explosive political force."[4]

But to what sort of danger did these declarations refer? Clearly it was not yet a matter of any Palestinian presence in the Gulf, but the smell of oil was already there. Take for example Arthur Z. Gardiner, Economic Operations Advisor, Department of State, who said bluntly: "The Russians are fishing in these troubled waters, and the presence of the refugees is a threat to many of our important installations, both commercial installations, oil pipeline and other important things."[5] The same official said a little later, speaking in particular to the representative from Ohio:

> I was there last autumn. I saw the Tapline. The Tapline, Mr Vorys, is 40,000 tons of oil a day going to Europe. All this title 1 business[6] depends in large measure on the oil coming through that pipeline. Within a stone's throw of that pipeline there are refugee camps of 15,000 people. If those people chose to take certain actions you might not have the Tapline. Those people could damage our interest if we do not do something for them...[7]

[2] *Ibid.*, p. 164.
[3] *Ibid.*, p. 762.
[4] *Ibid.*, p. 963.
[5] *Ibid.*, p. 773.
[6] Reference to the US programme to strengthen Western European security under NATO, a programme which cost almost 4 billion dollars for the year 1952-53.
[7] *Ibid.*, p. 780.

The Palestinians were dangerous not only because of their potential for direct action, but also because their cause itself inspired anti-Western feeling. Their presence alone "serves as a constant reminder to the Arab world of what is considered anti-Arab intervention of the West in the Palestine case. The refugee is therefore a symbol about whom all dissidents can rally."[8]

This falls squarely into the Eastern Arab perspective, (the Mashriq perspective, as we shall call it in this paper) even though it is expressed in this instance by a US official. But let us go on and see what the same official has to say concerning the specific case of Syria:

> Syria is another key to the solution of the Palestine refugee problem... It is in Syria, however, that we face the most difficult political problems. First of all, there has been extreme instability in Syria's Government − 4 coups d'état in 4 years. This has not provided a favourable atmosphere for the Agency's [UNRWA] negotiations. In an unstable situation public opinion has been at the mercy of ultra-nationalistic and xenophobic agitators. Large numbers of Syrians are convinced that the implementation of the 3-year [resettlement] program in their country would constitute an admission of Israel's defeat of the Arabs.[9]

There is no need to agree with the terms used (xenophobic agitators) to grasp the extremely thought-provoking nature of the US administration's observation in 1952. We do not wish to suggest, however, that no change has taken place under the sun in the last 30 years, although developments in the eighties have, as we shall see, made the "potential Palestinian danger" even more acute: Israel's continued intransigence, the increasingly central position of the Middle East in the global confrontation, growing disparities between indicators of strength and indicators of weakness in the Arab world..., not to mention the failure to integrate the refugees into the host

---

[8] *Ibid.*, p. 769.
[9] *Ibid.*, p. 771.

countries and their transformation into an actual "explosive political force"[10] under the leadership of the PLO.

The purpose of this paper is to study the Mashriq perception of the link between the Palestinian cause and the Gulf. Although Palestine is an integral part of the Mashriq, the Palestinian movement will not be studied as such. In order to avoid confusion and in order to deal with the question objectively and directly, we shall consider two levels. The first concerns the common perception, or the popular perception. We shall try to see how the Gulf is integrated into Arab nationalism and the image of the struggle against Israel. Three stages between the fifties and the present day will then be distinguished. Before passing to the second level, we shall explore whether the popular perception has any influence on the policy of Mashriq regimes and whether it has an operative character. That will lead us to pose the problem of the legitimacy of power in the Mashriq in particular and the Arab world in general. After that transition, the second level, concerned with regimes, will be dealt with. We shall see how official policies in the Mashriq and the Gulf have become linked and how this mutual influence operates. Here we shall devote special attention to the Syrian case. Finally in our conclusion we will present candidly the problems and dilemmas facing the Mashriq and the Gulf.

The popular perception

The popular perception, as we conceive of it here, is the Mashriq's "vision of the world," a collection of truths, which it is not necessary to prove to be convinced of, and which, without being cut off from reality, forms a particular reading of it. As far as our subject is concerned, the common Mashriq perception can be summarised by the following ideas:

---

[10] To use the expression employed by Bingham above.

1. Imperialism covets the Arab world and seeks to dominate it by any means: direct control, carve-ups and divisions, installation of puppet regimes, economic exploitation...

2. Zionism is an imperialist movement in its sharpest form, one that includes conquest, settlement and expulsion. The West is responsible for the creation of the state of Israel and the violation of Palestinian rights. Israel constitutes not only a forward post for the West, but is also part of the West's cultural universe.

3. The Arab world constitutes a single nation of which Palestine forms a part.

4. The West exploits the oil which should belong to the Arabs.

5. The liberation of Palestine, the unification of the Arab world, the defeat of imperialism in the Arab world, the control of oil wealth and its utilisation in all Arab regions without discrimination and the overthrow of pro-imperialist regimes are articles of faith.

6. The link between the Palestinian question and the Gulf is perceived quite naturally on two levels. The enemy is the same: Israel and the West are two faces of the same imperialism. The cause is the same: Palestine and the Gulf region are Arab lands, sharing the same Arab character. From the first level it follows that if the enemy gets stronger in one area he gets stronger in the other. From the second level, we may deduce that gains in the struggle in Palestine contribute towards the struggle in the Gulf and vice versa.

7. The Arab world belongs neither to the East nor to the West. It rejects all military bases, alliances and axes which limit its sovereignty or its neutrality.

The themes formulated here in their simplest form as "self-evident" constitute the (sometimes distorting) prism through which reality is perceived. Local and international events are cited to corroborate what is already perceived as obvious. Facts which appear to contradict the received ideas are rejected as insignificant or as pure camouflage. Thus, to take a very recent example, the news concerning strategic cooperation between the United States and Israel (September 1981) only serves to confirm what the Mashriq Arabs have "already known" for several decades, while the criticisms articulated in the US and in Israel concerning the meaning and implications of such a strategic agreement are spontaneously minimized or ignored.

It would be possible to discuss at length how much the themes delineated above conform with reality. It would be easy for outside observers to put forward counter-arguments which might be more convincing and more objective, but which might also be less convincing and less objective. Some would be quick to invoke the argument of Zionism as the solution to the Jewish question, to point to the intrinsic and fundamental nature of inter-Arab divisions, to the non-existence of a single Arab nation, to the community of Arab-Western interests against the Soviet danger... Others would go even so far as to say that the ideas set forth above are far from being shared by all Arabs. But it is nevertheless true that beneath any differences, these ideas constitute a basic perception around which clusters a spontaneous consensus in the Mashriq. They determine the scale of values and norms, the ideal of justice outside which justice itself would appear to be meaningless. Considered from the cultural angle, these ideas (along with other factors, especially history, tradition, language) bolster the feeling of common identity. Seen from the political angle, they form the bedrock of Arab nationalism in the Mashriq, "the beating heart of Arabism." From this viewpoint, the mission of the Mashriq, its "mission civilisatrice" in the Arab world, if we may venture to say so, has been to spread these values and to raise consciousness of them more and more, so as to convert and mobilize the Arabs of the periphery. Even the emigration of Mashriq cadres to the

Gulf can be regarded in this perspective.

It is therefore the Mashriq which establishes the scale of values, which determines what is good and bad and which formulates the criteria of "orthodoxy". Proof is not required; the burden of proof falls on the periphery. It is up to the periphery to adopt the norms of the centre and to prove that its behaviour conforms with orthodoxy. It is thus not accidental that the parties with a pan-Arab mission (Ba'th, Arab Nationalist Movement) were born in the Mashriq and from there have tried to win over the periphery. Nasserism itself, the charismatic pan-Arabism of Egyptian origin, tried the experiment of unity with Syria in 1958 and went astray in the Sinai in May 1967 purely in response to the wishes or criticisms of the Mashriq *Weltanschauung.*[11]

However, one should not assume that the popular Mashriq perception remains glued to a simplistic analysis of the nature of the enemy or to a summary determination of priorities and of the best means whereby to advance the cause. Yet arising out of the common perception, there is a process of increasing sophistication and differentiation through which the complexity of reality and the limits on the means available seem to be better perceived if not better understood. It is unnecessary to stress the role played by emerging elites in this process. Three stages may be discerned here.

The first stage preceded the 1967 war. In that period of political decolonization, popular mobilization seemed to be a panacea: it would vanquish imperialism, overthrow the monarchies, nationalize oil[12] and impose the unity of the Arab nation. Israel, forming part of imperialism by definition, did not seem to require a specific approach in the implementation

---

[11] Centre and periphery here refer only to the creation of values, not to strategic-political weight. This is especially true in the case of Egypt.

[12] See for example, David Hirst, *Oil and Public Opinion in the Middle East* (London: Faber and Faber, 1966).

of the means of struggle. Whence the famous slogan: Arab unity is the path to the liberation of Palestine.

The second stage is obviously the one which accompanied the deep "crise de conscience" undergone by the Arab world following the 1967 defeat. We will not rehash here the various currents of opinion which contributed to the wave of Arab self-criticism: from revolutionary Marxism to militant Islam passing by technological positivism.[13] But we will note what is of concern to our argument, namely that the struggle against Israel was no longer perceived as being mediated by the long wait for Arab unity, nor by popular mobilization on the strictly psychological level. Street demonstrations can at best overthrow regimes or even chase out a decadent French or British colonialism, but they are obviously incapable of stopping a military invasion mounted by tanks and fighter aircraft. The struggle against Israel, which after the occupation of new territories could no longer be postponed indefinitely, demanded separate attention. Some put their hopes in armed popular struggle, others in adequate preparation for classic warfare. Conversely, the field of struggle against imperialism shrank. It was not so much imperialism itself that was now opposed, but rather imperialism insofar as it propped up Israel. The order of the day in this regard became: use oil as a weapon in the fight against Israel. The link between Palestine and the Gulf became an immediate necessity. However, at the same time, the conservative regimes gained a reprieve since the reputedly radical regimes were themselves the object of popular disenchantment.

The third stage, which began with the 1973 war, was the theatre of a confused succession of illusions and disillusion-

[13] This was done quite recently by Fouad Ajami in his very suggestive study, *The Arab Predicament: Arab Political Thought and Practice Since 1967* (Cambridge: Cambridge University Press, 1981). See also Walid W. Kazziha, *Palestine in the Arab Dilemma* (London: Croom Helm, 1979), Chapter I.

ments. After several months of ambitious hopes which were swiftly disappointed, the ceiling of achievements that seemed possible of attainment in the medium term fell markedly. Faced with the inextricably knotted divisions between the regimes, the theme of "Arab solidarity" gained in legitimacy what the idea of pan-Arab unity had lost in terms of mobilizing dynamism. The idea of a negotiated settlement of the Arab-Israeli conflict now claimed to command as much respectability as that of the liberation of Palestine. The conservative Gulf regimes, however weakened from inside, not only won a reprieve in the Mashriq perception, but with their petro-dollars nurtured the ambition of taking part in the definition of the Mashriq scale of values, which in practical terms meant lowering it. The theme of oil as a weapon in the fight against Israel had to compete with the rival theme of newly-acquired Arab bargaining power. This bargaining power, born in the Gulf, claimed the ability to win for the Mashriq concessions on the Palestine question from the West and hence Israel, without the need for a shot to be fired or a new oil embargo imposed. As for the Mashriq regimes themselves, their image in the popular perception did not improve; on the contrary, a deep split appeared between civil society and the military- political regime.

Does this loss of illusions, the chagrin provoked by the rise of the "Saudi era"[14] (which is sometimes accompanied by a resigned willingness to snap up the manna which comes not from heaven but from the sub-soil)[15] signify a dislocation of the basic perception as it was summarized in the seven ideas

---

[14] Refer for example to the work of Sadiq Jalal al-'Azm, *Carter's Policy and the Theoreticians of the Saudi Era* (Beirut: Al-Tali'a Publishing House, 1977), (in Arabic).

[15] Reference here is to the numerous gifts offered by the Gulf countries to social (and other) enterprises in the Mashriq.

detailed above? We do not think so.[16] We believe that the primary spontaneous perception which forms the feeling of Arab identity, the bedrock of Arab nationalism, still remains valid. This primary perception is perhaps more unrealistic than ever. It may in some measure be lying dormant under a confused heap of contradictory and disconcerting images, but it is there, ready to explode at any moment and in the most unexpected guises, including that of religion. If we are so sure that this perception still enjoys Mashriq consensus, it is because it is otherwise impossible to understand the frustrations, noted by all observers in the Mashriq, which are in fact caused by the paradoxes of external reality: the power and precariousness of Mashriq and Gulf regimes, the military strength and political weakness of the state of Israel. Do not the popular Mashriq reactions occasioned by the assassination of Sadat (6 October 1981) bear witness to the force of these frustrations and at the same time to the force of the basic perception?

The Operative Character of the Common Perception

It would clearly be possible to cast doubt on, or at least to minimize, the bearing of this basic perception on the practical policies of the Mashriq regimes. It would not be hard to list the factors which act against the impact of pan-Arab nationalism on these governments:

• The "rational pragmatic" interest of states within their present frontiers may in the short or medium term run counter to the interest of a hypothetical Arab nation.

• States sometimes have to compromise with external reality and to lay aside their values because respecting them would entail unbearable sacrifices.

---

[16] Unlike Fouad Ajami, "The End of Pan-Arabism," *Foreign Affairs* (Washington) Winter 1978/79, LVII, 2.

• The existing regimes care more about survival and staying in power than about the achievement of pan-Arab aspirations or respecting their people's values.

• The social classes which form the mainstay of the existing powers have an interest in maintaining the status quo, whereas pan-Arab nationalism implies a profound radicalization and the overthrow of the social structure.

• The regimes have gained such a qualitative and quantitative mastery of the media that they are now able to *manipulate* popular perceptions. To take a non-Mashriq example, we could refer to the anti-Palestinian campaigns in Egypt at the time of the Sinai agreement in September 1975 and Sadat's visit to Israel in November 1977.

• The regimes can exploit the weariness of their people with the costly perpetuation of the Arab-Israeli conflict, or even use the consolation provided by petrodollars and the prospect of economic well-being, or even raise high the banner of specific mobilizing themes (religion, ethnic or regional particularisms...).

Many of these criticisms are undoubtedly well-founded. However, it has never been our intention to argue that the basic perception should enjoy the status of sole determining factor in the political decision-making process. Studying the relative importance of perceptions in the decision-making process is not new. It has already been done in the case of Israel[17] , and more recently in the case of Syria[18] . Nevertheless, we may take note of the special problems concerning the

[17] Michael Brecher, *The Foreign Policy System of Israel: Setting, Images, Process* (New Haven: Yale University Press, 1972); and more recently, from the same author, with Benjamin Geist, *Decisions in Crisis: Israel, 1967 and 1973* (Berkeley: University of California Press, 1980).

[18] Adeed I. Dawisha, *Syria and the Lebanese Crisis* (New York: Saint Martin's Press, 1980). Dawisha, who applies Brecher's model in his work, seems to assign undue importance to the influence of values on political decisions.

Mashriq (and the Arab world).[19]

In the unstable Arab world, and especially in the turbulent Mashriq, the primary problem for each political regime is its *legitimacy,* both internal and external[20] . From the *internal* point of view, a regime's legitimacy can be brought into question by two groups of reasons. Firstly, we may cite slurs on democratic ideals; not that these ideals are clearly defined, or that a model of democracy, a Western-style model for instance, is felt to be necessary. All that is meant here is the kind of violations perceived spontaneously as such: repression, non-respect for individual freedoms, a growing margin of socio-economic inequality. The second group of reasons whereby the legitimacy of a regime can be brought into question in the internal sphere concerns the failure to appreciate and act according to the values of Arab nationalism.

From the *external* point of view, the regime's legitimacy is that accorded to or withdrawn from it by Arab public opinion in other countries and by its Arab neighbours. This kind of legitimacy is obviously linked more to respect for the values of Arab nationalism than to conformity with the rules of democracy. Overall, the non-legitimacy of a regime can be punished internally by the growth of an opposition movement, leading either to a vicious circle of opposition-repression, or to the overthrow of the regime. Externally, regimes may be punished by propaganda campaigns against them, supplying the internal opposition with all forms of assistance, a more or less systematic official boycott (breaking diplomatic relations, economic sanctions, for example, Jordan 1970-73; Egypt 1977-).

It seems clear to us that no Mashriq regime can afford the

---

[19] See for example, R.D. Mclaurin, Mohammed Mughisuddin, Abraham R. Wagner, *Foreign Policy Making in the Midde East: Domestic Influences on Policy in Egypt, Iraq, Israel and Syria* (New York: Praeger Publishers, 1977).

[20] For the importance of the concept of legitimacy, see Michael C. Hudson, *Arab Politics: the Search for Legitimacy* (New Haven: Yale University Press, 1977).

luxury of ignoring, systematically and simultaneously, all three sources of legitimacy: the democratic aspirations of the people, the pan-Arab sentiments of public opinion, and the possible sanctions of the Arab world.[21] With democratic aspirations already posing a problem (here the Arab regimes show similarities with many Third World countries), Mashriq regimes have no choice but to appeal to the values of Arab nationalism in order to legitimize their power. We may go as far as to say that the more regimes worry about their survival, and the more they sacrifice democratic principles in order to ensure it, the more they have to protest their loyalty towards the values of Arab nationalism. This affirmation of loyalty may of course be false, perhaps only verbal, but how long can credibility be maintained at this level? Besides, the very fact that the government feels the need to justify itself when its acts are not in line with its words shows the extent to which the values of Arab nationalism remain alive. The survival of the regime, the struggle for power, very often seem to depend on them. Similarly, opposition to a regime only acquires popular legitimacy when it claims to share the values of the basic perception, and when it bases its criticism of the existing government on the latter's transgression of those values. In fact the opposition, in its criticism of the regime concerned, may easily appropriate for itself almost the same arguments as those cited at the beginning of this paragraph concerning the factors running counter to respect for pan-Arab nationalism by governments. It might also reproach the regime for having over-sacrificed the "raison de la nation" to the "raison d'Etat"[22]

---

[21] Even in the case of Egypt, it is probably not a matter of chance that Sadat was assassinated precisely when he was sacrificing the last component of legitimacy which was left to him (through internal represssion).

[22] To use some expressions expounded by Walid Khalidi who cites four "raisons": raison d'Etat, raison du statu quo, raison de la révolution and raison de la nation. See: "Thinking the Unthinkable: a Sovereign Palestinian State," *Foreign Affairs*, LVI, 4 (July 1978).

and to the "raison du régime." And as we have suggested, the opposition has more chance of gaining Arab support from the exterior if it bases its criticism of the authorities on the way these authorities have betrayed pan-Arab nationalism, than if it attacks the government for its record of violating democratic liberties.

What may we deduce from all this? From the operative point of view, we may say that the basic perception is one factor among others in political action, and that for Syria and Iraq at least, it impregnates the élites in power and has been the driving force in their ascension.[23] The action of governments sometimes conforms with the scale of values mentioned and sometimes diverges from it. Let us say rather that governments spontaneously orient their actions according to their vision of the world and the values accepted by their people, as long as overriding and urgent considerations (territorial integrity for example) or substantial advantages (the law of cost and benefit) do not dictate or suggest to them actions in the opposite direction. Governments themselves, in the sometimes confused mixture of values, can also choose to emphasize those which seem the most appropriate to the demands of day to day action. They can still act in accordance with the principle of apparent non-contradiction, i.e. try to compromise between values and interests, and thus to make use of the greatest room for manoeuvre just within the threshold beyond which the contradiction with the basic values becomes too obvious or untenable. They can, for example, send out rather equivocal "signals" concerning their readiness to recognize Israel on certain conditions (e.g. pending on appropriate quid pro quo). On the other hand, the regimes are all the more sensitive to the spontaneous values of their people when the events justify their original fears. A "signal"

---

[23] Even in the case of the Jordanian dynasty, the pan-Arab component of the basic perception is not absent.

sent out towards the US and ignored by that country or understood as a sign of weakness, leads to the government in question taking a U-turn back to the position it started from, and discovering that its initial anti-American vision of the world has been confirmed by the facts.

What then does this amalgam of facts and values contribute to the perspective and policy of regimes?

The perspective of the regimes

Whether they like it or not, the regimes daily find themselves confronted with the Arab-Israeli conflict. Pressure from the popular perception demands the adoption of clear nationalist positions. Palestinian militancy or any internal militancy requires control and the prevention of any overflow. The occupation of Arab territories by Israel calls for military preparation and sustained diplomatic activity. The risk of Israeli aggression necessitates caution, internal crisis management and external alliances. The development of the international and inter-Arab scene, advice and pressure from countries which might be more or less friendly, or more or less hostile, suggest the opportunities to be seized, the reefs to be avoided or the low profile to be kept.

It is not the purpose of this paper to study each of these considerations which face the regimes. But we should touch separately on the Gulf factor as an input to the political process. In other words, we should study how the rise of the Gulf on the Arab and international scene has influenced the policy of the Mashriq regimes towards the Israeli-Arab conflict and towards the various actors in the conflict, including the two super-powers. For us that means inferring the governmental perception, even when it is not expressed, from observed governmental action. Although the analysis which follows is based on close observation of events, it should be recognized that parts of it are speculative for lack of access to the necessary sources of information.

The time has long gone when certain Mashriq regimes, along with their public opinion, could call for the overthrow of the Gulf monarchies. The 1967 defeat brought to an abrupt end any such campaign and any tendency in that direction. In this context, many observers have put forward the idea that the Israeli attack was aimed at (or at least had the effect of) diverting the "radicalizing" energies being expended in the Gulf by the Mashriq countries (and Egypt, in Yemen for example) towards the unshakable rock of Israel. Since the Khartum summit of August 1967, the policy of the confrontation countries has been to give priority to the struggle against Israel and to freeze any interference in the affairs of the Gulf in exchange for some tens of millions of dollars a year. Even though the confrontation countries were calling for the oil weapon to be used in the fight, it does not seem that they were able or willing in the 1967-73 period to give this appeal an immediate or clear character as to its bearing or conditions. In spite of the strategic importance of Gulf oil going back to long before the creation of the state of Israel, the Gulf regimes in the early sixties had neither the Arab nor the international stature which they enjoy today. They were barely perceived as entities just emerging from the control of the oil companies, and having at their disposal crumbs (royalties) from their vast subterranean resources. As for the confrontation regimes, they were very much weakened by the defeat, both militarily and politically, and had lost much of their leverage.

Slipshod as it was in many respects, Saudi-Syrian-Egyptian coordination in preparation for the October war exceeded all that its architects could have expected in terms of results and consequences. In relation to Israel, the front line states gained military credibility. With regard to the US, they acquired political credibility and an American concern to avoid superpower polarization over Arab-Israeli issues in the future. Internally, the front line states were substantially strengthened. There is no need to add to this picture the radical transformation of the status of the Gulf countries. But as we shall see, the stature gained in this way was not only the source of a new strength, but also the source of renewed weakness, and the frontline states tried to turn both the strength and the weakness to their advantage.

We shall restrict ourselves here to the Syrian viewpoint.[24] The leaders of Syria, like many observers, took note of the implications of the new-found strength of the Gulf oil countries. The embargo was a gesture that these countries had to make, for internal and external considerations, towards regimes which had just launched a war as a last resort and which had in addition taken them into their confidence. When the strategic results of the embargo went beyond all expectations, the obligations of the oil-rich monarchies towards the cause increased proportionally. In spite of themselves, these monarchies became the repository of hopes and expectations. Their power underwent a forced transformation. Ideological and emotional reasons (the Islamic character of Jerusalem, for example) aside, their newly-acquired power could only be translated into influence in the Arab world if it was used to advance the Arabs' main cause, that of Palestine.

By the same process, Arab prestige became a question of survival. What we said above on the subject of the legitimation of Mashriq regimes now became valid for the Gulf. The tensions born from extremely rapid social change, the need for a foreign and Arab labour-force (Mashriq and Egyptian), the over-conspicuous alliance with the US, all worked together to destroy the old consensus and reveal the anachronism of state structures. In order to legitimize their hold on power, the Gulf

[24] For a point of view which does not take into account or seems to minimize the Gulf component in Syrian policy, see: Elizabeth Picard, "Les militaires syriens devant les accords de Camp David," *Défense Nationale* (Paris), Août-Septembre 1981.

countries seem to be forced to prove the positive use of their power, in other words to work for tangible results in Palestine.

Moreover, the very course which the Arab-Israeli conflict took after the 1973 war greatly boosted the influence of the Gulf regimes and multiplied the responsibilities and constraints which that influence entailed.[25] Whereas in the aftermath of the war Syria was (and still is) interested in retaining an Arab military option, the course followed by Sadat has resulted in the effective neutralization of any military pressure on all fronts at the same time (Sinai, Golan, Jordan, Lebanon). By this we do not mean that Syria was interested in a new Arab-Israeli war, but merely that it considered (and considers) that strategic parity with Israel is essential to any real and fair progress towards a solution of the conflict. Being unable to exert any pressure on Israel in an immediate, direct and autonomous sense, Syria thought to prepare the ground for the eventual possibility of this by a rapprochement with Jordan (1974-77), an active role in Lebanon (1975-   ) and even a reconciliation with Iraq (1978-79). As for the Gulf regimes, it seems clear that they are not interested in a renewal of hostilities. An oil embargo cannot be imposed every day. Moreover they shudder at the prospect of a new military test, whatever the outcome. This would either result in the strengthening of the front line states, and a corresponding fall in the relative importance of the Gulf within the Arab system; or the front line states would be hard-hit and a protective shield between the Gulf states and Israel might shatter, perhaps irremediably. Moreover, as we shall see later, the mere outbreak of hostilities would lead to polarization and radicalization in the Arab world in general, and in the Gulf in particular.

---

[25] For a different point of view, at least for the period following 1978-79, see Paul A. Jureidini, R.D. McLaurin, *Beyond Camp David: Emerging Alignments and Leaders in the Middle East* (Syracuse: Syracuse University Press, 1981).

Whatever the outcome, the vacuum created by the freeze in the Mashriq on any progress in the area of the Arab-Israeli conflict and by the absence (whether objective or intentional) of an Arab military option could only be filled by the oil countries' diplomatic role. The non-military trend gives a preponderant role to the Gulf regimes, since they alone are perceived as being capable of doing something. Their responsibility is even harder to bear and the weakness of the monarchies consequently even more conspicuous, because gains achieved by the diplomatic path alone are a mirage or at least extremely difficult to obtain. For seeking to obtain concessions from Israel solely by virtue of Gulf-US bargaining is unduly optimistic. However, it is precisely that which in the Mashriq is perceived as the minimum task of the Gulf monarchies;[26] and consequently on that endeavour rest the prestige, stability and survival of these monarchies. The more the international and American situation allows the Gulf countries to hold up the shimmering prospect of being able to obtain results in the short term, the stronger the Gulf regimes feel internally and on the Arab scene, and the more they are tempted to play a "moderating role." Inversely, the more improbable progress appears, and the closer the US appears to be to the Israeli arguments on the Arab-Israeli conflict, the more the Gulf regimes lose their internal and Arab credibility, and feel obliged to proclaim their attachment to the most orthodox Mashriq positions. One only has to compare on the one hand, the confidence with which the Gulf regimes encouraged the Kissinger-sponsored disengagement process on the Egyptian front in January 1974 and on the Syrian front in May of the same year or Carter's efforts in 1977 to convene the Geneva conference with the possible participation of the PLO, with the fright engendered by the separate Israeli-

---

[26] See for example an editorial by Bilal al-Hasan "The American Ally from Begin to Fahd," in *al-Safir* (Beirut), September 13, 1981.

Egyptian agreement on the other. The Americans themselves were not mistaken when they sought to offer the Gulf regimes the protection of a new security system to compensate for the internal and Arab weakness which they themselves brought about with the Camp David process. But they were well and truly mistaken in thinking that their readiness to intervene militarily could replace what these Gulf monarchies need most to ensure their prestige and survival, namely the protective bosom of the Mashriq Arab consensus.[27]

The efforts of the Gulf monarchies on behalf of Palestine, such as they are, are not then a free gift, but more like the payment of tribute. For this reason a country like Syria does not feel that these efforts (financial assistance, diplomatic activity) constitute a real instrument of pressure on it. A case study of the famous Syrian missile crisis in Lebanon in spring 1981 enables us to pinpoint how it is that a Mashriq country can judiciously turn the power of the Gulf to its own favour and in favour of Arab-Israeli political-strategic parity.

For the Syrians, moving the missiles into the Beqaa in response to Israel's breaking the status quo in Lebanon was a calculated risk. The Syrian move could only be deemed legitimate by Arab public opinion in general and by the Gulf regimes in particular. After all, the Syrians were only defending a vital security region. Even if their gesture was a challenge to the (extremely elastic) Israeli concept of security, it could not be considered an act of provocation. Apart from Sadat, who in any case was only able to speak from outside the Arab consensus, nobody in the Maghrib or the Mashriq could accuse the Syrians of being irresponsible or of offering

---

[27] Concerning Saudi Arabia, see among others: Bruce R. Kuniholm, "What the Saudis Really Want: a Primer for the Reagan Administration," *Orbis*, XXV, 1 (Spring 1981); William B. Quandt, "Riyadh between the Superpowers," *Foreign Policy*, No. 44 (Fall 1981); Ghassan Salamé, "Arabie Séoudite: Une vocation de puissance régionale servie par l'Alliance avec l'Amérique," *Le Monde Diplomatique*, No. 331 (October 1981).

the Israelis a pretext for an attack which would simply further weaken the Palestinian cause. Conversely, Syrian panic in face of the challenges hurled directly against it by Israel would have been perceived not only as a sign of weakness, but would also have initiated an inevitable process implying at least the return of Syria to its modest pre-1973 stature, its withdrawal from Lebanon, and a considerable weakening of the PLO.[28] The legitimate and essential nature of the Syrian initiative was therefore bound to guarantee it at least verbal support from the Gulf countries.

One could obviously ask what use this sort of support would have been to the Syrians in the event of an Israeli military riposte. The sympathy of brother countries after a severe Israeli-delivered blow is slim consolation indeed. It is clear that the Syrians were counting on much more than that: (1) they were counting on the Soviets to save them from the worst outcome and to minimize the costs; (2) they were counting on the Saudis to take advantage of the best outcome and to maximize the advantages.

The worst case was what the Israelis naturally wanted: to teach a military lesson to Syria. To deal with this possibility, the Syrians took the precaution of protecting their rear. For a long time (and especially since Camp David) they had counterbalanced the strategic imbalance caused by Egypt's defection with a "qualitative" improvement of relations with Moscow. In October 1980, they had even signed a treaty of friendship and cooperation with the Soviet Union. Although the Soviets hinted that their obligations under the treaty in principle extended only to Syrian territory proper, they could

---

[28] The ins and outs of the Lebanese crisis do not fall within the scope of this paper. For a correct understanding of the vital nature of the Syrian initiative constituted by moving the missiles into the Beqaa, see in the Israeli press: Zeev Shiff, "War in Lebanon: New Dangers for Syria and Israel," *Ha'aretz,* May 3, 1981; Haim Herzog, "As Blind People in Lebanon," *Ma'ariv,* May 8, 1981; Eytan Haber, "A Useless War," *Yedi'ot Aharonot,* May 14, 1981.

not allow an Israel emboldened by the accession of messianic Reaganism to the US presidency to deliver humiliating blows to their friend in Lebanon. Besides, immunity for Syrian territory itself is not something to be sneezed at.

It would certainly be interesting to know if the Soviets' encouraged, coordinated, restrained, braked or disapproved of the Syrian gesture. For our part, we believe that Moscow played a role from the outset which was firmly in favour of the Syrians and restraining at the same time. But that is not of great relevance to us here, since in any case the Syrians would have had a crucial role to play in arriving at a decision on an issue which vitally concerned them — since they, more than anyone else, would have had to pay for any of its awkward consequences. Besides this, the Soviets, afterwards, had no choice but to support the Syrian initiative — an important factor of which the Syrians were aware from the start.

There was a time, the 1967-73 period for example, when the US would have spontaneously viewed any such Syrian initiative as being the work of Moscow, would have considered it an intolerable challenge, would have encouraged Israel to respond and would have considered a corresponding streng- thening of Soviet influence as a pretext for still more vigorous responses. But this time, despite the bitter anti-Sovietism of the new US administration, the US feared that an Israeli riposte would provoke an uncontrollable spill-over[29] which might have endangered the delicate political situation in the Gulf region.

This brings us to the second consideration borne in mind by the Syrian leaders when they decided to move their missiles into the Beqaa during the night of April 29. The Syrians in

---

[29] For an interesting development of the idea of spill-over, see the chapter, "The Politics of Protracted Conflict: Resistance Organization and the Middle East System," in John W. Amos II, *Palestinian Resistance: Organization of a Nationalist Movement* (New York: Pergamon Press, 1980).

fact must have known that the missile crisis would provoke profound apprehension amongst the Gulf countries, not only at the rational level (as for the Americans) but also at the "gut" level.[30]

The Gulf monarchies had to do more than give Syria their verbal approval. They had to do everything in their power to forestall an Israeli military initiative. Such an initiative would have meant a serious blow to the Syrian army. For the Gulf monarchies, that would have led to an increased Soviet presence in Syria, or in other words the decisive failure of the entire political process begun in the aftermath of the October war. That would further intensify frustrations in the Mashriq in particular and in the Arab world in general, leading in turn to radicalization and polarization. In the medium term it would imply the accentuation of inter-Arab conflicts and of the US-Soviet confrontation in the Middle East. The Arab countries, and especially the West-leaning ones, would find it more difficult to claim non-alignment. They would have to choose, officially and irrevocably, one camp or the other. For the Gulf regimes, the dilemma would be intolerable. One alternative would be to bow to US pressure and proclaim an alliance with a country which has become more than ever convinced that Israel is a strategic asset against Soviet "satellites" such as Syria. As a result, they would have to enter the famous strategic consensus along with Israel (and implicitly against Syria and the Palestinians).[31] The other alternative

---

[30] At this "gut" level, the new US right wing would not have been unhappy with a blow against a Moscow "ally". The contradiction between "knee-jerk" and measured reaction (or between "vision of the world" and perceived interest) in the US governmental élite seems to us to have been demonstrated further at the time of the bombing of the nuclear reactor in Baghdad and during Israeli operations against the PLO in Lebanon.

[31] For a conservative American view which would like this to happen, see Robert W. Tucker, "The Middle East: Carterism without Carter," *Commentary*, LXXII, 3 (September 1981).

would be to accept the urgings of increasingly "radical" countries and, without aligning themselves in an alliance "against nature" with Moscow, make a rapprochement with the Soviet Union, condemn the pro-Israeli policy of the US, and risk American armed intervention. Such an impossible choice between contradictory pressures would lead at best to a retreat within themselves, isolation and weakness while waiting for better days to come; and at worst it would lead to destabilization and a change of regime.

It goes without saying that all these implications were not a direct and immediate part of the missile crisis. The crisis merely unveiled them, brought them out into the open, and even perhaps exaggerated them. It is the prospect of these implications which lies behind the urgent quest of the Gulf countries to persuade the US to curb Israeli activity in Lebanon, to understand Syrian preoccupations, and instead to try and "recuperate" Damascus. That would appear to be the direct origin of the Philip Habib mission.

Prevention of an Israeli riposte thanks to Saudi fears and (American) fears for the Saudis was therefore a gain for Syria. Without wishing to exaggerate the significance of this gain, we may say that the Syrians scored a point off Israel: they made inroads on the credibility of Israel's threats, and limited its direct intervention in Lebanon's internal affairs; they practically succeeded in freezing the status quo ante as it was in Lebanon from 1978-80. To do this, Syria had to take risks which would not have been possible if the only consideration had been the disproportionate military capacities of the two countries in the battle-field. The risk was possible because of the Saudi-Soviet conjunction, which is paradoxical in more than one respect. In passing we may note that the PLO tried to benefit and did in fact benefit, from the situation created by this conjunction, when it "dared" to respond from South Lebanon to the Israeli army's campaign launched in July 1981 to destroy its military infra-structure.

The Saudi-Soviet connection is paradoxical for several reasons. Here are two countries, the Soviet Union and Saudi Arabia, supporting a third for apparently opposite reasons: the former in order to hold on to its position and prevent greater US influence in the region, the latter to prevent increased Soviet influence. But when analyzed, the reality turns out to be more complex than that. For the Soviets, Arab solidarity embracing Syrians and Saudis amongst others is not such a bad thing, as long as this Arab solidarity is directed against Israel and broadens the Arabs' (and Saudis') room for manoeuvre with regard to the Americans.[32] As for the Saudis, even though they fear "communist subversion," they clearly cannot criticize the Soviets for defending the Arab cause or the Syrians for seeking Soviet military assistance.[33] As has been repeated time and again throughout 1981, the Saudis are more apprehensive about the "Israeli danger" than about the "Soviet danger."

The Syrian initiative during the missile crisis does not therefore in itself, or in its direct consequences, contain the germs of a radical new orientation towards one or other superpower. In the most extreme conditions, i.e. if the internal constraints imposed above all by the popular nationalist and non-aligned perception are left aside, the two options remain equally open for Syria. But in practical terms, things look a bit different. For, on the one hand, since it is impossible to leave aside these internal constraints or the world vision of the leaders themselves, Syria *could not* decide to conclude a separate peace with Israel together with an alliance with the US at the expense of the Palestinians. And on the other hand, Syria *would not* wish to be driven to losing the advantages

---

[32] See supra, pp. 194-6, in Rashid Khalidi's paper on "The Gulf and Palestine in Soviet Policy."

[33] David Hirst, "Time May Force Reagan's Hand," *The Guardian,* August 12, 1981.

which it derives from the power and the weakness of the Gulf countries. Therefore a tighter alliance with Moscow in conjunction with a confrontation with the Gulf countries under the pretext of these countries being under US domination is not considered desirable. Let us note here that neither Syria nor the PLO signed the Aden treaty concluded between South Yemen, Libya and Ethiopia on August 19, 1981.

If Syria is profiting (or suffering, depending on the observer) from the consequences of pursuing a middle course between Moscow and Riyadh, this middle course has a certain effect in the Gulf itself. This point is underlined for instance by the two essential preoccupations of the Gulf Cooperation Council set up in May 1981: (1) the affirmation that Gulf security can only be assured by the countries belonging to the area, and that it requires opposition to any attempt to intervene in the affairs of the region on the part of the great powers; (2) the affirmation of the primacy of the Palestinian question,[34] as if that primacy formed an integral part of the Gulf's security.

The credibility of the non-alignment idea perhaps still remains to be proved. We may note in this regard, however, the very significant rapprochement between the Soviet Union and Kuwait and observe that the affirmation of non-alignment took place at the same moment as the US was talking about the Gulf as a region of vital interest, about the Rapid Deployment Force and about a strategic consensus in the Middle East against the Soviet Union. As for the affirmation of the primacy of the Palestinian question, it is of such great importance to the Gulf that it gave birth to the Fahd plan (August 7, 1981).

---

[34] See for example, the Council's communiqué, at the end of its meeting at foreign minister level, in Taif, on September 2, 1981, in *al-Nahar,* (Beirut), September 3, 1981.

The eight points of the Fahd plan are the most striking and the most explicit example of the gradual advance of the Gulf towards the centre of the Arab scene on the issue of the Arab-Israeli conflict. It is inevitable that this move of the periphery towards the centre, high-lighted by the Fahd plan, should provoke a certain uneasiness, friction and more or less concealed criticism in the Mashriq.[35] For the Mashriq peoples and regimes, the uppermost question does not seem to concern the content of the Fahd plan so much as the fact that it was formulated by a Gulf country without prior consultation.

The reader will have noticed that the regimes' view of the links between Palestine and the Gulf has been expounded mostly in relation to the case of Syria. Let us finish by saying a few words about Jordan and Iraq. In order to ensure its survival the Jordanian regime has to perform a balancing act between all its neighbours at the same time: Syria, Iraq, Saudi Arabia and Israel. The result is the paralysis of any initiative in the area of the Palestine question. Iraq, a country belonging to the Mashriq and the Gulf at the same time, confirms, however indirectly, our analysis of Syria. Iraq gained stature in the autumn of 1978 when in a masterly fashion it reintegrated into the official Arab camp by convening an Arab summit in Baghdad and by accepting official Arab terminology in relation to the Arab-Israeli conflict. Its growing influence with the Gulf countries and on the development of the Arab-Israeli conflict seems however to have been lost when Iran again became its main preoccupation. But like it or not, as Israel's destruction of the nuclear reactor in Baghdad recently showed, Iraq is and always will be destined to be part of the Palestinian question.

---

[35] See for example, the criticism of Muhammad Haidar, the Syrian Ba'th Party spokesman for external relations, in *al-Safir*, October 16, 1981; and the AFP report from Amman about some lukewarmness in Jordanian-Saudi relations, because of the Fahd plan, in *al-Nahar*, October 22, 1981.

Conclusion

Whatever the possible divergences of analysis on this or that aspect of the questions raised, the preceding study emphasizes the complexity and indeed the autonomy of the Arab system. The Arab world is not an aggregate of well-knit nation-states with nothing in common except a few frontiers and some characteristics of language and religion. Rather it forms a system, or a unique container with contents that may be diverse, but which in the eyes of the Arabs appear to converge towards a unified consensus. The interaction which goes on within the system does so not only between states, but also between state structures, peoples, trans-Arab elites, parties and media at the same time. The Mashriq-Gulf interaction concerning the Arab-Israeli conflict forms only one aspect, admittedly an important one, of the total interaction within the system.

This study has also brought up several dilemmas facing the Arab world today.

The first dilemma concerns the Arabs' vision of the world, basis of their identity. There is such a gap between this vision of the world and the actual policy of regimes, between the popular perception and the constraints of reality, that we may speak of a crisis in the Arab system, or a crisis of Arab ideology. By this we do not want to imply a criticism of the Arab vision of the world or a questioning of the components of the basic perception. Such criticism or questioning belong to history. Here we are concerned with the problem of the absence, or at least the non-articulation, during the seventies and early eighties, of élites and counter-élites which would have emerged from the base, would have been organized and structured, and would have been intermediaries (by their position and by opposition) between peoples and governments, between perception and reality. What is missing in other words, is political parties with programmes of action to deal with society, the state, resources, Palestine, and external alliances. Fortunately, there is one exception – the Palestinian movement in several of its trends.

The second dilemma concerns those who wish to lead internal opposition in the various Arab countries. How can a regime be weakened and overthrown without weakening the country? How can a government be de-legitimized without allowing the perceived enemy (Israel, imperialism) to take advantage of this? The extreme experiment of Iran is perhaps a demoralizing one. The Arab-Israeli balance is so delicate and is made up of so many political, non-military components, that any modification of the internal status quo in any country can have decisive effects (positive or negative) on the development of the conflict.

The third dilemma consists of the paradox presented by the regimes: extraordinary sophistication in international relations and judicious tactical manipulation of regional and international rivalry on the one hand; and internal weakness and precariousness on the other. The result of this for the regimes is a succession of ups and downs, of victories and nasty surprises. This dilemma in terms of the Arab-Israeli conflict in particular becomes: what to do so that the struggle for Palestine is the expression of popular will and capacity, and not the always ephemeral result of the regimes' desire for prestige or survival?

The fourth dilemma is specific to the Mashriq in its relations with the Gulf. How to avoid turning the Gulf into a milk cow with the unfortunate social and economic consequences of this, (decrease in exploiting one's resources, adoption of unbridled-consumption models, "nouveaux riches" attitudes...), while at the same time calling for an equitable distribution of Arab resources? And in particular for the radical Arab regimes: how to take advantage of the power of the Gulf in the struggle for Palestine without legitimizing and strengthening the regimes in that area?

The fifth dilemma concerns, for the regimes, the objectives

to achieve and the means by which they may be achieved, above all in the area of the Arab-Israeli conflict. In the medium term, what is the Mashriq and Arab solution to the Palestinian problem? What role does military preparation play in the conflict? What is the post-Camp David role of Egypt? What are the possibilities and limits to the Gulf's contribution to the progress of the Palestinian cause? Does the progress of the Palestinian cause stem essentially from a struggle against Israel, or from a confrontation with its American protector?

These questions do not require individual answers but rather orientations and approaches, which should be formulated by the regimes and Arab political forces. It would be unfortunate if these answers should be dictated from outside as a result of the active policy of other powers, under the pretext of the instability and instrinsic divisions of the Arab world. Or more correctly, it would be unfortunate if the Arab orientations were to develop more or less thoughtlessly, more or less automatically, in reaction to the active policies of outside powers. However, let us add, as the previously-mentioned American testimonies of 1952 would suggest, now less than ever, can any external force impose lasting trends on the Middle East if it ignores the primacy of the Palestinian cause in Arab perceptions and policies, and ignores the link between the Gulf, the new centre for global rivalry, and that cause.

Program of the Seminar on
"PALESTINE AND THE GULF"
November 2-5, 1981

FIRST and SECOND SESSIONS : Introduction and Background
THIRD and FOURTH SESSIONS : International Actors
FIFTH and SIXTH SESSIONS : Regional Actors and Conclusion

Monday, November 2

FIRST SESSION

Moderator: **Constantine Zurayk**
Chairman of the I.P.S. Board of Trustees
Opening of Seminar.

Camille Mansour
Introductory Remarks.

Michalis Papayannakis
"Western Economic Interests in the Arab World".

Pierre Terzian
"The World Energy Balance and the Gulf".

SECOND SESSION

Moderator: **Marwan Buheiry**

Frank Barnaby
"The Global Arms Build-up".

Mohamed Al-Rumaihi*
"Factors of Social and Economic Development in the Gulf in the 1980's".

Tuesday, November 3

THIRD SESSION

Moderator: **Elias Shoufani**

Michel Tatu*
"Palestine and the Gulf: A European Perspective".

Marwan Buheiry
"The Atlantic Alliance and the Middle East in the Early 1950's and Today: Retrospect and Prospect".

Rashid Khalidi
"The Gulf and Palestine in Soviet Policy".

Wednesday, November 4

FOURTH SESSION

Moderator: **Camille Mansour**

Robert J. Pranger
"The Emergence of the Palestinians in American Strategy for the Middle East: Issues and Options".

Oleg V. Kovtounovitch*
"The Present Situation in the Middle East and the Policy of the Soviet Union".

FIFTH SESSION

Moderator: **Sami Musallam**
             Institute for Palestine Studies.

---

* Contributor did not attend conference, but seminar paper was presented to IPS.

Shafiq al-Hout
"Palestine and the Gulf: A Palestinian Perspective".

Elias Shoufani
"Israel and the Gulf".

Thursday, November 5

SIXTH SESSION

Moderator: **Rashid Khalidi**

Camille Mansour
"Palestine and the Gulf: An Eastern Arab Perspective".

Rashid Khalidi and others.
Concluding Remarks.